THE LOST SON

A LIFE IN PURSUIT OF JUSTICE

BERNARD B. KERIK

NEW YORK CITY'S 40TH POLICE COMMISSIONER

ReganBooks

HarperTorch

An Imprint of HarperCollinsPublishers

This book is based on my experiences, notes, and memories, along with research from the New York newspapers: *The New York Times, New York Post, Daily News, Newsday, The Village Voice,* and *The New York Observer;* from *New York* magazine, *The New Yorker, Spring 3100,* and *City Journal;* and the following books: Fleming, Thomas, *New Jersey: A History.* New York: W. W. Norton, 1977; Jeffers, H. Paul. *Commissioner Roosevelt: The Story of Theodore Roosevelt and the New York City Police, 1895–1987.* New York: John Wiley, 1994; Lardner, James, and Thomas Reppetto. *NYPD: A City and Its Police.* New York: Henry Holt, 2000; Mackey, Sandra. *The Saudis.* New York: Houghton Mifflin, 1987; Nahm, Andrew C. *Introduction to Korean History and Culture.* Elizabeth, N.J.: Hollym International Corporation, 1993.

PHOTOGRAPH CREDITS: Text: all photographs courtesy of the author except for the one on page 233 by Paul Brown; first insert: all photographs courtesy of the author; second insert (color): all photographs by David Fitzpatrick; third insert: photographs on pages 1, 2, 3, 4 (bottom), 5 (top), 6, 7, 8–9, 12, 13, 14–15, 16 by John Botte; photographs on pages 4 (top), 5 (bottom), 10, 11 by David Fitzpatrick.

HARPERTORCH
An Imprint of HarperCollins*Publishers*
10 East 53rd Street
New York, New York 10022-5299

First HarperTorch paperback printing: September 2002
First HarperCollins hardcover printing: November 2001

HarperCollins ®, HarperTorch™, and ❤ ™ are trademarks of HarperCollins Publishers Inc.

Printed in the United States of America

Visit HarperTorch on the World Wide Web at www.harpercollins.com

10 9 8 7 6 5 4 3 2 1

An astonishing story of bravery and honor: one man's quest—against incredible odds—to make a stand against crime . . . and to uncover the painful truths of his own life. Here is the story of an American hero.

THE LOST SON
BERNARD B. KERIK

FOR CELINE CHRISTINA AND
JOSEPH MICHAEL ANTHONY,

AND TO MY HERO,
DONALD RAYMOND KERIK, SR.

THE LOST SON

SOME THINGS YOU MUST ALWAYS BE UNABLE TO BEAR.
SOME THINGS YOU MUST NEVER STOP REFUSING
    TO BEAR.
INJUSTICE AND OUTRAGE AND DISHONOR
    AND SHAME.
NO MATTER HOW YOUNG YOU ARE AND
    HOW OLD YOU HAVE GOT.
NOT FOR KUDOS AND NOT FOR CASH.
YOUR PICTURE IN THE PAPER NOR MONEY IN THE
    BANK, NEITHER.

                    JUST REFUSE TO BEAR THEM.

                              —WILLIAM FAULKNER
                              Intruder in the Dust

CONTENTS

PART THREE - THE CITY

AFTERWORD

ACKNOWLEDGMENTS

IN March of this year I walked into Judith Regan's office to discuss what I thought would be a very simple project. I wanted to capture my life's journey in a book for my children to read and have forever, and for others to learn from. What I didn't know then was that it would be one of the most heart-wrenching and painful journeys in my entire life.

Looking back on one's life is never easy. Our own instinct allows us to ignore the bad and retain the good, and writing a memoir usually requires us to reflect on both. As I did so, I realized that there were many unanswered questions about my life, questions that I would have to answer on my own or with the help of others, some of which I would enjoy, but most of which tore my heart out. It is mostly with the help of others that I survived this process to tell my story.

Perhaps even the best of authors sometimes need a little help in telling their stories. I, on the other hand, needed a lot, and I got it from Jess Walter, a distinguished writer whose thoughtful guidance was invaluable. He will be added to the list of people whom throughout my life I will consider a mentor and true friend.

I can never repay Sergeant Lenny Lemer and Detectives Bobby Hom and Jimmy Nuciforo of the New York City Police Department for spending so much of their own time trying to uncover the truth about my past. Chief Steve Hilbert of Plain City, Ohio, and Chief H. Darrell Pennington and Captain Al Zelner of Newark, Ohio, all dedicated not only their own time but staff as well to a murder investigation that we all anticipated might never be solved. Sergeant Ken Hinkle and Detective Steven Vanoy of Newark, Ohio, led an investigation with no stone unturned in an attempt to find the truth. And special thanks must also go to Sergeant Gary White and members of the Dayton (Ohio) Police Department for their assistance and tireless efforts.

For eight years I've worked for Rudy Giuliani during one of the greatest times in New York City's history. He has been a true friend and mentor and a tutor and counselor. He was also the first person I spoke to when I learned about my mother and didn't know where to turn. His support gave me the encouragement to get through the pain and embarrassment of my unknown past, and for that, a mere thank-you will never be enough.

To John Picciano, Joe Dunne, and Joe Esposito, everyday heroes who run the NYPD under my command: I thank you for picking up the slack when my mind, heart, and soul were in Ohio. You never asked or interfered; you just got the job done. And to my personal staff, there is none greater: Lowell Stahl, Jim McCabe, John Clifford, Gerry Kane, Peter Friscia, Tom Antenen, Tom Fahey, Chris Rising, Eddie Aswad, L'Tonya Meeks, Renee Herriott, Nancy Walker, Carol Ratchpaul, and Janet Fitzpatrick. And I can't forget Leslie Crocker Snyder, Jerry Speziale, Kate Moran, Nathan Berman, and Simon Cohen for being such great friends and sounding boards when I just needed someone to talk to.

To the detectives assigned to my detail, Sean Crowley, Donny Trenkle, Hector Santiago, Craig Taylor, Bobby Picciano, Sonny Archer, Mike Jermyn, Mike Sanchez, Gary Combs, Vinny Gericitano, Lynne Silver-Meriwether, John Giammarino, and John Cumbo, thank you for the cold readings, the feedback, and the soul-searching we did together. And thank you for protecting my heart when I needed it.

Thanks must go to Paul Brown for his artistic genius in presenting my story in a stunning visual image, to John Botte and David Fitzpatrick, spectacular artists and photographers, and to all of the ReganBooks staff, including Kurt Andrews, Cassie Jones, Paul Olsewski, Jennifer Suitor, Conor Risch, Carl Raymond, Carla Parker, and Josh Marwell, for their hard work and dedication.

To my mom and dad, sisters, Vickie and Terry, and brother, Don: Without your support, this would have been much, much harder. I could never have gotten through this process without the support and encouragement of my wife, Hala. As if my job weren't enough, every bit of my spare time has been put into this memoir, which has taken away from time I could have spent with her and my daughter, Celine.

My son, Joseph, turned out to be one of my strongest supporters. At sixteen, he listened and learned, as did I, about the mysteries of my childhood and my life before he was born. He never judged me or my past. As I prepared to head to Ohio for the first time in forty-one years, it was his words that gave me the energy to move forward. "Call me as soon as you find out something. I love you and good luck."

And finally, the person who is really responsible for making this all happen is Judith Regan. She clearly demonstrated her editing and publishing genius in helping me tell a story I never knew, and then helped me get through the pain, heartache, and understanding of the story once the information started rolling in. In addition to writing the book and running the largest municipal police department in the world, I was trying to conduct a thirty-seven-year-old homicide investigation from four hundred miles away, and at times the stress and pain were just unbearable. It was more than I could take. She eased the pain through her guidance and support and was extremely generous with her time and understanding. Throughout this book you will read about courage and honor, dedication and loyalty. You will read about true everyday heroes. But there is one hero who is missing from the text. Her name is Judith Regan.

THE LOST SON

THE DREAM

PART ONE

LIGHT *streams through the crack in the door. From the bed I hear voices on the other side and I desperately want it to be my mother or father. I slide out of bed, bare feet plopping onto the floor beneath me. I take a few steps and reach up for the doorknob. Light spills into the room and a woman's voice stops me at the door. "Go on, honey. Go back to bed." But it's not Mommy. It's the woman who lives in this house. I have no idea who she is.*

Sometimes there are other children here, but I don't know where they go at night. I play with them during the day, but when darkness sets in they disappear, and the feeling of loneliness is deeper. Where is my mother, and why won't she come and get me?

I cry myself to sleep believing that I will wake up in her arms. But in the morning I'm still alone. I drop out of bed again and trudge into the kitchen. The room is filled with the burned-hair smell of hair straightener. There are other people in the room, but I don't know them. I climb onto a wobbly chair and push myself up to the small kitchen table. Breakfast is a piece of toast with jelly on it, dunked into a cup of coffee.

I turn to the woman and ask her, "When is Mommy coming to get me?"

She looks at me and smiles gently. Her voice is not unkind. "Maybe today, dear." But quickly it is night again and the fear comes over me like a fever. I don't want to go back to that room.

The woman reaches out with a dark, worn hand, glistening and oily to the touch. She walks me to the room and guides me into bed.

I don't want to be here! I lie in bed, staring at that column of light through the crack in the door. "Where is Mommy?" I cry out, but no one answers. I'm afraid I will be here forever. My mother will never come for me. And I will never go home.

Suddenly I sit up in bed, drenched. I look at the clock; it is five forty-five in the morning. I'm not four years old. I'm forty-five, lying in my bed next to my wife. I've had the dream again, a dream I have never told her about, that I have never told anyone about. I've had this dream for forty years, and I know that it is tied to real memories. I just don't know how much. The parts of my life that I do remember— the trouble, the poverty and crime, the low expectations, the years of struggle, the fights and hassles, the unlikely achievements, the tragedy—these feel like dreams themselves. But this other dream is the one that haunts me—these vivid memories of an abandoned boy, of a son lost and waiting for his mother to return—this is my deepest mystery, a hole in the center of myself.

I can't believe that I had this nightmare today of all days. I shake my head as I climb out of bed and walk toward the shower.

It's August 19, 2000. In a few hours I will stand in the Blue Room of City Hall next to Mayor Rudolph W. Giuliani, as he announces to the world that I am about to become the fortieth police commissioner of the city of New York.

1

NEW YORK

MAY 2001

SOME fuckin' mutt in a tuxedo has stopped traffic by climbing to the top of the George Washington Bridge and threatening to jump. In Times Square, FBI agents and New York police detectives are having a shootout with a fugitive wanted for murder, robbery, rape, and kidnapping. And here in the Bronx I am climbing out of my car at the 47th Precinct—the Four-Seven in cop parlance—where a forty-three-year-old man has just been arrested for raping and strangling his eleven-year-old neighbor.

Outside the Four-Seven, photographers and angry neighbors form a tunnel of outrage during the perp-walk, when the accused murderer of the eleven-year-old girl is marched from police car to precinct house. The crowd shouts, "Killer!"

"I didn't do it," says the man, Clarence Moss. Then quietly he says, "I'm sorry." He tells detectives that he drank beer and smoked crack all day, and when eleven-year-old Tamiqa Gutierrez came to the door to ask if Moss's grandchild could play, he attacked her and raped her for almost a half hour. She struggled so much that he choked her and she finally passed out. When he was done with her, he dropped her in the hallway just outside her apartment, and when her father found her she was choking on her own vomit and blood. She died in the ambulance on the way to the hospital.

At the Four-Seven, I brief reporters on the case and go out of my way to credit the detectives, who did a tremendous job tracing the evidence back to Moss's apartment and getting him to confess.

I'm quiet as I leave the station house and climb into the backseat of my dark unmarked car. It doesn't matter how many times you see a crime like this; it gets to you, the things people do to children. It's almost 8 P.M. and I've been going since 5:30 A.M. Yet I'm not finished. I still have two dinners and one police event to attend. In the front seat, two cops from my security detail wait for the next order.

Sometimes I can't believe where I am. At my desk I will occasionally remind myself by pulling out the solid-gold shield of the police commissioner, the shield that once belonged to Theodore Roosevelt. Few people have any idea what it means to be police commissioner of the City of New York. I know there isn't another position like it in the world.

It's not just that I am in charge of the largest municipal police department in the nation—forty-one thousand officers, fifty-five thousand total employees in more than one hundred commands. More than that, I am responsible for the safety and protection of the eight million people who live in New York and the tens of millions of tourists and visitors who come to the city every year. Their safety was the most profound symbol of the resurgence of the city, its dramatic eight-year turnaround from near bankruptcy and out-of-control crime. When I got this job in August 2000, I promised to sustain and improve that resurgence, to lower crime even as national crime figures were beginning to creep back up. I also promised to improve morale among police officers and to repair relations with the community, especially minority communities, after the shooting death of Amadou Diallo.

I keep my promises.

So eighteen-hour days are common. I usually work six

days a week, and often I work seven. On this day in May 2001, I open my eyes from the catnap in the back of my car when the radio explodes with traffic.

Something has happened at the Carnegie Deli. At first it sounds like a robbery. The two cops in my security detail are handling the car's four cellular phones. Sonny Archer turns and leans over the backseat. "It looks like five are shot, boss," he says. "Two DOA. One likely." Two are dead and one is about to go.

I nod to Mike Sanchez, my driver. "Let's go."

Within minutes, we're roaring down the West Side Highway, lights flashing and siren blaring, veering in and out of traffic. At 57th Street, four wheels—police motorcycles—are waiting for us. They swarm around my car, two in front and two behind, clearing traffic and escorting us to the scene through an obstacle course of taxis and limousines.

The Carnegie Deli is a landmark in Manhattan, an old-style restaurant and tourist attraction on the street level of a building at Seventh Avenue and 55th Street, in the heart of midtown. Outside, it's like a street fair, police and reporters and diners and theatergoers and the usual people gawking. I get a quick briefing and then climb the stairs to the sixth floor, to an apartment above the deli.

Until an hour ago, a thirty-nine-year-old woman named Jennifer Stahl lived in this apartment, a former actress who supported herself by selling marijuana. On a door in the apartment was a cardboard sign listing six different types of pot and prices—from $300 to $600. On this night, May 10, 2001, she had been sitting around with some friends when a man rang her apartment from the street below.

She knew the man, a wannabe musician named Sean Salley. She buzzed him up but was surprised when she opened the door to see two men. The men had guns. They had Stahl's friends lie on the floor, and one of them began duct-taping their hands and feet while Salley allegedly took Stahl into a small room, which contained the marijuana and some money.

"Take the money, take the money. Take the drugs. Don't hurt anybody," Stahl said. Then there was a single shot.

"Why'd you have to shoot her?" asked the other man, who was duct-taping Stahl's friends in the living room. The next few minutes must have been terrifying for the four people in that room, who squirmed and tried to crawl away as the gunman walked around, held them each down, and shot them, one by one, in the head.

The living room of the apartment is a grisly sight—two young dead men on the floor. One of the men had just managed to wiggle one of his hands out of the tape when he was shot. As I stood over them looking at the carnage, I couldn't help but think about the people in this country that continue to say that marijuana is a victimless crime. Tell it to the people lying there in a pool of blood.

Jennifer Stahl is also dead, and another woman is seriously injured. Miraculously, one of the men was only grazed in the neck.

Back on the street I confer with Bill Allee, the chief of detectives, in front of a souvenir shop window full of Times Square snow globes and tiny replicas of the Statue of Liberty. I quickly brief reporters on what we know so far. We have security video from the stairwell showing two men climbing the stairs to the apartment.

For me this crime is a terrible reminder of what New York was eight years ago, when half the city's residents dreamed of moving away, when the crack epidemic raged violently, when crime and cynicism threatened to make this city fold up on itself.

It has been one of the greatest achievements of my life to be a part of New York's rebirth. Under Mayor Rudolph Giuliani, the New York City Police Department has managed a stunning reversal—a 63 percent drop in overall crime and an even greater drop in homicides—from 2,245 in 1990, to 671 in the year 2000. Even when the economy began to sour and national crime statistics began to flatten and even to rise, we managed to beat the numbers down here. We had even taken to calling New York the safest big city in the world.

WHEN he was police commissioner of New York City at the turn of the last century, Theodore Roosevelt was famous for his "midnight rambles"—venturing out late at night to check on his officers and feel the pulse of his city.

I find myself doing the same thing at least once or twice a week. I drive through the worst neighborhoods in the city, the blocks where crime is up and where neighbors may be complaining. On this night I'm patrolling with three cops from my security detail—Hector Santiago, Bobby Picciano, and Craig Taylor. The eleven police officers in my security detail are more than just bodyguards; they are the best cops I know and some of my best friends. They serve as a kind of Round Table, helping me keep an eye on the city, but also keeping me honest and inspiring me with their courage and resourcefulness. They are a cross section of the city they serve: black and white and Japanese and Italian and Latino, male and female. Highly decorated and battle-tested, they are the best this city has to offer, cops who have proved themselves to be as fair as they are courageous.

In the car behind me is Craig—six feet, five inches tall, lean and athletic, so quiet and unassuming you'd never know that he once had to shoot and kill two guys who tried to mow him down with a machine gun. With Craig is Bobby Picciano—Bobby Pitch—who still looks like the kid I trained as a West 42nd Street beat cop—fifteen years and two heroic gun battles ago.

And in my car is one of the best cops I know, my former partner, Hector Santiago. Hector's been involved in four shootings and was once shot in the arm by a drug dealer we were both chasing. Working with guys like Hector, with all the cops on my security detail, is the best part of my job.

Every day I am surrounded by heroes.

On this late spring night, we drive around West Harlem,

where neighbors have been complaining about an increase in drug dealing. I look for police presence, to make sure that we're going after the dealers and also to get a feel for what's happening out here, to see for myself what's happening on my streets.

We're driving east on 142nd near Amsterdam when I see two men running on the sidewalk. I've always had a knack for spotting such things, and my guys sometimes joke that I have X-ray vision. Hector sees the guys I'm talking about. It looks like one guy is chasing the other. Perhaps a robbery. They slow down as they approach a white van. Hector stops the car in the middle of the street in front of the two men and we jump out, yelling "Police, don't move!"

"Commissioner!" Hector says. "Stay in the car." But he knows I can't do that.

I put one of the two men against a wall. The other one runs on toward the white van. Beyond the van, Craig and Bobby are getting out of their car.

"Get out of the van!" I yell, but the second suspect has already started the motor, and he bangs into the cars in front of him and behind him as he tries to pull out.

"Shut the car off!" Hector and I yell. "Police!"

The driver keeps backing in and out, trying to clear space to get away. But when he turns to his left, he sees the barrel of Bobby Picciano's nine-millimeter handgun staring at him through the window. "Shut the fuckin' car off!"

At first the guys seem friendly, then confused. When we ask whose van it is, they point at each other. We run the license plate on the van, and it turns out to have been stolen off a different vehicle. When we run the vehicle identification number of the van, it comes up even more interesting. This van was recently taken at gunpoint in a carjacking in Virginia. The guys are no longer very friendly.

Then the description of the carjacker comes across, and we start to get some information on the two skells we've pulled over, Lloyd Triplett and Lydell Williams. It turns out that Triplett is a convicted murderer and armed robber who recently violated his parole. He perfectly fits the description of the shotgun-wielding man who stole this van.

Street cops and reporters always mention it when I'm involved in arrests like this, but being a cop is in my blood. A couple of months before, I helped stop a fight in the street between a man and his girlfriend; she was armed with a box cutter, he had a switchblade in his pocket. I also arrested a guy taking a piss alongside the road whose blood alcohol level was twice the legal limit.

As police commissioner, my focus and duties are substantially different, but I'm still a cop. In any profession, you should always lead by example—do what you'd want your officers to do and never ask them to do something you wouldn't.

By the time we finish with the stolen van, it's well after midnight.

Teddy Roosevelt once wrote that his own midnight tours brought him "in contact with every class of people in New York, and I get a glimpse of the real life of the swarming millions."

Some nights I can't sleep unless I've been out to see the streets. It's like a parent who has to go in at night to watch his child sleep, who holds his hand just above the child's mouth to feel him breathe.

That's what it's like, checking on the city. The night I was transferred to the Midtown South Precinct fourteen years ago, I went up to the observation deck of the Empire State Building and looked out. Being a cop and working in midtown Manhattan was a dream I'd had, and finally I was here, fulfilling my fantasy about working in the greatest police department in the world. Staring out at the city, I found myself thinking about the oath that I had sworn to uphold, and for the first time it was not just words, but a kind of promise I was making to the millions of people below.

SOMEONE once said I run an agency of fifty-five thousand people as if it were an office of ten. I think that's a good description of my management style. If a cop retires after thirty-five years, I'll be there to see him cut his cake. If a cop is seriously injured on the job, she's going to see me in the hospital. On Christmas Day I visited more than thirty precinct station houses between 4:00 and 10:00 A.M. to thank the cops who were working the holiday.

I expect my staff to be my eyes and ears when I can't be there, such as the day we dedicated a new display at the Police Museum, downtown on Broadway. The display showed the shields of all 572 New York City police officers who had lost their lives in the line of duty since James Cahill was killed on September 29, 1854. During the ceremony for the families of the slain officers, my chief of department, Joe Esposito, noticed an elderly woman standing alone, crying.

He went up to her and asked if he could help. A few hours later, Joe called to tell about this lovely woman he'd met, and as a result, I invited her down to One Police Plaza.

Her name is Helen Varecha and she is eighty-two years old. In 1968 her son John was a twenty-five-year-old patrolman, a promising young man midway through his second year in the NYPD. He lived at home with his mother and father. On October 7, 1968, John dressed for work, said goodbye to his mother, and went out on his last tour of duty.

That night, a car ran a red light in midtown Manhattan. Patrolman Varecha followed the car and pulled it over. What he didn't know was that inside the car were two low-level thugs, Albert Victory and Robert Bornholdt, who had spent the day shaking down nightclub owners for protection money and had just finished shooting up one club in an attempt to intimidate the owner.

No one knows what happened after John Varecha walked up to that car, but within minutes the two men had pulled out guns and begun firing.

They shot John Varecha seven times. He fell back into an alley and died there.

An off-duty police officer named Randy Jurgensen was hanging out nearby with his cousin, another off-duty cop named Joe Corcoran. They heard the shots and chased Victory and Bornholdt, who tried to run away on foot. They tackled the two men and eventually arrested them.

Even though it could have been a capital crime, Albert Victory got only twenty-five years for killing John Varecha. He threatened to kill the prosecutor and Jurgensen and even the trial judge. He escaped from prison in 1978 but was caught and sent back. And then, inexplicably, in December 1999, fifty-nine-year-old Albert Victory was paroled.

Randy Jurgensen would go on to become somewhat famous as a police officer, his exploits serving as the basis for the 1972 Al Pacino movie, *Cruising*. After that he worked as a consultant, writer, and actor for years, in everything from *The Godfather* to *Donnie Brasco*. To this day he uses a post office box as an address and keeps his eyes open because of Albert Victory's threat against him.

"I will never forget the sight of John Varecha lying in that alley or the sorrow and dignity displayed by his mother," Jurgensen said recently. He was stunned to see Albert Victory paroled in 1999. "To see that man walk out of prison, that was difficult to accept."

ON February 1, 2001, John Varecha's mother arrived at One Police Plaza and rode the elevator to the fourteenth floor. She was led through the outer offices and into my office. She carried herself with tremendous poise and dignity.

In my office, with my senior staff around me, I presented Helen Varecha with an inscribed copy of John's shield. She had told Joe Esposito at the Police Museum that she'd always wanted a copy of his shield. She thanked me and then stood.

"But there's more," she said.

I looked over at Joe Esposito and we both shrugged. Then she walked out into the hallway and returned with an old blue NYPD uniform, pressed and on a hanger. It was essentially the same uniform that cops wear today. She explained that her biggest fear was that she would die and someone would go through her things and not realize the importance of that simple blue uniform.

Helen Varecha pulled a small piece of notebook paper from her pocket. She unfolded the paper. "I am going to read," she said, "because my memory isn't what it used to be, and I want to make sure I do not forget anything."

"Thank you for this honor," she began, her fingers shaking. "I would like to explain what this uniform means to me. It hung in the closet for thirty-two years, neatly pressed, just as he left it, until today. This wasn't just some ordinary piece of clothing to be carelessly discarded. It was his uniform, a symbol of what he stood for—authority and respect. It represents our finest, the fallen heroes whose badges line the wall at the Police Museum.

"They gave their life to make our streets safe. I shed unashamed tears for them out of respect, just as I do when I hear our 'Star Spangled Banner.' For they have not died in vain. I hope this uniform will stand in honor of our finest, who day after day are out there to protect us." She folded up her little piece of paper and handed it to me.

I know there are some people in this city who have grown cynical about the police department. I know there are people who don't trust cops, who see them as lazy or corrupt or violent. And I know there are a handful of cops who rightfully deserve that reputation. But there was not a trace of cynicism in my office that day. Standing in my office with me, watching this strong, graceful woman who kept her son's uniform for thirty-two years, were Chief Esposito and First Deputy Commissioner Joseph Dunne. Together they had over sixty-five years of experience and were probably the best to ever hold the two top spots under the police commissioner. As cops they had witnessed every kind of depravity and violence and sadness and heroism, and yet right now, all three of us just stared at the ground, humbled and moved, crying openly. My own eyes stung with tears as she presented us with the crisp blue uniform of her lost son.

I ordered the uniform to be sent to the Police Museum for

display. We should treat it with the same respect that we treat those shields displayed on the wall, perhaps even more. This uniform covered his flesh, felt his heartbeat, and acted as a public reminder to everyone who saw him wear it that he was there to keep them safe from harm. We should never forget that. We should never forget John Varecha.

ALL day, every day, my security detail and my senior staff flow in and out of my office, briefing me about what's going on out there. A day in my office could fill a television network's quota for tragedies and heroes, scandals and absurdities. All day my office on the fourteenth floor of One Police Plaza buzzes with meetings and phone calls and the lightning pace of decisions.

A suspected serial killer is working at a local hospital as a nurse. The detectives want a few more days to investigate before they arrest him. But I don't want more victims, so I tell them to pick the suspect up immediately. Meanwhile, two Arab men are seen taking pictures of federal buildings near where two Islamic terrorists are on trial for the 1998 bombing of the U.S. embassy in Kenya. The two men are questioned and point to a third man, living in the Midwest, who has suddenly disappeared. I order increased security near the courthouse where the men are being tried. The chief of Internal Affairs comes in with a case against a cop who may have fixed a car dealer's criminal problems in exchange for a new Mitsubishi, and another case against some other cops who had a few beers too many and tore up a golf course. We take steps to whack the cop who got the car and make the golfers pay for their damage.

All day my staff comes to me with stories of knifings in school (one not likely, two collars), car accidents involving police officers (minor injuries, no fault), and brewing political problems (the Hispanic fraternal group wants a promotion for an officer I don't think is deserving). A woman is stabbed to death walking to her car on Staten Island. A cop is charged with racking up huge bills on the credit cards of other cops. Two bodies are found alongside the Hudson River. It goes on and on.

LATE one afternoon, the private telephone line in my office rings. It is Lenny Lemer, a sergeant assigned to the Intelligence Division and a longtime friend.

"I got some information on that thing you wanted."

I grip the phone. "What've you got?"

"Looks like it's her," he says. "Maybe we shouldn't talk about it over the phone. Maybe I should come down there."

"It's okay. We're on a hard line. Just tell me." I can hear papers shuffling in the background. "She had a pretty substantial criminal record," he says and hesitates.

There's something he doesn't want to tell me. "It's all right, just read it."

He sighs. "She has ten aliases: Joann Evaline Bailey, Patricia Joanne Curtis, Joann Evaline, Patricia Joann Fletcher, Patricia J. Bailey . . ."

After reading me the tenth, he says, "And there are three arrests," and he hesitates once more.

Again I've got to push him to continue.

"Three arrests," he says, "two for prostitution and one for escape. . . . I really need to come down there for the rest."

"Okay, hurry up and get down here." I sit back in my chair, staring at the portrait of Teddy Roosevelt, drifting into a daze. My intercom buzzes and my telephone rings several times but I don't answer. I feel like I can't move.

After about ten minutes there is a slight knock at the door and Lenny walks into the office. I can tell by the look on his face that it isn't good.

"I have the coroner's report," he says.

"Is it worse than I thought?"

Lenny shifts uncomfortably in his chair. "Yes." Then he reads the summary.

" 'This is the case of a female . . . who apparently received multiple traumatic injuries, resulting in multiple bruises of the left eye, left buttocks, thighs, and lower legs.

The bruise to the eye resulted in a cerebral hemorrhage . . . causing her death.' "

"Anyone arrested?"

"No," he says. "That's the weird part. I don't even see any sign of a homicide investigation. There's definitely something wrong here."

"Why wasn't there an investigation?" I ask. Lenny, not knowing what to say, just sits there, staring at me.

I hear stories like this ten times a day, 365 days a year. I hear about so many victims like this woman, it becomes hard to keep them straight. But this one I've got to investigate myself. And I won't rest until I find out why this woman was killed and who killed her. My stomach is in a knot.

I look down at the coroner's report again. It's dated December 14, 1964. Patricia Joann Bailey Curtis, a white female, thirty-four years of age, was found dead in Newark, Ohio. She was beaten to death.

She is buried under one of the ten names listed on her arrest record. When I say it out loud, I nearly lose my breath.

"Patricia Kerik."

My mother.

2

NEW JERSEY

1955

I was born September 4, 1955, in Newark, New Jersey, at St. Michael's Hospital—named for the patron saint of cops. So maybe I never had a choice.

My father, Donald, was one of ten children of my grandmother, Viola, and my grandfather, Steven, who had emigrated from Russia and ended up in Frederickstown, Pennsylvania, a small coal-mining town where the night shift limped past the day shift on their way to replace them in the hole. When he arrived in the United States, my grandfather's name was Cmesahi Kapurik. Shortly after his arrival, someone told him that Americans didn't like long names, and wanting to fit in, he became Steven Kerik. And like so many immigrants, Steven Kerik became an instant American.

The miners came from everywhere you could imagine, and working in the mines my grandfather learned to speak thirteen languages. My father heard all these languages being spoken around town, but when he asked his father to teach him Polish or Russian, my grandfather would say, "What country you in, kiddo?"

"America," my father said.

"Then that's what you speak." It took my grandfather more than twenty years to become a citizen, and he was fiercely patriotic and proud of his adopted country. He passed nothing of his homeland on to his children—neither religion nor food nor customs.

In Frederickstown, he worked hard, and drank harder. Sometimes my grandmother would have to send the kids down to the local watering hole on paydays to get his money before he could spend it all on booze. The kids, including my father, would approach him one at a time to ask for money to see a movie, then take the money home to their mother. She'd keep sending them back until they got all the money, or got caught. Once in a while he would realize what they were up to and he'd say, "Hey, weren't you here already?" but my father would insist he hadn't been and then he'd scat home to his mother with whatever he could get.

Coal mining was difficult, dangerous work, and my grandfather was covered several times by slate falls—the ceiling of the mines caving in on him and the other miners. He worked with bruises and broken bones, and it wasn't unusual for the morning to begin with my grandmother taping up his busted ribs for work.

My father had no idea what he wanted to do with his life, but he could see that he didn't want to spend it in a dead-end town covered in black coal dust. At thirteen he realized there was nothing in Frederickstown for him beyond the mines, so he packed up some personal belongings and left home with a friend, telling his mother and father that he was going off to Los Angeles to make his millions. Unfortunately, the City of Angels offered little to an uneducated, unskilled thirteen-year-old, and he made his way back to Frederickstown.

When he got home, he opened the kitchen door to see his father standing at the sink getting a glass of water. At first he was frightened about what his father would say or do. Although his father had never laid a hand on him, he felt that this time he had tested his patience.

My grandfather took a sip of water from his glass, looked over at his son, and said, "Well, did you make a million yet, kiddo?"

My father said, "No, Pap, not yet." His father took another sip from his glass, put the glass in the sink, and walked away into the living room.

When I think about my father's relationship with my grandfather, it sometimes reminds me of my own relationship with my father. Although my grandfather endured enormous pain and suffering, he also drank heavily, which ravaged his family. My father, scarred by his childhood, later carried much of that behavior into his relationship with his own family.

By sixteen he had dropped out of school and left Frederickstown for good. Twenty-one years later, when I was sixteen, I would do the same thing: drop out of school, run off to work, and continue the cycle.

After dropping out, my father worked his way west to Cleveland, and that's where he met Patricia Joann Bailey—a small, dark-haired, very intense woman whose own childhood had not prepared her for marriage or motherhood. She was one of eight children, four boys and four girls, whose father one day simply walked off and abandoned the family.

It was Patricia's eyes that caught my father's attention. You don't have to look very deeply into old photos to see those eyes as two round dark pools of suffering and trouble. To this day my father looks pained when he describes the woman he met; he just says she was "wild." She was twenty-one—three years older than my father—and had already been married twice.

They were married on August 28, 1952. From the beginning there were problems. He couldn't keep her out of the taverns and gin mills, and once she got inside those places he couldn't keep her away from other men. "We'd break up and get back together, break up and get back together," my father said recently. "She'd go off with someone, and then she'd call and say, 'Let's try again.'"

They tried geographic cures as well—moving from Milwaukee back home to Pennsylvania, to Ohio again, always trying to start a new life but never leaving their problems very far behind. In the late summer of 1955 they landed in Newark, New Jersey, where my father's sister Betsy was living. Pops got a job in a machine shop, and my Aunt Betsy's family seemed to be a calming influence on the young couple. That fall they were doing about as well together as they ever would, and at four in the morning on September 4, 1955, Patricia gave birth to a seven-pound, six-ounce baby boy, nineteen inches long. They named me Bernard Bailey Kerik, after Patricia's brother Bernard, with my mother's last name for my middle name. But everyone called me Beez or Beezy, because of the two Bs in my name.

Unfortunately, having a baby didn't make my parents' life any more stable, and they continued this awful pattern—my mother running off on some fling and then coming back a few weeks later, begging my father to reconcile. Sometimes she'd run back to Ohio, to see her family or some man she didn't want to give up. But a few weeks later, she'd drag me back to New Jersey and ask my father for a second chance. After almost five years of this, she finally ran out of second chances, and in 1957 my mother and father separated. Soon after that, they filed for divorce. I was two. Pops tried to get custody of me, but the lawyer told him that women almost always won custody battles like theirs. "You can probably prove she's an unfit wife," the lawyer told my dad. "But you can't prove she's an unfit mother."

In the end, that wouldn't be so hard after all.

BACK in Ohio, it didn't take Patricia long to find herself in the same old taverns, in the same old life of booze and derelict men. On those nights when she didn't come home, I stayed with a succession of relatives, friends, and acquaintances. Apparently she was working as a prostitute even then.

I have few pictures from the years before I was five, and

fewer memories. There is barely enough material to construct even the barest of childhoods—just some random
facts written during Patricia's stretches of sobriety: Beezy
got his first tooth at ten months; he weighed twenty-four
pounds at a year; his first sentence was "I don't want." At
three, Beez liked to practice quick-drawing his toy gun and
shooting someone named "Daddy Jack."

My father came to visit a few times in Ohio during their
separation and pending divorce. During his visits, my
mother wouldn't let him see me alone, insisting that her
brother's girlfriend watch us so that he didn't take me back
to New Jersey.

Then in 1958, just after my third birthday, Patricia was ordered by the courts to spend twelve weeks in a hospital or
institution of some kind, in an attempt to get control of her
alcoholism. I stayed at least part of this time with an aunt.
The hospitalization didn't stop Patricia's drinking for
long—if it stopped it at all. She may even have left the hospital early. Somewhere in there, she began a relationship
with a man named Claude Curtis. Claude was black, and
most of Patricia's family didn't approve of her being with
him. While she and Claude were out drinking and running
all over town, she left me with Claude's mother, near
Columbus, Ohio. It is this woman's hand that reaches out to
me in the recurring dream I have, and it is her house that I
see at night, the place in which I feel so lost and alone. Had
it not been for her kindness and gentle touch, the months I
spent there would have been much worse for me in many
ways. I will never forget her.

Sometimes I wake up and I can almost picture the room
where my mother left me, and the woman she left me with. I
can recall smells and sounds and light through the doorway—a handful of sensory memories that add up to a feeling of hopelessness and fear. I remember other children in
the house teasing me, and I remember wishing they would
stop. But most of all, I remember going to bed every night in

a strange room, wondering when my mother would come for me.

It's sad that just as my own memories were coming into focus, my mother's life was fading out, becoming as sketchy and unreliable as the dream that still haunts me.

Like the dream, my memory of that place and time doesn't have a beginning or an end. It's almost as if the little boy in that dream has been there forever. As if he's going to be there forever.

MY Uncle Bob had seen enough. He was my mother's older brother and also my godfather. In one of the two pictures I have of him, Uncle Bob is facing the camera, small and dark like my mother, wearing a white shirt with a jacket buttoned over it. He has a tight-lipped, slightly disapproving look on his face. It's not hard to imagine my mother on the other side of the camera.

In 1959 my father was working in New Jersey when he got a call from his old brother-in-law, Bob Bailey.

"Don," he said, "you'd better come back and get hold of Beezy. Pat's really fucking up. She ain't taking care of him. She's moved in with a black guy and is leaving the baby with this guy's mother while they run around drinking and carousing."

My father was suspicious. Patricia's family had always taken her side in the past. They were always supportive of Patricia and deeply attached to me; they ended up watching me much of the time. So why would Bob risk losing contact with me and at the same time hurt his sister?

"Come on, Bob," my father said. "You and I both know blood's thicker than water."

"Maybe to the rest of the family," Bob said. "But you come back here, Don. I love that boy and I know you'll take care of him."

"You know if I come get him, that's it," my father said. "You ain't gonna see him anymore."

"I know," Bob said. "But if you don't come now, he'll be lost forever."

And so my father made his way back to Ohio. It took him about three months to get custody. I was living with Claude's mother outside of Columbus when the police found me. My father followed the police to the tiny house. I seemed healthy, and he remembers the woman treating me very nicely. He said I called her "Grandmother." Although she had cared for me, she was more concerned about her son, who had a long and violent criminal record and was off somewhere with Patricia. As they took me away, the woman pleaded with my father and the police not to take it out on her son.

My father never did.

The police placed me in protective custody and put me in foster care for about six weeks, until the judge could hear the case. While my father waited in Ohio to find out if he would get custody of his son, Patricia called him one day and said, "Don't do this."

"Pat, it's already done," Pops said.

"I'll get even," she said to him.

"Do what you have to do."

On the day of the hearing, Patricia was nowhere to be found. Apparently she couldn't show up in court because she was wanted on a warrant for escaping from the hospital where she was sentenced by the courts to tackle her alcoholism. So she stayed away in some dank apartment above a tavern while the judge took away all her rights as a parent and awarded my father full custody. In the brief custody hearing, the judge told my father to pack my things and get me out of town.

Later that evening, at Claude's mother's house, Patricia heard the news and became so enraged that she punched a hole through the glass in the kitchen door and nearly severed one of her fingers.

I never saw or heard from her again.

I have to imagine that when my father took me away, it

only accelerated the end for my mother. I've spent so many years being angry with her, angry at the thought of her leaving, so many years wondering why she never came back for me, that I never really thought what it must have been like for her: to be so low and then to lose the only connection she had to a normal life.

It's hard now, looking down at a stack of papers and seeing a person's life, my mother's life, reduced to a rap sheet and a coroner's report. And part of my life is in those pages too. I often wonder how much of a person's personality is forged in early childhood, by events and people and feelings that we can't even consciously remember. I wonder sometimes if the traits that have allowed me to be so successful—a heightened sense of awareness and justice and duty, a deep need to protect people, an impatience with criminals, and a deep personal drive—are nothing more than a child's tools of survival and defense. Maybe what I've thought of as striving for a career and living a life of honor is actually just chasing the shadow of my own abandonment.

There are so many things I don't know, questions that haunt me. Was Claude Curtis my mother's pimp? Did he beat her? Did he have anything to do with her death? And if not, who killed my mother?

I spent a lot of time avoiding the legacy of my mother. And now it has shaken me. I've always been a person who moved forward, who didn't dwell on the past. I find myself crying now, for no reason. I find myself wondering if my strength is nothing more than a result of my weakness. At forty-five, I find myself thinking about a woman I haven't seen since I was four.

I suppose there is a part of me that worries that I somehow let her down and that if she had stayed in my life, I could have helped her in some way, protected her from herself, from the horror of those last four years of her life. I know it's ridiculous; what could a child do? Yet people are protected in strange ways, sometimes by nothing more than having something to live for. In March 1960 I was put in foster care and my father filed for custody. As I was about to start my new life, thirty-year-old Patricia Joann Bailey, divorced four times and having lost her only child, was arrested for the first time and charged with prostitution. She had four more years to live, but in some ways, I think she'd already reached the end.

3

NEWARK

1960

DAD and I returned to Newark at an amazing moment in time, the beginning of the 1960s and the tail end of a tidal wave of people fleeing to the clean, unspoiled suburbs of New Jersey. Between 1950 and 1960, New Jersey's population swelled by 20 percent—1.2 million people. As new houses were built in the Jersey suburbs, the Irish, Italian, Polish, and Jewish immigrants abandoned the inner city, their places taken by Latinos and African-Americans hoping for better jobs and security. As many as 130,000 black people moved to Newark between 1950 and 1970, most into the slums of Newark's Third Ward, into the row houses, apartments, and tenements that the earlier immigrants had left behind. In the 1960s Newark "tipped" and African-Americans became the majority. But the power structure remained white and terribly corrupt, and there were precious few economic and social opportunities for Newark's black citizens By the mid-1960s crime was at an all-time high, and the city felt like a pot about to boil. In 1967 the city would erupt in riots, four days of fighting, burning, and looting that would leave twenty-three dead and give Newark a reputation that has taken decades to repair.

In 1960 Dad and I moved in with my Aunt Betsy and Uncle John and their four children—John David, who was a year older than me; Bobby, who was a year younger; Steven, three years younger; and Nancy, four years younger. I liked living with them. After the hard, desperate scramble of life with Patricia, moving from house to house and man to man, her troubles never far behind us, this was at last a real home—kids and neighbors, a kitchen table and a brand-new Cadillac. After feeling alone for so long, suddenly I had an instant family and four cousins who were almost like siblings.

We'd been there about three months when my dad went away for three or four days—the longest I'd been without him since he came to Ohio to get me. About the third day he was gone, he called me up and said, "I'll be home tomorrow and I've got a surprise for you." I was five years old, and a surprise to me meant a toy truck, candy, toy guns, or a guitar. *Wow,* I was excited. I couldn't wait.

When he got back the next afternoon, he came into the room I shared with my cousins, looking very pleased with himself.

"Beezy," he said, "are you ready for your surprise?"

Overjoyed with anticipation, I stood there while he opened the bedroom door and presented me with a lively, pretty, blond-haired woman.

"Your new mother," he said.

I was surprised, but I was also disappointed. To a five-year-old child who has been tossed around for nearly three years and abandoned by his mother, accepting a new mom wasn't easy at first. I didn't want another mom who would leave me, and I didn't want to share my dad. I was the only one in his world at that time, and every night he'd sing Hank Williams and Everly Brothers songs to me before I went to bed, songs like "Bye Bye Love" and "I'm So Lonesome I Could Cry." And he would cry. All the songs he sang to me were about broken hearts, cheatin' hearts, and loneliness. I was afraid I would lose him too now to this new woman in his life.

Her name was Clara Dent, and she was my Uncle John's sister. Her husband had recently died of cancer, and as strange as my father's pronouncement may have been, he was right when he said, "Your new mother." From the moment they were married, Clara stepped in and was my mother, and when I think of the word *Mom,* I think of her.

Clara was one of twelve kids who grew up in Richeyville, Pennsylvania, which had a population of only a thousand people. There too the primary employment was either coal mining or working in the steel mills of Pittsburgh. Her father, William Dent, had been an orphan, and my mother's memory of him is clear: he was brutal and beat her viciously with his thick coal miner's pit belt.

One day while visiting Clara's parents, I was the victim of his rage too. I was about eleven or twelve years old, and Clara's sister Vickie was dating her present husband, Jack. I made a smart remark in front of everyone that my Aunt Vickie was also dating someone else. Before the sentence was completely out of my mouth, Clara's father slapped me so hard across the face that he knocked me to my knees.

Clara just stood there looking stunned, defenseless, and frightened. She was a grown woman with three children and she was still deathly afraid of him. Even talking about that incident now torments her. His temper still haunts her. And maybe it was what caused her sometimes violent temper. What I've learned from my own family history and from my work is that, tragically, violence often begets violence. Children who are abused often become abusers. But fortunately, the cycle of violence can be broken.

Although she went through a painful period of time in which she had a violent temper, Clara also had a greatly loving side, which came from her mother, my Grandmother Dent, for whom I'll always have a special place in my heart. I loved her and she loved me. She would make me breakfast and buy me doughnuts when I visited her. At night I would stand behind her as she sat in a chair, and I would brush her long silver hair with a metal-bristled brush, massaging her scalp.

After we moved out on our own, and away from Aunt Betsy's, I got to see my cousins John David and Bobby and Steven all the time, and we stayed as close as brothers. One summer day a few years later, we ventured away from their house near Barringer High School in Newark and found ourselves walking along the tree-lined paths that led into the middle of Branch Brook Park. It was like the Central Park of Newark—four miles of old swampland converted into a rambling stretch of streams, trees, flower gardens, a lake, bridges, and vast lawns. And like Central Park in the 1960s, it attracted every kind of criminal—bullies and thieves, drug dealers and perverts. It was no place for little kids to be alone. But there we were anyway, venturing in past the cherry trees chasing one another and screwing around. Our parents had told us over and over not to go into the park, but before we knew it we were miles from home, in the middle of nowhere. That's when we noticed eight boys, older and bigger than us, coming our way. We waited as they surrounded us, knowing what was next. One of the biggest kids stepped forward. "You got any money?" We didn't answer. "Come on, give it up."

A flurry of slaps, punches, and kicks followed that question. In the end, my cousins and I were beaten up and knocked down, and the kids stepped in to rip the money from our pockets. One of the kids paused over me for a moment, then reached down and took a ring off my hand. I fought back only to be beaten down again. It was a white gold and blue star sapphire ring that my mom, Clara, had given me for Christmas. That ring was very important to me. It was the nicest gift I had ever been given.

We picked ourselves up, wiped our bloodied noses, and limped back home, beaten and a little scared. It was just such a normal thing then in Newark to get into fights, to get beaten up, you almost expected it. It was a way of life. Every kid was expected to fight, to protect his lunch money or his reputation or his girlfriend or simply because he looked the wrong way at the wrong guy. But that day in the park felt different. That day in the park, they took something from me that I cared about, and I didn't like that feeling at all, the feeling of having no control over the outcome and not having anyone there to protect me. It was the same feeling of vulnerability that I had lying in bed in that dark room waiting for my mother to return.

I was probably in more than a hundred fights before I turned eighteen. But that day changed my life forever. I didn't like being a victim, feeling vulnerable like that, and I was determined never to let it happen again.

IN the meantime, my dad was drinking every day. A hard worker, he toiled nights at Tech Tool, a small tool and die shop where he was one of eighteen employees. Eventually Tech Tool landed a large contract for atomic submarine parts, and when the company was busy like that, Pop would work twelve hours a night for months at a time, and that pulled him even further away from the family. I remember him most days sitting in the dining room or living room, exhausted, the lights off and a Budweiser in his hand, staring off in the distance. He'd drink one or two six-packs, and by early evening he could construct a couple of pillars from the empty cans. He never got angry or violent when he drank; he was too sweet and wasn't that kind of an alcoholic. He just became more and more detached, more distant, as if he could pull away from the world one beer at a time.

As a child, I had no understanding of his problems. All I remember is feeling embarrassment and shame, not wanting anyone to come to the house. I didn't want anyone to see what I saw. I didn't understand that he had his reasons. He was a man who struggled with his own demons, a man incapable, as his father was, of showing his affection and revealing vulnerability in any way. He retreated instead. Now, as a man looking back at my own father's life, I see his goodness and grace. He was the father who came for me, who took three months of his life to fight for me in court in Ohio. He was a young, twenty-two-year-old father during the 1950s. He answered the phone call when my mother's brother said, "If you don't come and get your son, he'll be lost forever."

I have only recently come to understand that that single act was an act of heroism, of fatherly love. And I know that despite his flaws, despite the years that created such distance between us, fed by can after can of beer, despite all that, he came for me. He fought for me. And he brought me home.

WHEN I was six, Clara and Dad had their first child together: my sister Vickie Lynn. Two years later, I had another sister: Terry. And three years after that, a brother: Don. I was excited to have siblings, and I immediately became protective of them. I was there the day they were born, and I helped raise and take care of them. There is only one difference between my relationship with them and the relationships of all the other siblings in the Kerik and Dent clan. My sisters and brother and I are closer.

I was a tough kid growing up in tough neighborhoods and I was in a lot of trouble. I feel bad now about the way I tested Mom's patience. But she held her own, and sometimes she could be downright mean, smacking me around or, worse, using psychological warfare. Once, when little Terry was acting out, Mom told her that she was such a bad little girl she'd have to go live with the nuns at a nearby church. To prove her point, she threw us in the car and drove to the church on Madison Avenue in Paterson. She pulled up in front of the church and told Terry to get out of the car and go tell them she was moving into the church, that she couldn't live with her family because she was a bad girl.

Terry walked slowly up to the church, but when she got to the steps, she turned around and came running back to the car. I know Mom was thinking that she'd achieved some sort of miracle and that Terry had learned her lesson, but instead

Terry, who wouldn't let our mother get the better of her, even at four, said, "Mommy, will you tell Santa Claus where I live now?"

BUT the younger kids were saints compared with their older brother. Vickie, for instance, was an A student and a Goody Two-shoes. I, on the other hand, couldn't go a day without getting into some kind of petty trouble. My parents just saw their little hazel-eyed boy and had no idea how finely honed my survival skills were, even then. For me, every day became a quest to get money. My parents didn't have money for themselves, and they sure didn't have any spare money for me. Like everyone we knew, we were poor, living paycheck to paycheck and as often as not falling a bit further behind each week. The world was tough—a place where you had to scrap and fight just to survive, where you had to figure out your own way to get money to buy the things you needed.

In Newark, we lived on the ground floor of a small two-story house, and our landlord, Mr. Shane, an Orthodox Jew, lived on the second floor. Down the block, Mr. Shane also had a neighborhood grocery that I walked past to get to school in the morning, and Mom would sometimes send me there to get a quart of milk or a loaf of bread. Because Mr. Shane lived in the neighborhood, he extended credit to all the local families until the end of each week. One day when Mom went to pay Mr. Shane the rent and square up our bill at the grocery store, he told her it was thirty bucks—four or five times what she expected. As for most of our neighbors, thirty dollars might be the sum total of our savings at any given time, and my mother was shocked at the bill.

"Mr. Shane, there must be some mistake."

"No mistake, Mrs. Kerik," he said, and began to go over the bill with her. "Your son stops here every morning on his way to school and buys doughnuts, pretzels, potato chips, candy, and gum." I was feeding my entire second-grade class every morning on my parents' dime. Mom was furious.

And I guess it didn't make any difference that I was sharing all the goodies with my friends.

The following year, in the third grade, we were learning about banks, and the teacher had us set up bankbooks and savings accounts to teach us about interest and how to save money. Mom would give me fifty cents every Thursday to put in my account at school.

"Beez, did you put that money in your account?"

"Yeah, Mom."

"You sure."

"Yep."

That went on for a while, and then she asked me to bring my bankbook home so she could see how my account was doing. But the next day—"Beez? Where's your bankbook?"

"Oh, the teacher forgot to give it to me."

The next day—"Oh, I left it in my desk."

This went on until one day she was dusting behind the radiator in my bedroom and found this old, dusty bankbook. She opened it. There was one entry in it, but nothing after that deposit.

As often as I could do so without getting caught, I took money from her purse. When she bugged me to take out the garbage, I ignored her and went down the street instead, to take out the neighbor's garbage for two bits. Pops had a coin collection—old silver dollars and silver certificates, old dimes and nickels—and I'd skim a few off the top of that every few weeks too. He always figured I was the one getting into his little metal box, but he could never catch me, and he didn't want to accuse me. Years later, when I was in the army and home on leave from Korea, I admitted that it had been me. He went downstairs in the basement and returned with something in his hand.

He said, "I have something for you that you have always wanted but never got." He opened his hand. It was an antique one-dollar silver certificate from the collection.

"Here," he said, "it's the only bill you didn't take." I explained to him that the only reason I hadn't taken that one was its blue seal. I just assumed it was fake. We both stood there laughing. I still have that bill today.

Later, when we lived in Paterson, I got a part-time job cleaning up at a neighborhood drugstore. One of my jobs was to take the garbage out of the basement to the side street. There weren't many Thursday nights that I didn't add some goody to the garbage that I would return later to retrieve.

Once my mom found a big box of Duncan yo-yos in the crawl space underneath the stairs of our house. She marched upstairs and asked my sisters where the yo-yos had come from, but they weren't about to rat out their big brother. They just shrugged. Meanwhile, every kid on our block was walking around yanking the string of a new yo-yo.

One day when Mom was cleaning up my room, she picked up my pea coat and found a big lump in it. She reached into the inside pocket and came out with a wad of singles, surrounded by a rubber band. It was my stash from the yo-yos, the coin collection, and Mom's pocketbook. She was waiting when I got home that day. She dragged me into my room by the ear and held up the wad of cash.

"Where'd you get this?"

"It's mine, Mom."

"Where'd you get it?"

I didn't even hesitate. "Shoveling snow."

"Jesus, Beezy! It's June!"

My father says he remembers exactly when he realized that I was a different kid from the one he'd been imagining. He'd always give me a buck or two and send me to the store to get milk or bread. And remembering the gang that had jumped me in Branch Brook Park, he'd always warn me, "Beez, if someone tries to take your money, don't fight back, just give it to 'em."

"Aw, Pops, I—"

He'd interrupt me. "Beez, I can get another dollar. I can't get another son. If anyone stops you, you just give 'em the money."

"Okay, Pops," I said.

"You promise."

"Yeah."

And so I'd return every once in a while, shaken. "They jumped me again, Pops. I had to give 'em the dollar."

"It's okay," he'd say, rubbing my shoulders and wishing he could do more to protect me. "You did the right thing."

Then, one night when I was thirteen, Dad was playing shuffleboard with some buddies at an old gin mill where he'd sometimes hang out. The men would bet as they played, and that night Pops was lucky or skilled or whatever, and he took a couple hundred off his friends. He was walking home when someone came up behind him, bashed him on the head, knocked him down, and stole his cash.

A couple of days later, a rangy kid from the neighborhood—two or three years older than me, with a real tough-guy reputation—came running up to my dad, looking scared.

"Mr. Kerik," he said, "you gotta help me. I'm hiding from Bernie. He's looking for me. He's gonna beat me up."

"Why?"

"He thinks I mugged you. You gotta tell him it wasn't me."

My dad says he stood there shocked that this big tough kid with a reputation for mugging people was afraid of his little boy. And I guess for him it was one of those things you know but don't admit to yourself. He thought about all those times I came home without the grocery money pretending someone had taken it from me.

The truth was that no one was going to take a nickel off Bernie Kerik. It wasn't the old man protecting his son but the other way around. I was out investigating who had jumped my father, and I was prepared to knock the piss out of my most likely suspect—a thug who was older and bigger than me. That, he says now, is when he realized there was something different about me. Or something scary, he wasn't quite sure.

That night my father sat me down and told me that he knew who had mugged him and it wasn't that shaking kid and to leave that kid alone. I said I would. Dad looked at me like he wasn't quite sure he knew me. And in a lot of ways, he didn't. None of them did. Looking back, I can see that it was all kind of tied up together, my stealing money and my wanting to protect my father, to fight the bullies from Branch Brook Park and Ohio and all the other dark places. As I try to figure out now why I did what I did, the excuses are endless. I could blame my behavior on stupidity, trying to get attention, being angry at the world, or the sheer need for survival. But the bottom line is that there is no excuse. My petty thefts were wrong and unacceptable, and I will always regret and be ashamed of them.

The ironic thing is that when my parents caught me with money, they rarely asked why I needed it. They didn't ask and I didn't tell. It took a few years before they figured out where all my hard-earned and hard-stolen money was going.

The martial arts.

4

PATERSON

1969

PATERSON, New Jersey, was in a lot of ways an even tougher place than Newark. An old textile town, Paterson grew up in the mid-1800s around the silk industry of New York because it was close to the city, with a river and cheap land for the immigrants needed to run the factories. The mills hired mostly women and children and made them work thirteen- and fourteen-hour days. For decades the mill owners got rich and the workers got nothing until just after the turn of the century, when the unions set up shop there. Paterson was also home to the most notorious group of anarchists in the United States, and in the teens and the 1920s, it was the scene of bloody strikes and riots. It would forever be associated with violence and forever be known as a blue-collar, rough-and-tumble town.

By the time we moved there, in the mid-1960s, there wasn't much left of the silk mills beyond their brick husks, but the city was just as rough-and-tumble. My neighborhood was almost two miles from the old textile mills that surrounded Great Falls, where the Passaic River plunged over a shelf of rock and formed a deep pool. Just beyond the falls was the freeway, elevated above town as if the very act of getting out of Paterson required raising oneself up. And at the other end of that freeway, just out of view, was New York City.

Our neighborhood was mostly stooped storefronts and tight row houses, most of which contained two or three families. We lived on the second floor of a three-story row house on Broadway, the main drag through Paterson, a long stretch of neighborhood businesses: mom-and-pop stores, delis, fish markets, pharmacies, windowless bars, and soul food restaurants. On the first floor of our building was an insurance company, and on the third floor, a couple of rooms that were always for rent.

I think most kids who move around the way I did have one house that they remember as "home," and for me it was the house on Broadway in Paterson. My friends and I would hang out on the corners and get into fights or steal eggs from the grocery to throw at cars. My dad says now that I was a "perfect boy," which I think means I was in trouble most of the time, but rarely was it anything serious enough to drag him down to the police station.

By the time we arrived, Paterson had undergone the same sort of racial shift as Newark. Our part of town was probably 90 percent black, although I never looked at it in those terms. Looking back, there weren't many other white families in our neighborhood, two perhaps, but everyone seemed to get along just fine. My parents knew we weren't better than anyone else. The neighbors were poor. We were poor. Everyone around was poor. Skin color was never an issue. It never occurred to me that most of my friends were black. And if the first time some kid at school met me they asked about the "cracker" or "whitey" or "the honky," it never seemed to come up a second time.

Not that I didn't notice occasional cultural differences. One summer I was playing with one of my friends and we were racing around the way we always did, in some kind of mischief, running up and down alleys, over fences, through yards, between and through houses. I raced up my friend Rick Harris's steps and through his house, from front door to back door, and I was right behind him in the kitchen when all of a sudden I stopped dead in my tracks and turned. I must have looked like I'd seen a ghost. My friend's mom was heating some stuff and putting it on her hair with a medieval-looking rod. Back then, my father and I rarely talked about life with my mother Patricia. He hadn't yet told me that when he found me I was living with a nice black woman whose son was off somewhere with my mother. And so I stood there openmouthed, dumbfounded, and mystified, staring at that rod and smelling that burned-hair odor of hair straightener, wondering how the smell from my haunting nightmare had somehow made it into Rickie Harris's house. It would take me almost thirty-four years to figure it out.

IT wasn't so much that I was a bad student; I wasn't a student at all. I'd done pretty well in elementary school, but by the time I got to junior high, I was bored out of my skull. Why should I be tied to a desk while some old guy droned on about the Revolutionary War or the value of X in some equation or which part of the sentence was the predicate? I wanted to be out on the street, hanging with my friends, fighting and seeing the world. Looking back I see that if I'd put half the effort into school that I spent getting out of school, I could have been an A student.

In junior high school, I forged notes from my parents to get me out of class. Don had just been born and Mom was at home with him, so whenever Vickie and Terry had field trips for school, Mom wouldn't be able to go with the class. So I'd sit down and write, "We would like our son Bernie to accompany his sister Vickie on her class field trip," and I'd show up at their grade-school class and go with them. In part I went because I knew the mothers usually accompanied the class and I didn't like to think of my sisters without someone there for them. I was extremely protective of my little sisters and brother. But I also believed that a field trip to the most boring museum in the world beat sitting around in a classroom.

At first my parents didn't catch on that I was cutting classes. But by eighth grade, I had to take an extra period to make up for the classes I was failing by skipping school. One day my father came home after working the night shift and found me on the couch at nine o'clock in the morning.

"Aren't you supposed to be taking eight classes?" he asked.

"Yeah, I finished 'em all," I said.

"Oh, I must have a genius for a son," he said, and went to bed.

Despite my flair for truancy, teachers just kept passing me up to the next grade until I reached the notorious Eastside High School, the school portrayed in the movie *Lean on Me*, in which Morgan Freeman plays the tough but loving principal Joe Clark, who cleaned up Eastside by treating it like the war zone it was.

Unfortunately, I went to Eastside before Joe Clark began patrolling it with a baseball bat. The halls of my Eastside were filled with garbage and graffiti, and the bathrooms smelled of marijuana and cigarette smoke. It was commonplace to see a kid get beaten or stomped by ten kids over lunch money or a nice sweatshirt. A day didn't go by without a fight or a drug bust, and you got used to seeing the flashing lights of Paterson police cars parked in front of the building.

When *Lean on Me* came out in 1989, I was trying to convince some detective friends that I actually went to that tough, miserable school before Joe Clark cleaned it up. I appealed to my dad to prove it to the guys. "Hey, Pops, tell these guys. Didn't I go to Eastside High?"

My dad, without missing a beat, said, "Occasionally."

Eastside was a low-slung, fairly modern school surrounded by worn grass and announced by a chipped sign that read Welcome to Eastside High School, Home of the

Mighty Ghosts. That sign was about as far as I'd get. In the mornings I'd meet up with my friends and we'd walk to the deli across from the school, grab a couple of sandwiches, and sit on the stoop, watching the cars cruise in and out of the parking lot, waiting for someone to yell at us or look at us the wrong way, looking for any excuse to get into a fight. We might go hang out in the park or wander downtown or just hang out on the stoop all day, anything to stay out of school.

The school called Mom in to talk about it all the time. She'd yell at me or smack me around, but there was nothing she could really do. One day Pops came home after a twelve-hour shift at Tech Tool and found another note from the principal's office. He dragged me down to the school and told the principal, "You keep sending these notes home for my wife and me to come in, and I'm sick of it. If you can't handle him, I give you my permission to whip his ass. I'll sign a paper for you to whip his ass instead of you sending this paper home to my wife all the time."

The principal explained that they couldn't hit me, even with Dad's permission.

"Okay," he said, "then I'll tell you what you do. Get the whole school together, and I'll whip his ass in front of the whole school."

No, the principal said, they couldn't do that either.

But most of the time the notes came to Mom, and it killed her to see that her bright, friendly son was in so much trouble. It finally reached the lowest point when I was fifteen. The school called Mom in because I had skipped thirty-five days in a row.

Mom and I sat down with a guidance counselor and a social studies teacher whom I'll call Mr. Johns, who explained that school wasn't for every kid and that they ought to face facts: I was probably a lost cause. He produced a permission slip that would allow me to drop out of school right then and there. No way, Ma said, was I going to drop out of high school at fifteen. She held steadfast, but Mr. Johns kept trying to convince her.

"You might as well just sign it," he said. Then he nodded over at me. "I hate to tell you this, but your son is going to be nothing but a vegetable."

LIKE a lot of people who grew up in the sixties, I am a child of television. Many of my ideas of the world, my sense of myself, even my ambitions were influenced and sometimes shaped by TV shows. But I can honestly say that only one show changed my life. It came on every Friday night in 1966 and 1967 at 7:30 P.M.

It was called *The Green Hornet*.

The Green Hornet was really a wealthy newspaperman named Britt Reid, whose secret identity was known only to his secretary and the district attorney. *The Green Hornet* TV show was like a cooler version of *Batman*. Every week some supervillain or cabal of bad guys threatened the world and Britt Reid would have to put on his green mask and race around in the modified 1966 Chrysler Imperial that he called Black Beauty. But the best character on the show, as everyone knew, was Britt Reid's trusty sidekick and bodyguard, the mysterious martial arts expert Kato. Bruce Lee played Kato, and the best episodes always climaxed with him kicking and chopping and flipping waves of bad guys into submission.

My friends and I talked nonstop about the show, and later about Bruce Lee's movies. We emulated his high kicks, his roundhouses and vicious punches. In 1969 karate was suddenly cool, everyone I knew was into kung fu movies and magazines, and all at once half my friends were out in their yards trying to bust boards with their hands. But there was one kid in the neighborhood who wasn't just playing at being Kato. His name was Steve Jones, and he was four years older than me, seventeen when I saw him stretching and shadowboxing at the gym at Eastside, when I began hearing that he was seriously studying the martial arts. Intrigued, I started hanging out with Steve. He liked how seriously I took it, and he began to train me himself. I learned quickly, and I also saw that to get better, I would need to find other teachers. I started at a school in nearby Clifton, New Jersey, and I could feel right away that I had a talent for this, that it was something I wanted—more than I'd ever wanted anything in my life. I hadn't been into sports in school; I tried to play soccer for a while but was kicked off the team for fighting. Here was a sport where you couldn't get kicked out for fighting. Hell, it *was* fighting. And even more important, with martial arts I found something that tapped into deep pools of strength and self-discipline that I was just then discovering in myself.

By ninth grade, every spare cent that I earned and scammed and stole from Mom's purse was going to martial arts school. I moved from school to school, devouring all that the teachers had to offer, taking the things I liked from each master's style and adapting it to my own. At fourteen and fifteen, I'd hang out at Eastside with all the other kids, then run off on my own, jump a public service bus, and ride it through the sprawl of New Jersey towns, across the Hudson River and into Port Authority in Manhattan. Once off the bus, I'd take the A train to Canal Street, come up out of the subway, and walk from Canal Street to 1 Crosby Street, a dingy storefront with beaming Japanese characters on the door that read The Shanghai Dojo. My instructor there was the great master Peter Urban, one of the pioneers of Goju karate in the United States. My parents had no idea that while I was supposed to be in school, or at least somewhere near it, I was twenty-five miles away in the heart of New York. And if the city was no place for a fifteen-year-old kid to be alone . . . well, that just never occurred to me. I loved the city, its vitality and its size. Before karate classes, sometimes I'd catch a movie, and after class, hang out in the Village and then grab the bus back to Paterson.

My parents knew I was getting into martial arts; there

wasn't an unbroken board or brick anywhere near our house. I'd take bricks and cinder slabs up to the vacant apartment above ours and demolish them. I even began going to martial arts tournaments—again without telling my parents. In my first tournament, as a fourteen-year-old white belt, I was disqualified for hitting my opponent in the face. Soon I was winning most of the tournaments, at least the ones in which I wasn't disqualified. Trophies began piling up.

But my parents had no idea of the extent to which I was working, or that I was taking a bus into New York two or three times a week for training in the arts. I worked out so hard that sometimes I'd fall asleep on the ride home and miss my stop, waking up in the bus terminal in downtown Paterson, two miles from my house, on an empty bus. I'd have to walk home, trying to think of an excuse for why I was so late. Then one night I screwed around in New York too long and missed the bus entirely. When I realized the next bus wasn't until after midnight, I had to call my parents and explain that I was in New York at a karate school and wouldn't be home until after 1 A.M.

When I opened the door at home, Pops was waiting, finally fed up with all the notes from school, the stealing and skipping and lying. He snatched me by the arm and dragged me into the house, swinging for my head. I was ducking and blocking and ducking and blocking, and he chased me through the house and into the bathroom. Cornered, I slid down into the bathtub, and Dad leaned over and slapped the shit out of me. He wasn't a violent guy; that was maybe only the third or fourth time he ever hit me.

It certainly wasn't enough to convince me to stop training. The martial arts were exhilarating. The more I learned, the more I wanted to learn. Part of that had to do with learning to fight, obviously. My school was very tough, and we were expected to fight all the time. But once I began training, I really didn't have to fight as often. It only took a few fights before I had earned a reputation as someone to avoid and the actual fights became rare. If the guy on the other end of the argument knew my reputation, the fights had a way of evaporating before I had to do anything.

I think a lot of students start out the way I did, trying to become better fighters and realizing that fighting is only one part of the martial arts. I was slowly being transformed by the athleticism, the discipline, and the purpose that the arts gave to my life. Usually it takes a person three to four years of intensive training to become a black belt. It took me a little less than two and a half.

For the first time in my life I had ambition and drive and I was inspired. But it didn't all come from within. I had great teachers, and one of the greatest was Keith Keller, a tae kwon do instructor from Paterson, who was the first man to take a personal interest in me. It wasn't about money. It wasn't about business. He believed in me. And because he believed in me, I wanted desperately to live up to and to exceed his expectations. I would train and train until I was covered in blood. I'd push myself beyond the physical pain. I'd push myself into extreme fatigue and exhaustion. But I'd always come back the next day. I wanted more than anything to prove to him that I was worthy of his approval, that I would honor his hopes for me, that I would measure up and win, in every way, his respect and ultimately his love. I was a young man who was given the gift of guidance, a young man in dire need of direction and discipline. And he gave it to me.

The arts were the first bridge I saw out of Paterson, out of the miserable life that everyone saw for me, that I was making for myself. Mastering the arts was the first thing that began to fulfill me, the first thing that seemed to come easy to me. But I think it also was an answer to all those people who only saw me as a truant and a troublemaker, who couldn't see past the poor and uneducated street thug, and to Mr. Johns, the teacher who predicted I'd be nothing more than a vegetable.

5

THE SWEET SHOP

1971

I have always wanted to be a cop. At four and five I was practicing my quick draw. By six I was bugging my parents for a Dick Tracy holster and handgun. I have wanted to be a cop for so long, I don't even know where the idea originated. If a television program featured a cop, I couldn't turn the channel. I especially loved *Kojak,* with Telly Savalas as an NYPD detective squad commander who sucked on a lollipop as he barreled around Manhattan in a gray sedan, always in a race against time—to save the hostages taken during the Brinks truck heist, to clear the name of his dead partner, to find the dirty cop who tipped off the drug dealers.

When the movie *Serpico* came out, I must've seen it twenty times. Some cops didn't like it because in their minds it was about a guy who ratted out his fellow officers, but I don't see it that way at all, nor do I believe that most cops feel that way. To me it's a movie about integrity, honor, and courage, and when Al Pacino is shot in that hallway and he falls back on that tile floor, it is probably one of the most powerful scenes I've ever seen in a movie: a man paying the price for his belief in justice. That's what it means to be a cop. Narcotics undercovers in the NYPD—whether they like the movie or not, whether they agree with Serpico's cause or not—can surely relate to that scene. Every day they walk into buildings just like that one in an attempt to buy drugs from people they have never met. When they walk up to that door and knock, they don't know what's waiting for them on the other side. And sometimes, just sometimes, they pay the ultimate price in their own pursuit of justice.

I know that feeling, and it was my biggest fear as an undercover, the fear that I would die on one of those filthy black-and-white-tiled floors of some rat-infested tenement building. That image so disturbed me that each time I entered a building I would tell my partner, "If anything happens, just don't leave me there alone."

It wasn't just movie cops that I idolized. Even when I was a little kid, if a cop came into my neighborhood, I'd stop what I was doing and watch him. Some of my friends were nervous around the police, but I always felt comfortable talking to them, answering their questions and helping them out when they needed something.

I suppose one good thing about being a rowdy kid in the neighborhood was that I got to know all the cops in town. I'd see them on their foot posts, or they'd see me hanging out on some corner, and they'd wave me over. "Hey, Kerik. Get your ass over here."

I think they realized that even though I was a handful, I wasn't a criminal. I didn't drink or use drugs. I didn't mug people or steal cars or commit any of the serious crimes that many of the kids in my high school were already committing. And while my friends and I were fighting all the time, it wasn't like the fights of today. No one ever pulled a gun or a knife. There were broken noses and cracked ribs, but you didn't go to school worried that you might die that day.

For the Paterson Police Department in 1971, it must have been a relief to have a kid whose biggest crimes were skipping school and throwing eggs at cars. As I got older, some of the cops even became friends and wound up as martial arts students of mine.

A lot of the cops I knew used to hang out at a little café

that one of my friends' parents owned, a place called The
Sweet Shop. Cops ate there every day, having coffee and
pastries and sandwiches. Some were nicer than others, and
in a short time I got to know them well. There was one patrolman whom I especially grew to admire, Jerry Giamanco,
a big Italian cop who looked like Clemenza from *The Godfather.* The other cops called him No Neck.

One afternoon, No Neck was sitting in The Sweet Shop
eating his lunch. I was at the counter behind him, hanging
out with my buddies, laughing and being a nuisance, when
No Neck turned as slowly as that tree trunk beneath his head
would allow. "Hey," he shouted. "Shut up! You're making
too much damn noise. I'm trying to eat here."

"Man, please," I said, and turned my back to him. The
next thing I knew I was flying off the stool and landing upside down, my head on the floor and my feet in the air above
me. From the floor I could see No Neck chewing his sandwich upside down, staring at me.

"I am not going to tell you again," he said between bites.
"Shut the fuck up." I did. And when I'd see him anytime after that, it was always "Yes, sir" and "No, sir."

But the thing I remember most about those cops was
something that happened when I was fourteen and was
hanging out in The Sweet Shop with my friends.

Some guy walked in, and he may have been drunk or
stoned because he started hassling the woman who owned
the store, asking for money or free food or something. He
grew more belligerent and flipped over some stands on the
counter. I was just a kid, sitting there watching this, unsure if
I was big enough to do anything about it.

But before I could decide, a couple of the Paterson cops
came in and, as calmly as possible, grabbed the guy, handcuffed him, dragged him outside, and arrested him. And just
like that, it was over. No heroics or gunfire or blood, just two
guys doing their job.

But what a job! When someone did something wrong,
these guys actually did something about it. I didn't see any-

one else doing anything about all the things that were fucked up in the world. Not at home. Not at school. Not in Newark or Clifton or Paterson and certainly not back in Ohio, where there was no one to help my mother.

I watched these cops actually do something about the world, and I was happy that someone was taking care of people, that someone was watching and protecting them.

I liked most of the cops I met. They were funny and tough and eager to handle whatever problems came up. I saw myself in them, and for the first time I could imagine something I could do with my life that would be valuable.

Like any group of cops, a few were mean or lazy or took shortcuts. And maybe a few were downright corrupt, I don't know. But when it came down to it, the overwhelming majority of those guys went to work each day just looking for a chance to do the right thing. How many people can honestly say that?

One day when I was fifteen, hanging out on Broadway, a bus stopped across the street and an old woman climbed off. Immediately three older teenagers were on her. They took her purse and knocked her down. I was running after them before I realized it, up blocks and down alleys until finally I caught one of them and dragged him down by the shirt. We wrestled around until I got his arm behind his back and dragged him back to the corner. When the police came, I handed him over.

There wasn't any kind of reward or a newspaper story, nothing like there would be today, and I didn't expect anything for what I had done. But I do remember feeling the enormous surge in adrenaline and the challenge in the pursuit. I remember the pride in knowing I had done something good and, best of all, the fantastic feeling when the woman simply said, "Thank you." For the first time, I felt like a hero. I liked that feeling.

"JUST sign it, Ma."

She eyed me suspiciously. "But what is it?"

"I told you, it's a note to get me back in school." I explained again how I'd been suspended and that she had to sign this form for the registrar to acknowledge that she knew about my suspension and wanted me back in school.

I held it out to her, the top section covered by my hand. She leaned over the kitchen table and signed. That afternoon I took the form to the registrar's office at Eastside High and turned it in. I had officially quit school. No one in the office tried to talk me out of it. No one said a word.

And just like that, in May 1972, the spring of my junior year, I dropped out of high school. I was sixteen.

I came home right afterward and told my mother that the form she'd actually signed was my permission to drop out. She was furious. "You can't quit school!"

"I just did," I said.

When my father came home he was quieter but no less grave. "Okay," he said. "You do what you want, but you're not living here unless you find a job."

Luckily, I already had a job. The summer before, I'd gone to work for Frank Malatesta, who was in the process of making a small fortune with a cross-country moving company based in Paterson. I was a combination of gofer and muscle, running errands and helping to load the big tractor-trailer, then riding in the truck to places as far away as Florida and California and unloading. It was good hard work and it was a chance to see the country. They paired me with older guys who could drive, and I just rode in the cab, taking in stretches of countryside—mountains and beaches and scenes that were completely alien to a kid raised in Jersey.

Now that I was officially out of school, I went to work for Malatesta full-time. We'd pack the truck and leave Monday morning, drive to Palm Beach, Florida, or someplace, and return on Friday or sometimes Saturday or Sunday. Then on Monday morning we'd start out again. I was a good worker and got along well with the older guys. Early on, though, the idea of working every week began to wear on me, and one Sunday, when the weekend had seemed to last about two hours, I asked my mom to tell Frank that I was sick and wouldn't be able to go out with the truck on Monday.

She shook her head. "Beez, I never lied for your father. I won't lie for you."

"But, Ma—" I was interrupted by the phone. She answered it, keeping her eyes on me the whole time. "No, Frank," she said, "Bernie's right here." And she handed me the phone. And when I hung up, off to work I went. Both she and Dad remembered Mr. Johns's prediction that I would be nothing but a vegetable, and they worked hard to teach me about the work ethic I needed now that I was in the adult world.

My father even went so far as to get me a job with his company, Tech Tool. Mom had been asking him to get me a job there, but Dad was afraid I wasn't up to it, that maybe I'd embarrass myself or him. Still, he got me the job, and I started riding to work with him and his friend Ed.

The shop where he worked was small and was filled with presses, drills, lathes, and other machines for crafting metal parts. Guys would bend over these hot, oily machines all day—some of them, like Pops, for up to twelve hours at a time. Every day was the same. My dad, for instance, ran a turret lathe, and every day he sat at that lathe, machining the same parts over and over, hour after hour. I couldn't imagine spending the rest of my life bent over some machine, churning out bolts.

After I'd worked at Tech Tool for about four days, Dad looked up and saw that I wasn't at my post. He went into the bathroom. I wasn't there either. He walked over to his buddy Tommy and asked if he'd seen me.

"Yeah," Tommy said. "He's in the parking lot. He said to tell you he was tired."

My dad's jaw must've hung to the floor. "Tired?"

He waited until quitting time to come out to the car. "What's your problem?"

"I just didn't feel like working anymore."

He didn't look at me the whole drive home. The next

morning Ed picked us up, and we'd driven about half a mile
before my dad said, "Beez? You gonna work today?"

"Yeah. If I have to."

"What do you mean if you have to?"

"Dad," I said, "I hate this job."

He had Ed stop the car. "Get out," he said. I got out and
walked home. Dad went into work and told the foreman that
he'd fired me.

"You can't fire people," the foreman said.

"Oh, I can fire my own boy," my dad said. "But I'll tell
you what. I'll let you decide. Him or me?" When the foreman didn't answer, my dad went back to work. It amazes me
to this day how hard my father worked all those years. He
worked for that company forty years before it went bank-
rupt, and the pension that he'd worked for all those years
disappeared with the rest of the company. My father got
nothing out of those forty years except the right to keep
working. Sixty-seven years old now, he still works full-time.

My dad spent a lot of years worrying that I wouldn't in-
herit his work ethic, that I was lazy and lacked resolve. My
first few months out of school reinforced that worry in his
mind. His earlier warning echoed through the house: if I
didn't pull my own weight, I was out on my own. I was constantly trying to borrow money from him and Mom. Eventually my dad's patience ran out. He and I got into a huge
argument and I moved out. I cruised around and stayed with
different friends—a couple of nights here, a couple of nights
there.

In the afternoons I'd go to the grade school and see my
sisters and little Don because I missed them so much. They
were heartbroken to see their big brother and their parents
fight so much, to see their brother with no direction in his
life, scraping by with friends. For a couple of weeks, they'd
meet me near Eastside Park on the way to school and give
me their lunch money because they felt so bad. It was the
girls' idea, but Don gave up his money too, even though at
five he didn't understand what was going on.

Still, he has a vivid memory of those mornings near the park, mostly because of what happened one day. Three or four teenagers watched Vickie Lynn, Terry, and Don give me their lunch money. These guys swooped in, figuring they'd take the money off me. But I wasn't the kid from Branch Brook Park anymore. To this day, Don says, he remembers the flash of feet and hands, windmills and roundhouses, until all four guys were limping away, wiping the blood from their faces.

I don't think I realized until later how much Don idolized me. I was his hero, his black-belt big brother. He watched everything I did. When I later left home for the military, he wound up in the hospital because of ulcers that he got missing me and worrying about me. In a way he was right to worry. I look back now and see that I had no idea what to do with myself. As much as I hated high school, as terrible a place as Eastside was for learning, I dropped out and had nowhere to land. I was lost.

I'm not a person who spends much time worrying about his weaknesses. I don't see the point. But if I could go back and change one thing, I would finish high school and go on to college. I have never stopped learning and have found other sources of education—from the U.S. Army to a long line of mentors and role models, from the New York Police Department to Mayor Rudolph Giuliani. I have managed a great deal with very little formal education, and yet I will forever be saddled with those three terrible words: *high school dropout.* On one of the happiest days of my life, I was devastated when the Associated Press headline read "High School Dropout Appointed NYC Police Commissioner."

People sometimes use those words to marvel at all I have accomplished. I will forever be "the first high school dropout to . . ." I know people think they are complimenting me, but all I hear is the echo of a young man's failure, of decisions made before I had any idea what life was about, before I knew all that I was capable of doing.

* * *

"HEY, Ma, I joined the army."

"Sure you did, Beez." For months I had been telling Mom that I was joining the military. She wasn't buying it anymore. They'd had enough of my nonsense.

"Seriously. I leave in a week."

"Sure you do, Beez."

My parents had let me move back in after I'd stayed a couple of months with friends, but things were still strained between us. I wasn't earning very much money, and I was spending money—mostly my parents'—like it was free. They had moved to a slightly bigger house on 18th Street in Paterson, but the surroundings didn't change the basic fact that I was going nowhere. Off and on I kept working for Malatesta's moving company, but the thing I really wanted to be was impossible. I wanted to be a cop.

A lot of my friends were taking the police exam in New Jersey, and I watched them with envy because a high school dropout wasn't eligible to take the test. That's when I began talking to military recruiters about becoming a military policeman, and by 1974 I had begun to consider joining either the Marine Corps or the army.

"Pops, I'm joining the marines."

"Right. When are they coming for you?"

"Seriously, Pops. I'm gonna be in the marines."

"Sure you are."

I had turned eighteen, and it was as if Paterson were shrinking around me. I just couldn't take all the same old people, the fights and hassles, the lack of money and opportunity. I'd reached black belt in the arts and was competing and fighting at a rare level, going from teacher to teacher, but it wasn't enough. I felt that if I were going to continue my growth, I'd need to go east.

I talked to the army recruiter, and he said there was a definite possibility I could make it to Korea—the ancestral home of tae kwon do and the place where some of the best masters were teaching. At that time the Vietnam War was winding down, but the recruiter reminded me that there were no guarantees it wouldn't flare up again, and I might end up in combat. That was fine, I told him. While I didn't relish the idea of combat, I also knew I would be ready if it came to that, and would serve honorably.

On July 26, 1974, Mom was washing dishes in the kitchen when I came in and announced that I thought I had the best chance of becoming a cop if I joined the army and became a military policeman. She'd heard this so many times she didn't even bother looking up.

"Okay, Beez."

"I've already started processing," I told her. "I leave tomorrow."

"Right," Mom said. "You have a good time."

"I'm serious," I said.

"Sure you are, Beez."

I met Dad on the porch when he came home from work. "Dad," I said, "I'm going in the army tomorrow morning. Could you loan me twenty-five dollars so I can go out with my friends?"

"Oh, sure," he said, and walked right past me. But he stopped and turned. "Beez, you didn't really join the army."

"I did."

He stared at me for a long time, not believing me. He remembered my quitting at Tech Tool, and he didn't think I had the resolve and the discipline to make it as a soldier. "Okay, I'll give you fifty bucks," he said. "But if you're lying again, don't come home. And if you have joined the army, and you come home AWOL, I will turn your ass in."

"Don't worry about that, Dad."

All day I was packing up my duffel bags and Mom was laughing, amazed at how far I'd go for a joke.

"Ma, I'm really leaving."

"Sure, Beez."

"I'm telling you, I leave at eight in the morning. They're coming to get me."

She says that's when she was sure I was lying. "Beez, the army doesn't come to get you."

When the doorbell rang the next morning, Mom was making breakfast. She walked to the door and opened it. There was a staff sergeant in uniform. She immediately started crying. Dad came out, saw the man in uniform, and walked straight into the kitchen for a beer. With Mom tugging at my arm, I followed the staff sergeant out the door with my duffel bag and we climbed into a green Rambler with white government plates. We drove down 18th Avenue to Route 20, on my way to basic training. Like that, Paterson was behind me. And in front of me was a life—both good and bad—that I could never have imagined, a life that still seems to me as improbable as my joining the army must have seemed to my parents.

BOOT camp was pretty much what I'd imagined, reveille before dawn, popping out of bed as a drill sergeant yells an inch from your face that you're a maggot or a fucking pussy, and now you've got ten minutes to dress and shave and make your bunk before a five-mile run through the hot sand. And you haven't even had breakfast yet.

I can't say I liked basic training at the Army Infantry Training Center at Fort Dix, near Trenton, New Jersey. Who likes boot camp? But as I trained in the summer of 1974, it wasn't as hard for me as it was for some of the other guys. I had been working out pretty much nonstop in the arts and I was in tremendous shape, so the physical part wasn't hard. And the mental side—the discipline and the challenge—was something I had been craving without even realizing it. My father's concern that I was too soft or lazy or undisciplined turned out to be completely wrong. The military was the first time that life made sense to me—here was a code, a sense of honor and duty.

After basic, I went to Fort Gordon in Georgia for military police school. Of all the things I took away from my training there, the most important might have been my understanding of the power of the uniform. We always looked sharp. Our helmets shone like black glass. Our clothes were stiff as cardboard. We were charged with enforcing military protocol, so we had to be impeccable to be able to walk up to a guy and say, Your hat is cockeyed, or Your boots aren't shined.

Sometimes people outside the military fail to grasp the importance of the uniform. That's one thing I've stressed in every command position I've ever held. Sometimes you have to teach a person to respect himself, and the place to start is often with his appearance. If a soldier or a police officer—or a dogcatcher, for that matter—*looks* professional and capable, he's made the first steps toward *being* professional and capable. It was one of the things I learned in the military and one of the reasons I trace my transformation to the day I went ahead and took the plunge into the U.S. Army.

In the late fall of 1974, I finished up my MP training at Fort Gordon and came home for thirty days before leaving for Korea. I glided down the streets, full of the pride of the uniform and the change I could feel in myself. My parents had been to Fort Dix while I was in basic training, but as I strode into the house—my eyes forward and unblinking, the seam on my pants as straight as a midwestern highway—I could see the immense pride in their faces. But there was something more. They stood there staring at the son they had feared would be "nothing but a vegetable," and I think they saw for the first time the deep reserves of strength and commitment that I had. And so the look on their faces was not just pride but complete and total shock.

It certainly wouldn't be the last time I'd get that look.

6

KOREA

1974

I'D never been so fucking cold. The dead of night, December 21, 1974, and I was rattling around in the back of an army truck on my way to the frigid processing center at the army base on the edge of the Korean city of Pyeongtaek. Nineteen years old, about to be away from home at Christmas for the first time, I didn't know anyone and didn't speak a lick of Korean. In a few short months I'd gone from being a rebellious kid at home to being a soldier on my own in a foreign country. A cold foreign country. At the base, I stood off by myself watching soldiers move past in cold, huddled groups. Finally one of them paused and said, "Come on, we're going downtown."

"I can't," I explained, "I just got here and I'm restricted to base."

I spent the next two days sitting on a bunk in my Quonset hut watching my breath and filling out paperwork at brigade headquarters so I could be processed into my MP unit. I told myself it would have to get better when I got to my command.

On the afternoon of Christmas Eve, they moved me again, in the back of another cold, rattling two-and-a-half-ton truck. If anything, my actual command was worse, a tiny post—just twenty or so MPs guarding a nuclear missile battery on the edge of a tiny village called Sak Su Ni. I jumped out of the back of the truck in the middle of the night and looked at a frozen dirt field of Quonset huts that made the last base look like Atlantic City. Cold, disoriented, and uncomfortable, I knew I had made a mistake. All my visions of military life, of an adventurous foreign posting, of studying martial arts— all of this faded into a vision of two years spent huddling against the cold in lonely, remote villages.

And then I woke up and it was Christmas morning, the Quonset hut filled with light. It was sunny and warm and people were everywhere, smiling and friendly, saying "Merry Christmas!" to each other and slapping me on the back. I had breakfast, and then my houseboy, Mr. Lee, showed up and introduced himself.

"Where are your boots?" he asked. I handed them to him. "Your laundry?" I handed him that too. Later Mr. Lee brought the boots back polished so clean I could see my own smile in them. I hadn't understood the concept of house-boys, who were common throughout the military in the Far East. For a small amount of money, these guys would do all the grunt work. Like a lot of servicemen, I relied on my houseboy for everything. He knew more about military protocol than I did, more than anyone I met. He was the guy you went to if you needed something done. You needed a whistle? Mr. Lee knew the kind of whistle, where to get it, how much to pay.

Christmas morning, I explained to Mr. Lee that I was a black belt and wanted to study tae kwon do. Sure, he said, there was an instructor, whose name was also Lee, who would come to the base three days a week to teach. In New York City I had also studied with a Korean, Master Y. J. Chang, and I wondered if the native Korean teachers would be as good as he was. It didn't take long to answer my question. Master Lee was phenomenal. Humble and laid-back, when it came time to fight, he was devastating. I was ecstatic, and I think Master Lee was rather intrigued because I was something that wasn't supposed to be. Americans all over Korea were learning tae kwon do, but they never became as good as the Koreans. Most Americans just weren't limber enough and didn't have the powerful legs required of tae kwon do students. And there was something deeper, maybe in the nature of Americans, that didn't quite click with the Korean arts. But in me Lee found an American who had mastered tae kwon do, who could fight like a Korean. When I would go down to the village to study with Master Lee, locals would stop and watch, shaking their heads in disbelief. It was as if a Korean had come over to America, picked up a basketball, and started dunking.

Sometimes when Master Lee came to the base he'd bring his most promising Korean students to work out with me, and he'd watch with a kind of pride as his American student kicked the hell out of the best Koreans he could find.

Work wasn't always challenging, but I still loved the discipline of army life. I patrolled the perimeter of our small base or took my shift standing in a guard tower. It was as if something clicked for me those first months in the army, as if I'd found the thing I was supposed to do with my life. I felt myself growing more and more confident and believing for the first time that I might have leadership abilities inside of me, just waiting to come out.

The army was molding me into the kind of man I dreamed of becoming. My martial arts training was going well and I was fighting in competitions and winning just about all of them. This was exactly what I'd come to Korea hoping to find. Here I was, six thousand miles from New Jersey, and for the first time in my life, I felt like I was at home.

I didn't see Tibor Kerekes at first. I heard him. I was at dog training school, near Taegu, and was walking past a soldier putting his dog away when I heard a sound as familiar as my own voice. In fact, it was my voice, or my accent anyway, a perfect Jersey accent smack in the middle of Korea. It's one of those things you have no idea that you've missed until you hear it. I turned back. There was this skinny, athletic, wholesome, but slick-looking kid.

"Hey, where you from?"

He smiled at my accent. "I'm from Jersey."

"No shit! What are you doing here?"

"I just left the Presidio in San Francisco. I came to study martial arts."

"Yeah? Where you at?"

"Just started," he said. "I'm a white belt. How about you."

"Black belt," I said.

He didn't really believe me. He knew that mastering the martial arts involved not only fighting but also attaining humility and grace. To him I came across as brash and overconfident. But what he didn't know was that I wasn't bragging when I said I was a black belt; I just was.

Finding Tibor in the middle of Korea was like bumping into a brother I didn't know I had. As with brothers, there were things about us that were eerily similar. And also as with brothers, there were things that couldn't have been more different. Where I came across as brash, he was shy. Where my natural impulse was to take over every room I entered, Tibor's instinct was to fit in, get to know people. I liked the way he dressed and carried himself—quieter and with less impact than me, but effective in his own way. Later I'd help pull him out of his shell, and he'd serve like a brake when I wanted to run on some wild tear. And over time, we'd learn to balance our personalities perfectly to get things done: Tibor the politician and Bernie the bull.

But that first day, as we made plans to work out in the arts together, while I was excited to have found someone from Jersey who was into the arts, Tibor wasn't exactly sure he liked me. A few hours later, he was even less sure.

That night he took his patrol dog out on his shift, from 9 P.M. to 6 A.M., then put his dog away and climbed into his bunk. At 7 A.M. his door crashed open and he opened his eyes to see me standing there.

"What are you doing?" I asked.

He looked over at the cracked doorframe, then back at me. "Sleeping. What do you think?"

"Come on. Let's go, I thought you wanted to train."

He followed me down to the gym and we began stretching. Tibor admitted later that he had attributed my stories about being a black belt to my cockiness, and he figured that our skills would probably be about the same. He bent and twisted and stretched and prepared to spar with me. Meanwhile, I began stretching as always, dropping immediately into a Russian split, my legs going in opposite directions, my body still facing forward, chest and face now resting on the floor.

"Holy shit," Tibor said.

And then we sparred, but not for long. My kicks came at Tibor from every angle and he swatted at them like flies, trying in vain to keep up. But even though I knocked him around pretty good, he stood up to it. For two guys into the arts, this was instant bonding. Tibor could see that I was as deep into tae kwon do and as talented as I had professed to be. I could see that he had innate athletic ability, which made up in some ways for his lack of experience in the arts. By the time we were done, Tibor and I had become fast friends.

Three weeks and many ass-whippings later, we were sparring on a soccer field on the base. I was about to hit him with a spinning back kick when my left foot imbedded itself in a piece of glass, and as I turned, the glass cut around and through my middle toe like a can opener.

"Well," Tibor said with a smirk on his face as I lay there bleeding, "that's about the only way I'm going to beat you. Serves you right."

He and another soldier had to carry me a quarter mile to the nearest doctor, who yanked on the thread in a ham-fisted way and sewed up my foot while I sat there grimacing and fighting my urge to slap the shit out of him. Since I was just about finished with dog school, I was shipped back to Sak Su Ni so my foot could heal. I wasn't happy about leaving Tibor, but I had a feeling that we would remain friends throughout our time there and long after. Over the next eight months we hooked up at martial arts tournaments and visited each other's bases a couple of times.

Looking back, the pattern of your life emerges like a road in a rearview mirror. I see now that Tibor was the first of a handful of exceptional men of rare talent and courage who were slowly surrounding me and helping to build and mold the person I have become.

HOUSEBOYS weren't the only people eagerly awaiting American servicemen in South Korea. Everywhere an American base was built, a small Korean village would sprout in its shadow—a few stores, some bars, and dozens of small hooches, or huts, filled with women interested in meeting Korea's new residents.

By one estimate, one in every five women in South Korea worked as a prostitute in the late 1960s and early 1970s. Part of that was the culture of arranged marriage and male domination in which men weren't expected to be in love with their wives and prostitution was essentially looked upon as necessary—a kind of release from a very rigid social structure. Part of it was the economics of a country that was still healing from a civil war and trying to join the twentieth century sixty years late.

I'd had my share of girlfriends back in the States—very few of them serious relationships—and like a lot of young men running off to the military, when I was leaving for Korea I had even talked to the girl I was seeing about getting married upon my return.

But in Korea, my primary interest was in one thing and one thing only—the martial arts. At night, when the base was empty and every one of my friends was off doing his own thing, my mind would wander and loneliness would set in. Other guys in my unit would invite me down to the village, but because I didn't drink or smoke pot, there wasn't much there for me. I quickly came to realize that I needed companionship to keep my sanity. But I wasn't interested in chasing down one-night stands or working out some transaction every time I wanted to be with someone. I wanted to meet a woman who was interested in me, not in what little money I had.

After about four weeks, a girlfriend of one of the soldiers introduced me to a young girl named Yi, who lived in the village not far from the base. She was sweet, cute, very shy, and not at all interested in the nightlife in the village. It wasn't long before seeing her became a nightly ritual, and on some nights I would stay in the village with her instead of returning to base. Within a few weeks, we had moved in together and my life seemed complete. It was a simple domestic life, and we cared about each other. I would go to work and she'd stay home, and on my days off we would take short day trips around the countryside, and in the evenings she would watch me train. She loved to go to tournaments with me, loved the way Koreans watched me, surprised at the way I fought. She'd hang on my arm at those tournaments and reveled in the looks we got as we walked out afterward, trophy in hand.

As the months went by, things were going great. I was training like a lunatic, working harder than ever, and enjoying every day to the fullest. My mind was free of worry and nothing seemed to bother me. I felt like I was sitting on top of the world. That was all about to change.

IN May of 1975, I had volunteered for sentry dog school and been chosen out of five or six other candidates to travel to Camp Carroll in Taegu for school. But when I ran down to the village to tell Yi I had been selected and would be going off to school, she wasn't interested in what I had to say. She seemed distant, and when I asked her what was wrong, she didn't even have to answer. She gently took my hand, lifted up her blouse, and placed my hand on her belly. I stood there for what seemed an eternity looking at her and hoping I had misunderstood. With her eyes filling with tears, she said very softly in Korean, "There is a baby here." I felt my whole world had just come to an end. I'm ashamed now to recall how young and stupid and selfish I was then. I had no idea what to do, and I hoped that if I ignored it, the problem would go away. I tried to hide behind my youth and ignorance.

Over the next few days, I was preparing to leave for school but just couldn't get my head together. I couldn't concentrate on anything around me. I didn't want to admit that inside this woman's body was a baby—my baby.

I left for dog school, met Tibor, and returned to Sak Su Ni in mid-July. Yi's belly was growing, and so was her enthusiasm for having the child. As strong and courageous as I could be, I was scared to death of the situation I was in. Ironically, it was she who gave me comfort when I should have been comforting her. She would constantly remind me how happy she was that it was my baby and that the baby would always know who its daddy was. At some point I casually mentioned that perhaps I could take the baby to the United States and have my mom help out until we figured out exactly what we were going to do, and she snapped, "No way!" Then I was hit with another devastating blow.

I was transferred.

INCHON was some five hundred miles away from Sak Su Ni and Yi. As I prepared to go there, my head was spinning. Yi's belly was growing, I hadn't told anyone, including my parents, and Yi and I hadn't really talked about our future plans. I didn't know what to do. There wasn't anyone I felt I could turn to for help or guidance. I was confused and embarrassed and didn't understand the gravity of having a child. I felt as if my whole world were caving in.

We wrote to each other over the next few months, and Yi came to see me, her belly larger each time. I would get a note from her, and sometimes a woman from the village would come with a message about her condition. In the second week of October I received word that she had left Sak

Su Ni and traveled to be with friends and family in another part of Korea.

On October 25, 1975, Yi gave birth to a beautiful baby girl. About three weeks later, she brought the baby to Inchon to see me, and what should have been one of the happiest days of my life was the most heart-wrenching.

My baby was wrapped in a white and pink knitted blanket with only her face and dark hair sticking out. She was beautiful and soft and had the sweet smell of baby powder all over her. I cried as I held her for the first time. Again it was Yi who was our strength and comfort.

We agreed to name her Yi Sa (Lisa). Yi stayed for three days, and when she prepared to return to Sak Su Ni, I was sick. I was so distraught that I threw up. I would have given my arms or legs to have been able to relieve that pain. We both knew I was leaving Korea soon and promised each other to keep in touch. When I took her to the bus stop, I felt as if someone had taken a spoon and carved out a piece of my heart, a piece that is still missing today.

In early February of 1976, I was transferred to Fort Bragg, North Carolina. I spoke to Yi before I left and again tried to suggest that the baby would be better off in the United States with me, but she wouldn't hear of it. I cried on the telephone, afraid that I might never speak to her again.

It occurs to me now that our lives circle back and that the patterns can be relentless and downright cruel. A boy with nightmares of being abandoned by his mother grows into a man who re-creates the nightmare without a remote understanding of why. Even now, these are difficult things for me to admit. Here I was, doing to an innocent child something very like what had been done to me.

You devote your life to fighting for something as abstract and elusive as justice, and while much of the motivation comes from wanting to fix the outside world—all the bullies and bad guys—a major portion of it comes from within, from the fears and nightmares you have as a child. It kills me

to know that the first opportunity I had to undo some of the
sorrow of my own life, I wasn't strong enough to figure out
how to get it accomplished. This was a mistake I will always
regret, and I pray to God that one day I can make it right.

7

HOME

1976

MY brother, Don, used to dream that I was walking down the sidewalk in Paterson wearing my shiny dress uniform. He was eight years old and had trouble dealing with the fact that I was gone. I was as much a father figure to him as a big brother, and the doctors blamed his childhood ulcers on his missing me. So he didn't quite believe his eyes when he was out riding his bike one late-February afternoon and looked up to see me walking toward him, smiling, my head held back, my cap pulled down to my eyes.

"Bernie?"

I told Dad I was coming back, but I asked him not to tell anyone else. I snatched Don up in my arms and carried him to the house. Terry came to the door first and started screaming and crying, and then Vickie Lynn and Mom joined in, grabbing and pulling me in every direction, and I wondered for a moment if it might not have been safer to have told them I was coming home.

The first week I was home was total chaos because they were so happy to see me and impressed at the continued transformation from schoolboy hellion to crisp soldier. But it was hard for me to enjoy the time completely because something was tearing me up inside. I was a wreck, nauseated much of the time, and I had dreams of just crawling into a shell and disappearing.

I told Mom first. We sat in the bathroom, crying together, she on the edge of the tub and me cowering on the floor as I told her how it was killing me, having this baby that I wanted but couldn't see. I told her I wanted to stay in touch with Yi and the baby and hoped that over time we'd figure out what to do.

Soon after arriving back in the United States, I sat down over dinner with the girl I'd been seeing before I left. We had talked about marriage and a life together, but at the time we were young and immature and probably mostly influenced by my forthcoming departure for Korea. Her family was from a small town in Italy, and her father saw me as a rene-gade and constantly tried to convince her to find someone else. During dinner I told her about Yi and the baby, and she just sat there staring at me. I wasn't sure what was going through her mind, but it was apparent that she was stunned and in pain and extremely upset. I might have kept it a se-cret, but I couldn't lie to her. We never finished dinner. I paid the check, left the restaurant alone, and didn't speak to her for over twenty years. She went on to get married and have two lovely girls.

I tried to do the right thing. For a while, Yi and I stayed in touch, and she even sent pictures of the baby, but then sud-denly the letters and notes stopped coming. In late 1977, af-ter I had been discharged from the service, I got a letter from Yi saying she had married an American serviceman and moved to the United States. She sent me her telephone num-ber, and we began speaking once a week. She sent more pic-tures, and I began making plans to see Lisa.

Just as everything seemed to be going in the right direc-tion, Yi's husband complained to the military authorities that I was interfering with his family and harassing him and his wife. I assumed at the time that he was unaware Yi had been contacting me. Then I received a call from the federal au-thorities ordering me to leave Yi and her family alone. They also threatened to arrest me and lock me up if I contacted her again. I was shocked. At that point, instead of fighting, as I should have done, I backed off. Months later, when I was desperate to see my daughter and couldn't take it anymore, I tried to call Yi again, but the number had been changed. When I sent a note to the address she had given me, it was returned.

I never spoke to her again.

I have looked for her ever since. I've never stopped looking. I have searched and tried to contact people who knew her, and I have found nothing. For all I know, Lisa's mother and stepfather may have changed her name. Perhaps they told her that Yi's husband was her father and she doesn't even know I exist. Maybe Yi and the baby went back to Korea. I don't know. I don't even know where to start. Sometime in 1978 a letter arrived with no return address and no readable postmark, with a photo in it. Lisa was pretty and smiling, her hair at her shoulders, those big dark eyes beaming out at the camera. It's the last picture I have of her, and I keep it in my desk drawer.

I was a man when I came home from Korea. It was as simple as that. I felt different, complete in a way. The military had transformed me, taken all those random parts—toughness and resolve and a vague desire for something larger than myself—and crafted a soldier. The army put me on the path that I'm still on today. I joined because I wanted to study martial arts and to get a good job as a cop, but I returned with something close to a religious belief in the ideals of loyalty, duty, and respect. I loved almost everything about the army—the uniform, the lifestyle, the rigorous attention to detail. And I was good at it.

As military policemen, we were required to be impeccable in our appearance. At Fort Bragg, the MP who looked the best each morning got to take the day off from patrol. That MP was called *Numero Uno,* or Number One. I spent hours trying to become *Numero Uno.* It had little to do with taking the day off from work, because I actually liked to work. I just wanted to win. If there was going to be a "best" at something, then I was going to be it.

I polished my helmet and boots with cotton balls until they were black mirrors. I starched my pants so stiff I had to straighten a coat hanger to pry the legs apart before I could put them on. You could cut glass with the crease in my pants. The hardest part of the uniform was the cuffs of our pants, which we tucked into our boots, so I'd roll a piece of cardboard, attach two lines of pennies to the cardboard with masking tape, and then put it in the cuffs of my pants so they'd hang perfectly straight above my boots. Guys would stare at my pant legs, trying to figure out what made them so straight around the top of the boots.

I won *Numero Uno* just about every day. The sergeant would walk the line, looking up and down at twenty crisp, clean MPs before shaking his head. "Kerik. Looks like you've got it again."

The other guys quickly realized they weren't going to beat me, and as soon as the sergeant would announce that I'd won, I would look down the line and see two or three heads leaning forward, guys who desperately wanted a day off nodding and whispering, "Hey, Kerik. Pick me."

"Sarge, I'm gonna work for this guy over here," I'd say, and later that soldier would pay me ten or twenty bucks for my day off. It was perfect. I got to be the best. And I got extra pay to go on patrol.

After I'd been back a couple of months, I got a letter from Tibor, who was still in Korea. As letters go, it was pretty short, but I couldn't have been happier when I read it: "Please see attached orders. You're not going to believe this."

Tibor had been assigned to the Twenty-first Military Police Company, 503rd MP Battalion, Eighteenth Airborne Corps. At Fort Bragg, North Carolina. My battalion. My company. Of all the possible postings around the entire world, the chances that he would get the exact same command as me were unbelievable. He assumed that I'd arranged it, even though I was just a private. "If any grunt had that kind of pull, it'd be you," he said.

Tibor always said I had a quality that transcended rank— "a command presence," as he used to put it. During combat, soldiers say, rank sometimes falls away and soldiers instinctually know whom to follow. Even though I was fortunate enough to serve during peacetime, I always believed I had that kind of leadership, that people knew I wouldn't back away from anything, that I would find a way to get the job done. I think people naturally want to be led and will follow people who know where to go.

Tibor arrived in July, and it was like Butch and Sundance were together again. We continued training in the arts, worked together, and spent the rest of the time running around like the twenty-one-year-olds that we were. Fort Bragg was the perfect place for us—a big, prestigious base where the top soldiers were trained. As martial arts experts, we occupied a special position on the base. We even found ourselves training soldiers in the highest levels of Special Forces and other elite army units.

Occasionally Tibor and I would get assigned off-base to Fayetteville, the city outside Fort Bragg, where we worked as liaisons with the Fayetteville Police Department, helping them with rowdy and out-of-control soldiers from the base. We patrolled Hay Street, a long strip of topless bars and nightclubs where the soldiers were always getting into trouble. One day I was walking along Hay Street on patrol when I saw a crowd gathered outside a bar and, in the center of it, four soldiers surrounding a Fayetteville plainclothes cop. The cop was in his early forties, with a military haircut. He was big, maybe six feet, four inches tall, 250 pounds, with a big, round, bloodred birthmark that started at his left eye and ended below his mouth. You took one look at him and knew this was not someone to mess with.

He casually asked the soldiers to disperse, but one of them suddenly took a swing at him. In one quick move, the cop with the birthmark deflected the punch, stepped forward, and hit the soldier in the chest with the open palm of his hand. The kid went flying. The group quickly dispersed.

The cop's name was Billy Joe Turner, and he was a former Green Beret, from the army's Special Forces. He'd served three tours in Vietnam, but when the war ended there was a reduction in force (soldiers called it being "riffed"), and there was no further use for a fighting machine like B. J. He'd taken a job as a patrolman for the Fayetteville Police Department in the plainclothes unit, and his job was to do just what I'd seen, cruise around and defuse groups of drunken soldiers before they caused problems.

B. J. and I hit it off right away. I admired his toughness and loved hearing his stories about combat and the amazing guys who had served with him. He connected with us too, and I think he saw Tibor, and especially me, as throwbacks to the tough, confident soldiers he'd always served with. In the next few years I would learn more from Billy Joe than I could ever imagine, and he would show me parts of the world that I couldn't have found on a map if you spotted me the longitude and latitude.

A newspaper described me once as "a self-made man." That's partly true. I had to build myself from the ground up, but it wasn't from scratch. Along the way I borrowed ideas and was inspired by exceptional men like Keith Keller, Tibor, and Billy Joe, who helped show me what it means to be a man. There would be many more. I still had a long way to go.

THE car went by and I couldn't believe what I'd just seen. I turned to my partner, who was driving our Jeep. "That guy just flipped me off," I said. "Let's go."

We pulled the car over and I walked around toward the passenger side. The guy wore the uniform of the Eighty-second Airborne Unit, so I had every intention of giving him the benefit of the doubt.

"What's up?" I asked when I'd reached the car.

The guy in the passenger seat stared at me with utter disregard. "What do you mean?"

"What's with the finger?"

"This one?" And he stuck his middle finger right in my face.

So I broke it.

A few days later my lieutenant called me in. "Hey, Kerik. You have a problem with some guy while you were on patrol?"

"I didn't have a problem."

He looked at some papers on his desk. "Well, it looks like you broke some guy's hand. His boss lives next door to me, and he called me up and said, 'Your fuckin' guy broke my guy's hand.' He's talking about a court-martial."

"Bring me up on charges? For what? He flipped me off. Can't we bring *him* up on charges?"

"Let me try to work this out," he said. A few days later, he told me they wanted to charge me with assault. If I was found guilty, that would be the end of my army career.

"I didn't assault anyone," I pleaded.

"I know," my lieutenant said. Then he came up with a compromise. I'd been a few minutes late one day at a formation, so he decided they would give me an Article 15, a lesser form of disciplinary action, charging me with being AWOL from formation. "And for that, you're going to get demoted," he said.

"I don't want to get demoted," I said.

"Look, Kerik. Either you get demoted or you get court-martialed. One or the other. You can't go around breaking people's hands."

So I had to take the demotion from corporal to private first class. The truth is that I deserved my punishment. I was young and brash. Today, if one of my officers did what I'd done, I'd certainly bust him down.

But the result was tough. For all the success I'd had in the service, I was just one step from where I'd started. And although an Article 15 wasn't as bad as being court-martialed, there was a heavy price to pay. At the time, Tibor and I were thinking about reenlisting. We'd been training elite soldiers, and the army was just creating Delta Force—a highly trained, highly specialized fighting unit based out of Fort Bragg that would ultimately turn into the premier counter-terrorist unit in the world.

In 1977 I had been assigned to the All-Army martial arts team. I spent eight months on the team, fighting in competitions, giving exhibitions, training every morning, and then teaching self-defense tactics to ROTC summer camp cadets in the afternoons. I also taught classes in knife and stick fighting and weapons to Special Forces personnel at the JFK Unconventional Warfare Center. So if there was anyone cut out for Delta Force, it was I. But to get into the elite unit, you couldn't have any disciplinary actions on your record. And of course, I had the Article 15, the AWOL charge that was really about the guy with the broken finger. It seemed unfair, but there was nothing I could do.

No matter how much we liked the army, neither Tibor nor I wanted to spend the rest of our lives as grunts. And we were both feeling the travel bug again. So we decided not to reenlist. Tibor had gotten out already and was taking the test to be a police officer in his hometown of Carteret, New Jersey.

I was scheduled for discharge in July 1977. As the end of my army career approached, I wasn't sure what I was going to do. I knew I wanted to go into law enforcement, and I had applications in with the North Carolina State Patrol, the Paterson Police Department, and the New York City Police Department, but I had no solid leads. Then one day I ran into a couple of guys at Fort Bragg who were working on an investigation involving cigarette smuggling out of North Carolina, mostly to Florida.

"I know all about that shit," I said to one of the guys.

"How?" he asked.

I explained that I'd worked for a moving company after

high school and that we were constantly traveling south to Florida.

A few days later I got a call, and the guy on the other end wanted to know what I planned to do when I got out. I confessed that I wasn't sure yet. Then he offered me a job with the Interstate Revenue Research Center of Indianapolis—the guys I'd seen investigating cigarette smuggling.

They wanted me to help set up surveillance of the smugglers in Florida. "We just need to figure out how to get you inside," said the lead agent.

"That's easy," I said. "I'll hitchhike."

And like that, I had a job. Over the next ten months I'd hang around truck stops posing as a loader. I'd watch the truckers load up with illegal cigarettes, then I'd bum a ride south with them. I'd chat up the driver on the way down, then get out and call the agents in Florida and tell them all about the shipment that was coming down. It would turn out to be great practice for the undercover drug work I would do later.

But as I prepared to leave the army in July of 1977, I knew that I would be leaving a very important part of my life behind. The army had rescued me, had given me the tools and core beliefs that would guide me through the next twenty-five years. It also allowed me to go back to school to get that piece of paper that had prevented me from joining the Paterson Police Department—my high school diploma. But if I was sad to be leaving the military behind, I was also eager to get on with the next stage of my life, whatever that might be. In fact, the future seemed so near, I was caught a bit off guard when my past dropped out of the blue.

I walked into the barracks one afternoon and the guy at the desk said, "Hey, Kerik, your Uncle Bob called. He left a number."

"Bob who?"

I called the number, which had an area code that didn't look familiar.

"Beezy?" asked the voice on the other end.

It was the name my family called me, but I didn't recognize the voice. "Yeah, who's this?"

"It's your Uncle Bob, your mother Pat's brother."

My dad had told me a little bit about him, how he'd selflessly arranged to get me back to my father. But I had never been very curious. I suppose I just wanted to leave that part of my life behind.

Bob asked me how I'd been doing, and I told him about the army, about Korea and my martial arts training. He seemed genuinely pleased, and he told me how proud he was of all I'd accomplished. It felt strange to hear all this from someone I didn't know, and yet I felt something for him.

He said he had one other thing to tell me. "Beez," he said, "it's about your mother. I wanted to tell you. She's dead. She died in 1964."

I looked around, maybe to see if anyone was standing nearby, but I was alone.

"Okay," I said. It was the only thing I could think to say. And for just a second, I thought about what I had been doing in 1964 when she died—running around, playing with my cousins, being a brother to Vickie and Terry, being beaten up by those bullies in Branch Brook Park. As hard as I tried, I just couldn't connect her world to mine.

"Okay," I said.

Bob told me he was going to send me some things and wanted to know if he should send the package to me or to my parents' house. I told him to send it to my parents.

"Okay, Beez," he said. "I just wanted to tell you . . . how happy I am that you've done so well for yourself. You know, I've always thought about you."

I didn't say anything. After a few minutes, we hung up.

Two months later, just after I was discharged from the army, I drove up to New Jersey to visit my parents. I stood in the kitchen of my parents' house and my mom handed me a small box that was addressed to me. Inside the box there was an old dusty and dirty teddy bear and a small, simple baby album. There was a note from Bob that said that the teddy bear was mine and the baby book contained the only memories he could find. On the cover of the book was printed "Diary of Baby." I turned to the next page: "Our Priceless Gem." The next page had a picture of a baby boy, a dusting of dark hair on top of his head, his eyes closed peacefully. Alongside the picture was a woman's careful handwriting: "This picture of you Bernard Bailey Kerik was taken right after you were delivered into the world."

There were several more pages, but I didn't read them. I just couldn't. I closed my eyes and then closed the baby book. I placed the book in a plastic freezer bag and put it back in the box. I put the box in a drawer.

It would be twenty-five years before I would open the book again.

THE SHIELD
PART TWO

KERIK

IF WE TAKE THE GENERALLY ACCEPTED DEFINITION OF BRAVERY AS A QUALITY WHICH KNOWS NOT FEAR, I HAVE NEVER SEEN A BRAVE MAN. ALL MEN ARE FRIGHTENED. THE MORE INTELLIGENT THEY ARE, THE MORE THEY ARE FRIGHTENED. THE COURAGEOUS MAN IS THE MAN WHO FORCES HIMSELF, IN SPITE OF HIS FEAR, TO CARRY ON.

—GENERAL GEORGE S. PATTON, JR.
War As I Knew It, 1947

LAWRENCE Marcario stood with a team of cops in the cold hallway of the Ravenswood Houses public housing development in Queens. He stood behind two sergeants from the housing bureau, Darren Finn and James Hopkins, who knocked on the door of the first-floor apartment. A woman let them in.

It was December 1995 and the cops were looking for a twenty-eight-year-old man named Sean Pritchett, an ex-con who had recently finished a five-year sentence for killing a drug dealer. Released from prison two months earlier, Pritchett had immediately violated parole and was the primary suspect in the recent murder of a Manhattan bar bouncer.

As the cops looked around, Pritchett's fiancée excused herself to get dressed. She went into the bedroom and opened the closet to reach for a shirt. Behind her clothes in the closet, the cops could make out a man's leg. Moving the woman aside, Finn and Hopkins stepped into the bedroom, yelling: "Police! Don't move! Let us see your hands!"

There was a burst of gunfire from the closet. Two shots from Sean Pritchett's nine-millimeter handgun hit Hopkins and Finn in the chest and were deflected by their bulletproof

vests. Another shot grazed Finn in the armpit and another
tore through his hand. A bullet hit a medal on Hopkins's uniform and was deflected across his neck, and then finally one
of Pritchett's bullets found its target, ripping into Hopkins's
stomach, boring through his intestine, and lodging against
his spine. The injured Finn pulled himself from the room,
but Hopkins fell, his gun dropping next to him on the floor.

Other cops returned fire through the doorway, and for the
next twenty minutes the room became a war zone—nearly
seventy rounds going back and forth. Trapped in the middle
of it all was the wounded Hopkins. And it was during those
frantic first moments, with bullets flying back and forth, that
Lawrence Marcario ran into the room, with no thought for
his own safety. He fired into the closet as he shielded Hopkins with his own body, and eventually pulled him from the
room.

When it was over, Sean Pritchett had been hit seventeen
times in the shoot-out. Yet he lived and was sentenced to
eighty-six years in prison for attempting to murder these police officers. Hopkins and Finn also lived, but after multiple
surgeries and months of stress and pain, they each took early
retirement.

And Lawrence Marcario?

Five years after his act of sheer heroism, the NYPD
Medal of Honor winner pivots and crosses the stage toward
me, compact and proud in his dress blues, a white glove extended as he reaches out to shake my hand.

Lawrence Marcario is one of 141 detectives here in the
auditorium at One Police Plaza receiving his promotion to
detective second grade. Their families sit proudly in folding
chairs as each name is announced. Very few of these detectives will ever win the Medal of Honor—the NYPD's highest commendation—but these men and women are all
heroes, they all have the potential to run into that room, to
throw themselves into the breech.

Some cops seem to make a habit of such courage. A few
weeks earlier I had promoted a detective named Joseph Vi-

giano, a member of the Emergency Services Unit, who was awarded the Medal of Honor twice. In 1989 Vigiano and another cop responded to a report of "Shots fired," and when they arrived, two men ran into a building and one turned and fired a nine-millimeter pistol at them. Both officers were struck by bullet fragments. Vigiano fired back and killed the gunman.

Then in 1994 Vigiano was trying to question a man suspected of attempted murder and robbery when that man and an associate pulled guns and began firing. While other cops took cover to fire at the gunmen, Vigiano chased them into a stairwell, where one of the men shot him in the chest—the bullet deflected by his body armor—and in the arm. Wounded, Vigiano kept chasing the men to the rooftop of the building, where they escaped. The gunmen were later arrested.

Days like this are the best part of my job. Every few weeks, I have a promotion ceremony and get to reward people like Lawrence Marcario and Joseph Vigiano. I think these ceremonies provide me with a far greater reward than the one the officers receive. I leave humbled and inspired that these people have decided to devote their lives to being police officers, to selflessly protecting the people of this city. Days like this remind me why I first became a cop and why I now work long hours devoting myself—the way these cops do—to caring for the people of this city.

That's one reason I make such an effort to promote officers who may have been overlooked because of politics or whose value can't always be measured on paper. I am always watching out for deserving officers who have been unfairly passed over.

Last April a Brooklyn detective named David Carbone was called at home and told that he was on a list of officers to be promoted. He was told to put on his dress blues and go immediately to the chief of detectives' office. He was ecstatic. He'd been on the verge of being promoted to detective second grade in 1998 when he was in a car accident. Finally, he thought, his career was back on track. He'd just bought a new uniform for the Columbus Day Parade, so he raced off to headquarters.

But when he got there, his name wasn't on the list of promotions. He sat in the waiting room, feeling worse and worse as other detectives walked by in their dress uniforms. Was there a cop in his precinct who had it in for him? Apparently the phone call about the promotion had been a cruel prank. Demoralized, Carbone went home. But his story quickly made the rounds at One Police Plaza, and within an hour, David Carbone's personnel file was dropped on my desk. As I read about Carbone's years on the force, I encountered an exceptional cop—active, smart, conscientious—everything we ask our officers to be. I couldn't understand why he hadn't been promoted earlier.

I called him to my office. "I stand before you an embarrassed man," he said.

When I told him that he was being promoted to detective second grade, he was stunned, then excited, then took a breath and said he didn't want his promotion to be the result of some prank.

It isn't, I said. The prankster had done him—and me—a great favor by bringing his file to our attention. He was exactly the kind of detective who deserved promotion. The next day he was the first detective across the stage. "I'll never forget what you did for me today," he said when I shook his hand.

On the same day that Medal of Honor winner Lawrence Marcario is to be promoted, my chief of staff, John Picciano, comes to me with the story of a young detective named Dave Acres, assigned to the Gang Unit. In the first eight months of 2001, Acres has single-handedly taken thirty-two guns off the street. Taking guns off criminals was one of the things I excelled at as a young cop, and it is a part of policing that I stress, for one simple, inarguable reason: every time we take a gun out of a criminal's hands, we prevent a potential crime. And yet in all my years I've never heard of a cop taking thirty-two guns off the street in a year, let alone in eight months. Most cops won't take thirty-two guns in a whole career.

But on the morning of the ceremony, Acres's boss, Deputy Inspector William Tartaglia, whose three-year-old daughter suffers from brain cancer—called my office and explained that he'd been so overwhelmed by her illness, he'd forgotten to recommend Acres for promotion to detective second grade. He knew it was too late; he just wanted to make sure that Acres would be considered in the next round of promotions a few months down the road.

Like a lot of large agencies, the NYPD is a creature of process; there are rules and procedures and requirements to be followed for everything we do. With forty-one thousand police officers, it has to be that way. And so a promotion simply doesn't happen in a day. At least it didn't before I started. As my savvy chief of staff tells me the story of Dave Acres, he watches me out of the corner of his eye. He's been with me for six years and he knows what I will say next.

"Reach out to this guy."

"Acres, sir?"

"Yeah," I say. "Get him down here."

"Sure, Boss."

By noon, Dave Acres is standing in my office.

"You know why you're here?"

"I think so, sir," he says.

"We try to get the best guys for promotions, but sometimes we miss a few," I say. "We missed you. Your boss told me what you've done over the last eight months. You're doing a great job, and you deserve to be promoted."

I believe in rules, in their power to create order and affect performance. And yet laws and rules are made to serve people, not the other way around. At the promotion ceremony that afternoon, Dave Acres sits with 140 other detectives. As I look out at their faces, I don't need to look down at my speech. The words come naturally because I think them every day.

"Just ten years ago, I was sitting where you are today. Just ten years ago, I got my detective shield, and it was the proudest day of my life." I tell these detectives about the sorry state of New York City then, in the late 1980s and early 1990s, when crack cocaine flowed like the East and Hudson Rivers, when crime was three or four times as prevalent as it is now. "In 1994," I say, "the *New York Times* took a poll, and forty-five percent of the people said they wanted to move out of the city; they didn't want their businesses here; they didn't want to send their kids to school here.

"But in 1994, things started to change. And now, no longer do mothers have to teach their children how to duck from gunfire. No longer do mothers put their babies to bed in bathtubs to protect them from gunfire.

"When I started in this job, people told me I had to be careful because crime has gotten so low in New York City that it can't go any lower. Well, it has. And the credit goes to the men and women who are sitting in this room today. . . . It is because of you."

Then, one by one, they cross the stage, beaming with pride: Dave Acres, Lawrence Marcario, and 139 other heroes.

IN the NYPD, your superior is Boss (pronounced bu-oss). You aren't promoted, you're made. Bad guys are skells, perps, mutts, or mopes. You aren't fired or demoted, you're whacked. You don't call someone, you reach out to them. When you make an arrest, it's a grab, collar, or pinch. If you're a cop with connections or relatives in the police department, you got juice or a contract. An average day in my office might sound to an outsider like an episode of *The Sopranos*.

"So what do we do with this jerk, Boss?"

"This guy's a fucking zero. Whack him."

"But we just made him two months ago."

"Yeah. And now he's gotta go."

If the FBI were to tape the conversations that go on in my

office every day, it might take them a few hours to realize they weren't listening in on the Mafia.

It was one of those examples of life imitating art when in the 1970s, Mafia families began to speak and dress and act like the Corleone family from the movie *The Godfather*. But they weren't the only ones to be affected by a movie about crime and punishment. Cops too were taken in by the code of honor and loyalty that ran beneath the life-and-death world of *The Godfather*. The reality is that there was never loyalty and honor in organized crime. Most of those guys would cut one another's throats for forty bucks and rat one another out to fix a parking ticket.

But to most cops there is nothing as important as honor, loyalty, and family. We need a code of black and white that helps us do a job where the reality can sometimes be very gray. For us, Mafia movies are a kind of shorthand, a reminder of that code. One night I gather my whole security detail for dinner, and the laughter rolls up and down the long table like a wave. Every other line seems to come from *The Godfather*.

Dessert comes and someone says: "Leave the gun. Take the cannolis."

When someone talks about work: "Kay, don't ever ask me about my business."

Even my son, Joe, gets into the act, switching us from *The Godfather* to *Goodfellas*. "Hey, I hear things . . . things about your wife."

"You're funny," someone else says, which sends Pitch into a dead-on Joe Pesci impersonation: "But I'm funny how? Funny like a clown? I amuse you? I make you laugh? I'm here to fuckin' amuse you?"

My guys at the table lean on one another's shoulders and wipe their eyes.

Personally I've seen *The Godfather* maybe fifty times. And its lessons of constant betrayal and bloodthirsty politics have never been more pertinent than in my current job. The Mafia is softball compared with New York politics.

Every decision I make is analyzed, second-guessed, twisted around, and open to protest. There is literally a protest about something every day in New York. But most of the political game is played behind the scenes. On everything from promotions to discipline, I encounter normal office politics, but I also hear from the five unions representing patrolmen, detectives, sergeants, lieutenants, and captains; the civilians who work for the department; and the fraternal organizations and activist groups representing black, Hispanic, Irish, Italian, and every other ethnicity of officers. A hundred small decisions every day, each one with the potential to piss off the unions, the fraternal groups, the mayor's office, the courts, the jails, the lawyers, the state and local politicians, and the activists. And then, of course, there's the press. In the NYPD, public relations is a twenty-four-hour job.

Every morning and again each afternoon, the Toms come into my office to brief me on what reporters are sniffing around in. The Toms are my public information officers—my press guys. They are like an old vaudeville act—the suit, Tom Antenen, deputy commissioner of public information (DCPI), thin and dry as a martini, a civilian I brought over from the Department of Correction; and his uniformed counterpart, Deputy Chief Tom Fahey, a bulldog in a short gray flattop, a classic old-time cop who tells wonderful stories out of the side of his mouth while Antenen gives sarcastic commentary. Sometimes at the end of the day I look forward to my briefing with the Toms as if they were a favorite TV show.

The Toms give me a list of that day's media requests. It starts with a *New York Post* columnist, Jack Newfield, who is working on a piece about the warrant squad—police officers whose job it is to round up criminals who have violated parole or missed trial and are the subject of arrest warrants.

It's common sense, but this wasn't always a priority for the NYPD until Mayor Giuliani came along. It might not be obvious that you could lower homicides by picking up someone who has violated his shoplifting probation, but nothing could be more simple: Get criminals off the street. Crime goes down—12 percent this year alone. The homicide rate has fallen from 2,245 in 1990 to 671 in 2000.

In the afternoon, Mayor Giuliani and I share the dais at Madison Square Garden, presiding over the graduation of 1,121 new police officers.

In the wake of the divisive Amadou Diallo case, this is the first academy class in the history of New York that doesn't have a majority of white officers.

"For the first time, the NYPD graduates a recruit class where there is no majority group," I say to this sea of young faces seated before me, their shiny black caps pulled down to the tops of their eyes. "There are no minority groups, there is just a class of 1,121 dedicated individuals who reflect the city's population closer than at any time in the New York Police Department's one-hundred-and-fifty-year history.

"It's a remarkable achievement, another step forward for the NYPD and something that's certain to make us a better and more responsive police department.

"People can talk about job security, they can talk about the twenty-year pension, the benefits, the unlimited sick leave," I say. "I know and you know—that's not why you're here. You're here because deep inside, you want to make a difference. You're here because you're the kind of person who sees someone in trouble—someone who needs help—and you have to get involved.

"You're here because there is a hero inside just waiting to get out. Well, I'll promise you this—starting tomorrow, this city will find a way to put that hero to work."

It is overwhelming for me to stand up here and look out at these young police officers, at their proud families. I remember so clearly being in that seat at the beginning of my career. But these officers are coming in at a different time.

These young men and women will be caretakers for a city that has turned around 180 degrees in the fifteen years since I sat out there.

"It's an incredible thing to live and work in a city where confidence has replaced fear," I tell them. "It's an incredible thing to live in a city that belongs to the honest person, and not to the criminals. . . . That is the New York City of today. Tomorrow, I place it in your hands. Make sure you keep it well."

THE letter—dated May 11, 2001—was from a woman in Harlem named Evelyn Cunningham.

Dear Commissioner Kerik:

For the past two weeks, following my arrest for crossing the street against a red light, I have searched through my eighty-five years to try to identify any similar personal experience that could measure the depth of my pain.

She described being arrested during a sit-in at a Maryland roadside diner that "banned Negroes" during the 1950s. But she said that what had happened to her in New York two weeks earlier was in many ways worse.

In the year 2001, on New York's Broadway, between 148th and 149th Streets, it was not as civilized as it was in Maryland. Two weeks ago I was walking along Upper Broadway when I noticed a double-parked police van carrying three police officers. . . .

The officer at the wheel thrust his arm from the window, pointed his finger at me, got my attention, and shouted, "Hey you! Yeah, you, you! Get yourself over here!"

*I had assumed that officer's target was one or more
of the people standing around the area generally considered drug dealer territory.*

But this cop wasn't interested in the drug dealers. He was
yelling at an old woman crossing the street. So Ms. Cunningham walked over. The cop asked for her ID, and she
handed it over. A career journalist, she told the cop she
worked as a volunteer in the Three-O Precinct, writing
grants to pay for youth programs in the precinct area. She
told him that her brother was a decorated cop who had
passed away several years ago.

"And of course I told him I was eighty-five years old," she
wrote.

*He was not moved nor amused by my quick recital of
some of my former employers: a New York City mayor,
two governors of New York State, a Vice President of
the United States, and a President of the United States.*
*Clearly he had no concern about my résumé, or my
rights, and certainly not for the pride or dignity of an
eighty-five-year-old African-American woman who, in
her own way, was trying to help him do his job.*

Instead, this moron wrote Evelyn Cunningham a summons for jaywalking.

"Where do I go from here?" she wrote. "What do I want?"

*I want desperately for you, Commissioner Kerik, to
seek and find all the means possible and available to
make those men and women in your command understand fully and clearly that aged African-American
women are not invisible women who seem to exist as
only vehicles for fulfilling some cops' daily quotas,
and who must be protected from abuse of any kind,
from any source. . . .*

Finally, did I really walk past a red light? I don't know. It's hard to say. Those beautiful white blossoms that grow on New York City's famous callery pear trees have a short blooming time, usually no more than two weeks. During the short season, they grow in such profusion, one cannot always see the traffic lights—red or green.

When I got the file of the cop who wrote her the summons, I was floored. This guy had twenty-two incidents— twenty-two complaints like this from citizens. It was outrageous. There is no quota for traffic summonses in the NYPD. He and the other cops were in that neighborhood in that van because the police department has a drug initiative there, but rather than mess with drug dealers, this guy writes a summons to a dignified woman crossing the street. A woman who happens to work as a police volunteer! And for what? Is there some big jaywalking crisis in Harlem that I don't know about?

So I whack this moron. I can't really fire him, but I modify him, take away his gun and his shield and take him off patrol. This is one of the big reasons so many people in the African-American community don't trust the police. Obviously there may be a few cops who are racist or corrupt, just like a small percentage of the population at large, but often the problem between cops and people of color can be traced to something else: ignorance and arrogance.

In this case the cop yelled at her, "Hey, you! Get yourself over here!" Now maybe he has a problem with old black women; I don't know. What I do know is that he was arrogant and he was rude, and that kind of arrogance and rudeness is sometimes misperceived as racism. I don't tolerate racism, and I'm not going to tolerate arrogance that can lead to the perception of racism.

Of course, one of the big problems I inherited with this job was the fallout from two notorious cases: the beating and abuse of Abner Louima in a Brooklyn station house and, most famously, the tragic shooting death of Amadou Diallo, who was reaching for his wallet in the doorway of his Bronx home when he was shot to death by police.

These cases, and a few lesser ones, when put through the meat grinder of New York media, gave the impression that the New York Police Department was filled with violent, racist cops. Nothing could be further from the truth. Go to Harlem. Go to Bed-Stuy or East New York. Go to black and Latino and Asian neighborhoods, and you will find the best police work in the world. Put out a call over the radio that shots have been fired in a Harlem building, or that children are in a burning house, or that a rape is in progress, and watch the precinct house erupt. No cop will ask what race the victim is. It doesn't happen. The truth is that cops will go and risk their lives without giving a thought to race.

The truth is that the forty-one thousand officers in the NYPD had six million official contacts with the public last year, including three hundred thousand arrests. If you add the times a cop talked to someone on the street or in parades, the number of contacts becomes something like *thirty million*. And in all of those contacts in the year 2000, there were just four thousand civilian complaints, only two hundred of which were substantiated by the Civilian Complaint Review Board.

Of course, with forty-one thousand cops, there are a certain number who simply shouldn't be out there. We're constantly on the lookout for bad cops. Last year, Internal Affairs ran one thousand integrity tests, offering bribes and using other tests to weed out dirty cops.

But a far more insidious problem, I'm convinced, is this institutional arrogance and rudeness. When I ran the Department of Correction, I instituted civility tests in which we had officers secretly call the jail system and record how well they were treated. We went out of our way to find people with Jamaican and Puerto Rican accents. They'd say something like "Hello, my son was locked up last night and you took his property. How do I get it back?"

At first the results were terrible. "Just a minute," the correction officer would say, and the phone would drop to the desk and sit there for ten or fifteen minutes.

When we began, we'd do fifty calls a month and forty-five would be unacceptable. I began calling the supervisors in and really holding their feet to the fire. This is the key to my style of management: we did these tests exactly the way a Fortune 500 company would do market studies, gathering data and then holding the managers responsible for the results. By the time I left the Department of Correction, we were doing one hundred calls a month and getting one, maybe two unacceptable.

I recently conducted a survey within the police department, and the early results were similar to the early DOC results. Of the fifty calls, two cops performed exceptionally. Two others passed. And forty-six failed.

If I could just convince street cops of this one thing—that they need to be respectful, that they don't need to antagonize people—I'd cut complaints to the Civilian Complaint Review Board in half.

And maybe I could have spared Evelyn Cunningham what she called in her letter "a draining and deeply depressing day." So after I take care of the officer, I personally call Ms. Cunningham and ask if I can take her to lunch. I cancel a couple of internal meetings and drive to Harlem to pick her up.

"You have to excuse me if I seem a little nervous," she says after she gets in the car. "I tried my best to maintain my composure, but when I realized you were really coming up here, I have to say, I was taken aback."

The summons was torn up and thrown away, and the precinct commander stopped by to see her. Now I apologize again, tell her that I've disciplined the officer, and thank her for her wonderful letter. We talk about the unfortunate gap in perception between some cops and people of color. We have a great lunch. She is a phenomenal woman: brilliant, poised, and caring. When the lunch ends, I'm angry all over again, just imagining the impression this delightful woman had formed about the NYPD, about *my police department*. The quest for justice begins with fairness, with the belief that everyone will receive equal treatment and equal protection, regardless of their skin color or their religion or their address.

I find myself thinking about this at home one night as I dial the telephone number of another elderly woman, in Washington, D.C. "Hello," she says.

"Hi, this is Bernard Kerik. Do you remember me?" I ask.

"Sure I do," she says.

The woman's name is Anna Bailey. She was my mother's friend when they were kids, and ended up marrying her brother James. She was my Aunt Ann all those years ago in Ohio. Sergeant Lenny Lemer, still helping me dig into my mother's murder, tracked her down as one of the few people who might remember my mother's death. She lives with her daughter and son-in-law in D.C. now, but her memory of my mother in Ohio comes back crystal clear, as if she were remembering the events of only a few days ago.

"Patricia was very intelligent, very bright," Anna says. "As a child, she'd study for a day or two and ace the test." Patricia's family, on the other hand, was a train wreck. Her mother, Dorothy, didn't have much use for her eight children—four girls and four boys—except for the work they could do around the house. The two youngest, James and Patricia, had the worst of it. When Dorothy couldn't deal with them, she sent them to an orphanage for months at a time.

Most of the kids were alcoholic and their deaths were horrible. One of Patricia's sisters died in her thirties of typhoid. In 1952 John, the oldest brother, was robbed and beaten to death. Two of Patricia's older sisters, Helen and Virginia, were drunks who became prostitutes as teenagers. Virginia was a pill-popper who married a cop and then a transvestite.

Helen was vicious and violent and probably the one who pushed her little sister Patricia into prostitution.

"Those girls believed it was a way of life to become prostitutes," Anna says sadly. My mother began working as a hooker as a teenager, long before my father met her. She did it to make money to buy booze, Anna says, almost apologetically. "She was the smartest and the prettiest, but she was always in the wrong place with the wrong people. She just wasted her life. It was tragic."

I tell Anna that one thing from Patricia's file confuses me. "When we ran my mother's name in the records in Columbus, Ohio, we found a brief notation about the FBI. But there was no explanation."

On the other end of the phone, Anna hesitates.

"What is it?" I ask.

"One time your mother asked me to go down and see the FBI with her. They wanted to ask her some questions. They showed her a number of photos of girls," Anna says. "The pictures were of prostitutes involved in white slavery—young girls transported by a couple of Cleveland pimps over state lines to work in other cities as prostitutes.

"When we got outside, your mother turned to me and said she knew every girl in those pictures. She was deeply involved in it. She was one of those girls."

My own voice sounds raspy. "Where?"

"Back east. In New York."

I immediately flash on my years on patrol, walking up and down West 42nd Street, and the women selling themselves there. I try to picture my own mother in those sad faces. How many dozens of women like that did I arrest? Women like my mother.

"Your mother, she would do a good job raising you for a while, but she'd always give up and run off," Anna says. "You were a sweet baby, a very happy baby. She took care of you, cleaned you, and was good to you, but . . ."

"What is it?" I ask.

"It's just . . . I never saw her hug or kiss you the way that mothers should," she says. "I know she tried to be a good mother, she wanted to be a good mother. I just look at the way she was brought up, and I don't think she knew how."

The further my mother drifted into drugs and booze and prostitution, the less Anna saw of her. Eventually Anna lost track of her and didn't see her until her funeral. She can't help us with the details of my mother's last days or her murder. Her funeral was sad, Anna says. Patricia's own mother didn't even go.

I thank Anna for her help, and before I hang up I ask one more question about my mother. "So what made her happy?"

Anna answers quickly: "To look pretty and have a beer in front of her."

I remove the baby book from the box and the plastic bag where it sat undisturbed for twenty-five years, ever since I got home from the army, ever since I found out my mother was dead and this baby book arrived in the mail from Ohio.

I flip through the pages—family tree and birth certificate, heights and weights and footprints and a picture of a sleeping newborn with a woman's careful scrawl above the photo: "This picture of you Bernard Bailey Kerik was taken right after you were delivered into the world. Sept. 4, 1955."

She recorded the gifts that arrived—"4 checkered gowns, 2 doz. diapers, 2 shirts, 1 receiving blanket . . ."—and when I first raised my head (six weeks), first smiled (eight weeks), first sat up (six and a half months), and first held a bottle (seven months). As I read, I find myself looking for signals of her decline—for instance, on the page about my teeth, she wrote, "I couldn't keep track of every tooth, but I did get a few down."

First steps, first sentences, favorite toys—I read each section looking for . . . what? Some clue about what happened to her, some explanation for her death, or maybe just proof that she loved me?

"Bernie, you are very tiny for your first Xmas," she wrote. My first birthday and second Christmas passed uneventfully, and she seemed happy to simply list the presents. But on my second birthday we were in Ohio. What does it mean? It's frustrating trying to find meaning or direction in these simple bits of information ("We had a very nice party").

On my fourth Christmas, she wrote, "your real daddy flew down from N.J. & had Santa Claus bring you a Lionel Elec. Train . . . daddy Jack got you cowboy boots."

Ten months later, on my fourth birthday, her handwriting is loose and her thoughts seem disconnected, and I can sense a tone of sadness in her blind insistence that everything was perfect:

> *Beezy darling—You had a wonderful birthday party—*
> *You had 14 other kids besides Danny your nephew—*
> *There was nothing missing—You had a beautiful cake,*
> *table setting & many other things—Bob was with you*
> *100% . . .*
> *I love you truly Beezy–*
>
> *Mommy*

In the same handwriting, she noted:

> *Rose and Moma watched you Beezy for 12 wks while*
> *Mommy was in the hospital & you really loved to be*
> *there and always had a good time. . . . Each time*
> *Mommy came home on leave you had learned some-*
> *thing else. . . . You are a good little boy and very*
> *smart—You seem to remember everything—We love*
> *you very much—*

I think about what Anna said to me on the phone—that Patricia didn't know how to be a mother. For forty-five years, the vision I had of my mother was that she'd abandoned me and never come back for me. But the woman in the pages of the baby book is a mother who did love me, even if it was only for a short time. I suppose I want to believe that—or need to. It's something I have searched for my whole life.

The last pages of the baby book—my fifth, sixth, and seventh Christmases, the next three birthdays, along with "My first day at school"—are as blank as my memories of her. I think about all those Christmases and birthdays when I desperately wanted her to call, to come back for me. But she never did.

The new police chief of Newark, Ohio, H. Darrell Pennington, agrees with Lenny that there was no investigation into my mother's murder in 1964. He says that because she was a prostitute involved with a black man in a rough part of town, it may be that authorities back then believed my mother's murder just wasn't worth investigating.

Chief Pennington says my inquiries about the case have caused him to assign a detective to look into it, to see if anyone is still alive who might have some information. I thank him and tell him that I'll do whatever I can to help. And just like that, the investigation into my mother's murder is officially reopened.

Today is the anniversary of my appointment to the NYPD in 1986. I find myself thinking about my first days as a cop, about my excitement and my feeling of purpose. I saw myself as a kind of shield for people who had nowhere to turn, for people cast aside, for people in danger. It makes you wonder just how much your childhood affects you as an adult. Maybe I do have memories of my mother that I can't consciously reach—a woman so beaten by life that she was never able to defend herself. Maybe *she* is the person that I set out to help. Maybe in the end, my mother is the reason I became a cop.

Despite Chief Pennington's reopening the case, there is almost no chance of solving my mother's murder. I know that. It's been thirty-seven years, and most of the principals are long gone. But as I slide the baby book back into its box, I know that I will keep looking.

And what I might find scares me far more than any murderer.

9

SAUDI ARABIA

1978

I was ready for a change when Billy Joe Turner called. I was living in North Carolina, my short army career over. In some ways I was no closer to my dream of becoming a police officer. I had stowed my past along with the unopened baby book in a box at my parents' house. It was my future that was a mystery.

I enjoyed working for the IRRC, the federally funded agency that investigated interstate cigarette smuggling. I hitchhiked and hung around truck stops throughout the South, gathering information and helping to set up stings. It was a very good job. I had an undercover car and a radio. In the army I had made four hundred dollars a month; now I was making twelve hundred. For the first time I had money for the things I wanted. But after eight months, something was missing. I was at the peak of my physical conditioning, fully trained by the army, and here I was chasing cigarette smugglers across the Southeast. Yet I didn't even know anything was missing until that call from B. J. Turner.

The former Special Forces major and Fayetteville police officer was in a different business now, using his old military contacts to provide security and consulting for various projects in other countries. I was glad to hear from him. Strong, fearless, and always a gentleman, B. J. was the closest I'd ever come to a mentor. This time he cut right to it. "Bern, I want you to come to Nicaragua to work with me."

"Nicaragua?"

"That's right. I have a job for you down there."

"I have a pretty good job," I said.

"How much you make?"

"Twelve hundred a month."

"I'll pay you fifteen," he said. "And you can bring your boy, if you want."

"Tibor?"

"Yeah."

B. J. explained that he was in Nicaragua with two men I'd trained with in martial arts at the JFK Center—Mike Echanis and Chuck Sanders.

I got off the phone and wondered, Where the hell is Nicaragua? I had no idea that it was in the midst of political and social upheaval. I just knew fifteen hundred was more than twelve and that Tibor and I could work together again.

But before I could quit my job, B. J. called right back. "Hold up," he said. "It's kind of hot down here right now."

He said he was on the way back to the United States and he would call me when he could. Not long after that I got a call from a guy in Washington, D.C., named Richard Bratton, who said Billy Joe had given him my number. He said, "B. J. wants to know if you want to go to Saudi Arabia."

I called Tibor, "Hey, we're goin' to Saudi Arabia!"

"*You're* going to Saudi Arabia," T. said. He had just taken the test to become a cop in Carteret, New Jersey.

"You don't want to be a cop in Carteret," I said. "Come on, man. They got nine cops in the whole damned town."

"I'm staying," he said.

"They're paying fifteen hundred bucks a month. No taxes. No expenses."

"When do we leave?" T. asked.

We drove to Washington, D.C., to hear about the job. The building we went to was nondescript and unassuming, the office appearing to be that of a construction company. We met Bratton, one of those shadowy guys who acted as if he was involved in something dark and covert even when he wasn't. And in this case, he wasn't. Unlike Nicaragua, this job turned out to be pretty straightforward and safe.

The Saudi government, in its attempts to modernize the country, had contracted with the U.S. Army Corps of Engineers to supervise construction projects all over Saudi Arabia. In addition, American architects and engineers, construction crews, and security firms had been hired to oversee every aspect of the projects. We would be working on the massive King Khalid Military City at Hafar Al-Batin, a modern military base and surrounding city that the Saudis were raising from the empty desert near the border of Iraq. It would later be one of the primary military bases used during the Gulf War, but in March 1978 it was little more than a desert and a bunch of rolled-up blueprints. While the base was under construction, guards were needed to secure it and patrol its perimeter, and that's where Tibor and I and the rest of Billy Joe Turner's men came in.

Four weeks after meeting with Bratton, T. and I received our visas and flew over to London to meet B. J., who was waiting there for us. He took it upon himself to show the Jersey kids around, pointing out the Thames River and London Bridge. At Buckingham Palace, I was looking at something when B. J. yelled at me to turn around. When I did, all I saw was a big white hat, and while I watched it, B. J. took a picture of me—with Queen Elizabeth in the background.

We stayed in London for about three days. When it was time to leave, the three of us went to Heathrow Airport for our flight. At the magnetometers, T. and I laughed hysterically as B. J. removed one layer of clothing after another until he was down to his underwear. After three tours in Vietnam, his body was filled with odd bits of shrapnel, metal plates, rods, and pins. Springs. Bolts. Who knew what all he was carrying in there?

We landed in Dhahran, Saudi Arabia, and the intense heat

was a shock, like a slap in the face. I had never felt heat like that. And it was nighttime. We met with our contact, a guy who said we would fly out in the morning. He gave us the name of the place we were going—Hafar Al-Batin. I looked for it on the map but couldn't find it.

"Right there." He pointed to a blank spot on the map thirty-five miles south of Kuwait.

I looked again. "But there's nothing there."

"You're right," he said. "It's desert."

We flew out in an eight-seat airplane. I hate small airplanes, but it was either that or a nine-hour ride in a Suburban through the desert. We landed, and I stepped off the plane to find that my feet stuck to the tarmac. The soles of my sneakers were melting. It was 1 P.M. and the temperature was 110 degrees. We left the airstrip and started down a narrow dirt lane that passed for a road. I looked in both directions, but there was nothing as far as I could see. No buildings. No trees. Nothing. In fact, I saw nothing for miles until we came across a ragged-looking man standing alongside the road in sandals and the traditional white Saudi garment called a *thobe*. He waved, but we just drove past.

"We'd better stop," I said. "That guy needs help or something."

"Nah, he's a Bedouin. He lives out here."

I looked around. "He lives out where? Where does he live? 'Cause there ain't no houses out here. There ain't nothing out here. There's sand and there's sand and that's it."

Later I got to know more Bedouins, the small number of fiercely independent and nomadic Arab tribesmen who continue to live as their ancestors did, moving across the desert on camels, trading, and sleeping in thin tents. Often they camped in the desert near Hafar Al-Batin, and it was common to see a family—a man and his wife, fifty sheep, three kids, and a tent—living out there in the middle of 120-degree nothingness.

A few days after we arrived, T. and I were introduced to the rest of the security team. They were almost all in their forties, hard, lean retired Special Forces and intelligence experts. They introduced themselves: a former command sergeant major—one of only a handful in the whole army—Colonel So-and-so, Brigadier General Something-or-other. And then there was Tibor, a corporal, and myself, who left the army bucked down to a private first class. The other guys had all served heroically in Vietnam. We were kids. I looked at Tibor. "What the hell are we doing here?"

But Billy Joe told them we'd make great additions to the team, and that was that. Besides, we had something they needed. Dogs.

Since we'd trained and handled dogs in the military, our assignment was to set up a plan for dog patrols around the perimeter of the King Khalid Military City. We recommended Dobermans instead of German shepherds because of the tremendous heat. But even as we answered questions, both Tibor and I felt like we were bluffing. We didn't know what the hell we were doing there. I knew how to train dogs and train dog handlers, but here I was now twenty-two years old, and within days I had architects drafting plans for kennels—temporary and permanent—training sites, and air-conditioning units, faking it all the way. Finally we had a meeting, and we all had to submit our proposals. As architects and planners took their turns, the Saudis listened, nodding and saying, "Good. That's good." Then it was my turn. I began going over the plans for the kennels, but one of them stopped me.

"What is this?"

"The training site," I answered.

"Training for what?"

"The dogs. You hired us to do dogs."

He looked around the table. "What dogs?"

"The dogs. To patrol the fence line." He just stared at me. "You know, dogs can see at night. They're good for that."

"Dogs," he repeated.

"Yeah. Dogs. Arf, arf?"

He just stared at me. "You do realize this is a Muslim

country. To Muslims, dogs are like demons. You can't bring dogs here."

I looked over at Tibor, then across to Billy Joe and the others in the room. If they didn't need dogs, then they probably didn't need us. It looked like we'd just lost our high-paying new jobs.

Billy Joe stood staring at the architect's sketches of the kennel and the training area and all of it. Finally he scooped it all up. "All right. Fuck it. We ain't doing dogs. You'll do something else."

In 1978 the King Khalid Military City at Hafar Al-Batin was a giant construction site dotted with trailers and tents and surrounded by fencing. There were flags where the buildings would stand. The project was in its second year and wouldn't be complete until 1985. It would end up housing fifty thousand people and cost five billion dollars to build—a hundred thousand dollars for each person who lived there. Security was a mess at the construction site when we arrived, but we quickly pulled it into shape and set up a routine for patrols and for policing the people coming and going.

The other guys in security—about twenty-five of them—took to Tibor and me right away. Our first impression of these guys as former military heroes was completely reinforced as we got to know them.

It wasn't just the security guys that were former military. Everybody we met was either retired from the State Department, retired from the military, former Air America, retired CIA, actively in the CIA, or doing something they couldn't explain. I thought back to our original meeting with Richard Bratton at the construction company in Washington, D.C. I asked Tibor, "You ever see a construction company with magnetometers? With signs saying No Weapons Beyond This Point or No Cameras or Electronic Devices or No Recording Equipment?" When we'd asked one guy about his construction background, he'd just stared at us, as if he couldn't think of one just then. I smiled at Tibor. "I'm starting to wonder about that construction company."

But even if there were active intelligence agents all over Saudi Arabia, still the most impressive guys there by far were our team members.

Some of them carried the scars of combat, and not always scars you could see. I remember one guy named Herman Spencer, retired Special Forces, whom the others treated with special deference. He was the kindest and most peaceful guy, but you'd be talking to him and suddenly he'd skip like a record. He'd be saying what a good glass of water this was, and all of a sudden he'd give you an address in Switzerland. The other guys just seemed to ignore this, so Tibor and I did too.

It turned out that Herman Spencer and a few other guys had been involved in one of the most famous attempts to free POWs in Vietnam, the Son Tae raid, in which his team was sandbagged; the CIA's intelligence was faulty, so that when they arrived at the POW camp it was empty, and they had to fight their way out. The stories these guys told were amazing. They had been through it all. But when the war in Vietnam ended, there was nothing for them to do with their training and their gung ho personalities, so they found themselves working together—a clique of highly trained people who worked internationally as consultants and security experts and, in some cases, mercenaries. Out there in the middle of nowhere, we might've had the most highly trained and decorated little army in the world.

We were responsible for every aspect of security at the KKMC, including the huge residence and living quarters of the king and crown prince. Occasionally other members of the royal family would stop by, and we would coordinate security for them too. In addition, we acted as liaisons between the local police and the thirty-five hundred employees of American companies working on the project.

There was literally nothing but desert beyond the fences,

and the guys became like my family. They quickly took Tibor and me under their wings. We were martial arts buffs, strong and sometimes arrogant young men, and yet all that cockiness disappeared when we were in their company.

"Don't slouch," they'd say. "Stand up. Get your hair cut."

They taught me how to stand, how to talk, and what to wear. I was learning how to be a man from the best men around me, and from these guys I picked up an air of confidence and ability that I still strive for today. You couldn't invent a situation to panic these guys. They had been all over the world and they looked the part. Consummate professionals, they were classy and confident, always gentlemen.

For two and a half years, these guys took on the project of an unsophisticated kid from New Jersey. From manners and personal demeanor to table etiquette to vocabulary to proper attire, they remade me as one of them.

Once I bought some dress shoes, the only kind I knew, Florsheim. B. J. pulled me aside. "Don't ever buy those shoes again," he said. "Next time you go home, stop in Rome and buy Bally or Gucci, they're much nicer." So I did, even though the price almost stopped my heart. Soon I was taking trips to Europe to buy my clothes.

After about four months in the kingdom, I decided to buy myself a nice watch, so I went shopping in Dhahran with B. J. and another guy. I felt rich after four months of earning fifteen hundred a month, so I was ready to splurge. I had my sights set on a Seiko diver's watch. It was $110—more than I would normally spend, but I figured, hey, that's what money's for. B. J. stood next to me and just shook his head. "What are you doing?"

"I'm buying this watch. Isn't it great?"

"You're not buying that watch."

"What's the matter with that watch?" I asked.

He took me by the arm. "Come on." He dragged me out of that store and into another store, a Rolex store. I had no idea what a Rolex was. "See that watch?" he said. "That's a real diver's watch."

**RELATIVES SAY
I WAS A HAPPY BABY**

**WITH MY SISTERS,
TERRY AND VICKIE LYNN**

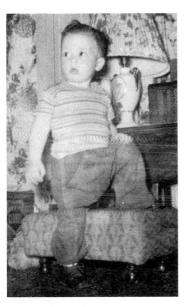

AT TWO YEARS OLD

**MY UNCLE, ROBERT BAILEY,
AND ME**

ABOVE LEFT: MY
UNCLE GEORGE
WITH MY MOTHER,
PATRICIA, WHO IS
PREGNANT WITH ME

ABOVE RIGHT: UNCLE
ROBERT BAILEY AND
DAD, AUGUST 1956

LEFT: THE KERIK CLAN
IN 1973 (CLOCKWISE
FROM LEFT): ME, TERRY,
VICKIE LYNN, MY DAD, MY
MOM, CLARA, AND DON JR.

OPPOSITE: U.S.
ARMY MILITARY
POLICE SCHOOL,
1974

CLASS OF
JUNE 196
SCHOOL NO
PATERSON

MY EIGHTH-GRADE CLASS AT P.S. 13 IN PATERSON, NEW JERSEY, 1969. I'M ON THE FAR LEFT.

PATRICIA J. KERIK
1930 — 1964

OHIO DEPARTMENT OF HEALTH
DIVISION OF VITAL STATISTICS
CERTIFICATE OF DEATH

Reg. Dist. No. _____

Primary Reg. Dist. No. **4501**

State File No. _____

Registrar's No. **576**

1. PLACE OF DEATH	2. USUAL RESIDENCE (Where deceased lived. If institution: Residence before admission)
a. COUNTY **Licking**	a. STATE **Ohio** — b. COUNTY **Licking**
b. CITY, VILLAGE, OR LOCATION **Newark** c. LENGTH OF STAY (in hospital) **3 DOA**	c. CITY, VILLAGE, OR LOCATION **Newark**
d. NAME OF HOSPITAL OR INSTITUTION (If not in hospital or institution, give street address) **Newark Hospital**	d. STREET ADDRESS **1941 E. Main St.**
e. IS PLACE OF DEATH INSIDE CITY LIMITS? YES ☒ NO ☐	e. IS RESIDENCE INSIDE CITY LIMITS? YES ☒ NO ☐ — f. IS RESIDENCE ON A FARM? YES ☐ NO ☒

3. NAME OF DECEASED (TYPE OR PRINT) First **Patricia** Middle **Joann Bailey** Last **Curtis**

4. DATE OF DEATH Month **Dec** Day **14**, Year **1964**

5. SEX **Female**	6. COLOR OR RACE **White**	7. MARRIED ☐ NEVER MARRIED ☐ WIDOWED ☐ DIVORCED ☐	8. DATE OF BIRTH **3/1/30**	9. AGE (In years last birthday) **34** — If Under 1 Year Months / Days — If Under 24 Hrs. Hours / Min.

10a. USUAL OCCUPATION (Give kind of work done during most of working life, even if retired) **housework**	10b. KIND OF BUSINESS OR INDUSTRY **home**	11. BIRTHPLACE (State or foreign country) **Ohio**	12. CITIZEN OF WHAT COUNTRY? **U.S.A.**

13. FATHER'S NAME **Faye Rodney Bailey**	14. MOTHER'S MAIDEN NAME **Dorothy Butler**

15. WAS DECEASED EVER IN U. S. ARMED FORCES? (Yes, no, or unknown) (If yes, give war or dates of service)	16. SOCIAL SECURITY NO.	17. INFORMANT'S NAME **Bernard Bailey-Columbus, O.** Address

18. CAUSE OF DEATH (Enter only one cause per line for (a), (b), and (c).)

PART I. DEATH WAS CAUSED BY:

IMMEDIATE CAUSE (a) *Cerebral Hemorrhage* — INTERVAL BETWEEN ONSET AND DEATH *12-14-64*

Conditions, if any which gave rise to above cause (a), stating the underlying cause last. DUE TO (b) *Traumatic* — *12-13-64*

DUE TO (c)

PART II. OTHER SIGNIFICANT CONDITIONS CONTRIBUTING TO DEATH BUT NOT RELATED TO THE TERMINAL DISEASE CONDITION GIVEN IN PART I(a) *Pulmonary Care Cerebral Swelling*

19. WAS AUTOPSY PERFORMED? YES ☒ NO ☐

20a. ACCIDENT ☐ SUICIDE ☐ HOMICIDE ☐	20b. DESCRIBE HOW INJURY OCCURRED (Enter nature of injury in Part I or Part II of item 18.) *Undetermined at this time*
20c. TIME OF INJURY Hour a.m./p.m. Month, Day, Year	
20d. INJURY OCCURRED WHILE AT WORK ☐ NOT WHILE AT WORK ☐	20e. PLACE OF INJURY (e.g. in or about home, farm, factory, street, office bldg., etc.) 20f. CITY, VILLAGE, OR LOCATION COUNTY, STATE

21. I attended the deceased from _____ to _____ and last saw her alive on _____ DOA. Death occurred at _____ m on the date stated in 4; and to the best of my knowledge, from the causes stated.

22a. SIGNATURE (Degree or title)	22b. ADDRESS **Newark**	22c. DATE SIGNED **12-16-64**

23a. BURIAL, CREMATION. (Specify) **Burial**	23b. DATE **12/18/64**	23c. NAME OF CEMETERY OR CREMATORY **Forest Grove Cemetery**	23d. LOCATION (City, town, or county) (State) **Madison Co., Ohio**

24. NAME OF EMBALMER **R.M.Warthen** (LIC. NO.) **4885 A**	25. FUNERAL DIRECTOR'S SIGNATURE (LIC. NO.) **5136**

26. FUNERAL FIRM AND ADDRESS **Criss Brothers,Inc. 179 Granville St. Newark,Ohio** (STREET NO.) (CITY) (STATE)

27. DATE REC'D BY LOCAL REG. **12-21-64**	28. REGISTRAR'S SIGNATURE **Margaret Thomas**	29. DATE REC'D BY SUB-REGISTRAR	30. SUB-REGISTRAR'S SIGNATURE

I HEREBY CERTIFY THIS IS A TRUE COPY OF THE RECORD ON FILE IN THE OFFICE OF THE NEWARK BOARD OF HEALTH, NEWARK, OHIO 43055

DATE *June 12, 2001*

Sharon Dalton

LOCAL REGISTRAR
Registration District #4501

SIDE KICK IN KOREA, 1975

ON SENTRY PATROL IN KOREA WITH K-9 KING

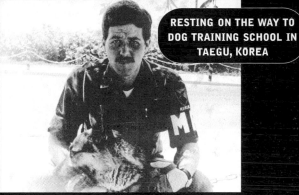

RESTING ON THE WAY TO DOG TRAINING SCHOOL IN TAEGU, KOREA

SECURITY DETAIL, KING FAISAL HOSPITAL, RIYADH, SAUDI ARABIA, 1983

BEING PROMOTED TO DETECTIVE
3RD GRADE BY FORMER POLICE
COMMISSIONER LEE BROWN,
SEPTEMBER 24, 1990

ESCORTING CONVICTED TERRORIST
SUSAN ROSENBERG, 1985

NYPD GRADUATION DAY WITH MY SON, JOE, DECEMBER 18, 1986

MEDALS DAY WITH MAYOR GIULIANI AND MY SON, JOE, SEPTEMBER 13, 1993

MAYOR GIULIANI WITH JOE AND ME, ST. PATRICK'S DAY 2001

MY DAUGHTER, CELINE,
AND HER GODFATHER,
MAYOR RUDOLPH GIULIANI

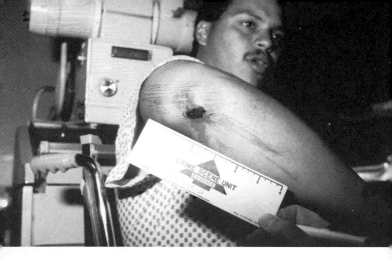

ABOVE: DETECTIVE HECTOR SANTIAGO AFTER BEING SHOT IN THE ARM

LEFT: THE CRIME SCENE OF HECTOR SANTIAGO'S SHOOTING, NOVEMBER 13, 1991

RIGHT: DETECTIVE MATTHEW MARTUCCI, JERRY SPEZIALE, AND I WITH MORE THAN A MILLION DOLLARS SEIZED FROM THE CALI CARTEL, 1993

IN JANUARY 1994, JOSÉ RUIZ DIAZ WAS EXTRADITED FROM SWITZERLAND. JERRY SPEZIALE (SECOND FROM TOP) AND I TOOK HIM INTO CUSTODY.

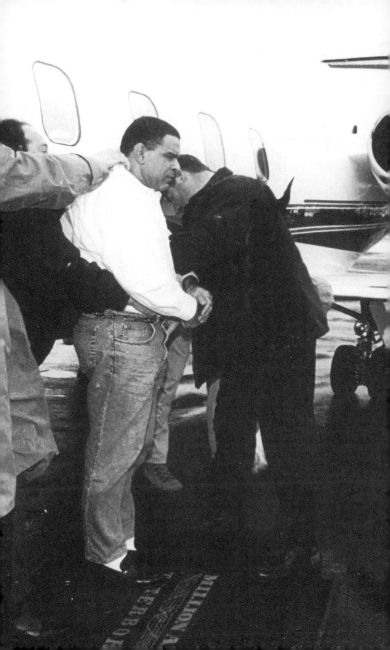

IN MARCH 2001, I WAS THERE WHEN PABLO ALMONTE LLUBERES WAS FINALLY BROUGHT TO JUSTICE FOR THE 1988 MURDER OF NEW YORK POLICE OFFICER MICHAEL BUCZEK

A FEW HOURS LATER I GAVE TED BUCZEK THE HANDCUFFS USED TO ARREST ALMONTE, THE MAN WHO KILLED HIS SON

DEA GROUP T-42 WITH 1,494 KILOS OF COCAINE, WORTH ABOUT $250 MILLION ON THE STREET JERRY SPEZIALE IS 7TH FROM THE LEFT. I'M THE 7TH FROM THE RIGHT.°

It was nice. And it had a cool silver band. "Okay," I said, "I'll take it."

While B. J. was looking around the store, I looked at the price tag. It was thirty-two hundred Saudi riyals—950 U.S. dollars. "That can't be right," I thought. I called out to B. J. and the salesman to figure out the real price. The salesman agreed that the price was wrong and that he would knock off one hundred riyals or thirty dollars. It was still $920.

"Are you out of your fuckin' mind?" I couldn't imagine how I was going back to Jersey and explain to my father that I'd just spent nine hundred bucks on a watch.

"You buy that watch or I'll buy it and take it out of your pay," B. J. said. You didn't win arguments with those guys, and I walked out that day with my first Rolex. I still have it sitting in a safe today, and I plan to give it to my son, Joe, when he turns eighteen.

AT noon, the people streamed from their houses and businesses and made their way to the mosque to pray. I was in Al Khobar—a suburb of Dhahran and the place where nineteen American marines would be killed by a truck bomb in 1996. When we had a few days off, we'd go to Riyadh or Dhahran to shop and eat and experience Saudi culture—at least the parts of it that were open to Americans.

When prayer was over that Friday, the people pressed into the square in front of the mosque. Something was happening. I walked to the edge of the square. Local police were making a big ring around the square and the people who had gathered there.

"What's going on?" I asked.

A guy told me, but I couldn't believe it. I didn't plan to watch, but when a black truck drove slowly into the square, I found that I couldn't look away.

The truck door opened, and out climbed a man from the Sudan, in a long *thobe,* his hands cuffed behind his back. He looked dazed, as if he'd been drugged. They pushed him down to his knees. My mind raced: they couldn't be doing this. Then the governor's bodyguard came out with a long thick sword. A marked police car with a loudspeaker mounted on its roof was parked in the square and a voice came from it, listing the man's crimes—including murder.

As they finished reading the charge, the bodyguard swung the sword from behind the defendant, at about a 45-degree angle, and the man's head seemed to slide right off his body. There was a geyser of blood, and his dead body pitched forward. I stood there for the longest time, unable to comprehend what I had just seen. I couldn't get it out of my mind. I would come across this scene repeated a couple of dozen times in the years that I lived in Saudi Arabia, and it would always seem surreal to me—beheadings for murders and rapes, dismemberments for thefts, and floggings for other less severe crimes. The dismemberments followed the same script, the executioner stepping forward, grabbing the defendant's right hand by the fingers, and sawing at the wrist until the hand came off.

No matter where you stand on the issue of the death penalty, to see an execution in Saudi Arabia is a chilling experience. In America it's become accepted that the death penalty has no deterrent effect, but that's partly because it is used so sparingly and it takes so many years of appeals and legal wrangling that criminals are hardly ever put to death for their heinous crimes. That's not true in Saudi Arabia, where murder, rape, and other serious crimes are extremely rare.

Obviously I don't think we should have a Saudi-style criminal justice system. The checks and balances and appeals of our court system make it the fairest in the world, but if the debate is simply about the deterrent effect of the death penalty, you need look no further than any town square in the Kingdom of Saudi Arabia on a Friday afternoon.

THE entire Islamic world was undergoing drastic changes in the late 1970s. The world energy crisis and high oil prices had flooded the Arab world with money for construction projects like the KKMC, and yet at the same time that modern buildings were going up, the Islamic religion was being dragged into the past by fundamentalist zealots. In Iran, the Ayatollah Khomeini had consolidated his power by criticizing the West, especially the United States, and eventually taking hostages at the U.S. embassy. Throughout the Arab countries, there was pressure from these traditional forces to overthrow their monarchies, which were said to violate Islamic law, and the pressure on people from the West, especially Americans, was constant.

In 1979 revolution came briefly to Saudi Arabia, the birthplace of Islam and the most stable country in the region. On November 20, while fifty thousand people prayed at the mosque in Mecca, three hundred or so fundamentalists took over the mosque, urging the crowd to overthrow the Saudi rulers and their government. It took government troops a week to root the rebels out of the mazelike mosque. More than one hundred were killed on each side, and a month later another sixty-eight alleged rebel sympathizers were executed.

I had been in Saudi Arabia for almost a year and a half when the director of security operations recommended me for another job. This one was at the port in Ras al-Mishab, where goods and products that were needed for the construction site were unloaded. I knew it would be hard to leave Tibor and this group of men that I'd grown so close to, but B. J. Turner had left several months earlier and was now extracting land mines from oil fields in Egypt. Later he'd end up on the Negev Air Base project in Israel. And as for me, I was beginning to crave new challenges.

So in July of 1979, I transferred to the coastal town of Ras al-Mishab and went from a highly trained and motivated staff of twenty-five to an office of one: me. I was the logistics officer, the only person from our company responsible for clearing shipments and cargo into the international port of call. It was learning on the run and I found I had a knack for it. I learned all about the vessels and barges. The ships would come in and I would go out to inspect them with the Saudi customs agents, give clearances, and work closely with the authorities to get the shipments approved. Customs in Saudi Arabia was a long, involved process, since the Islamic religion prohibits so many things from the West. Once we'd finished customs, I'd make sure the shipments got onto the right trucks to go into the desert.

I even taught myself to type the reports, using one of those books you flip upside down that has a picture of the keys you put your fingers on, while a tape recording tells you which letters to push. I loved the responsibility of managing something by myself, of running the entire operation at Ras al-Mishab for this company. For the first time in my life I didn't have a boss. I was the boss. I liked that.

By the spring of 1980, though, I began to feel as though my life in Saudi Arabia had run its course. I missed home. I had signed up for an eighteen-month contract and ended up staying two and a half years. Including my stint in Korea, I had been away from the United States much of the last four years, and in that time I'd felt myself grow more and more distant from the States. When I took vacations, I traveled to Europe or the Far East and rarely went home. I didn't pay attention to American music or fashions. I knew Jimmy Carter was the president, but that was about it.

With so little to do during my free time in Saudi Arabia, I had actually increased my physical training. Monday, Wednesday, and Friday I worked out hard in martial arts; Tuesday, Thursday, and Saturday I trained on weights; and every day I ran three to five miles. I left Saudi Arabia in the best shape of my life—with a thirty-one-inch waist, nineteen-inch arms, and twenty-eight-inch thighs. But my physical growth was nothing compared to the ways I'd grown professionally. I returned with two and a half years of experience in police work and security operations, including an education in areas that were nearly impossible for American cops to experience, such as international terrorism. But even my professional growth paled in comparison to what I'd learned as a person.

I had great teachers and mentors in Saudi Arabia: Billy Joe Turner and the twenty-five-odd members of our security team. In June of 1980 I stepped off the airplane reflecting their influence. Not the European clothing, but the way I carried myself—with a quiet, dignified confidence that came directly from them. I was like a sword, forged to a glimmering, hard point by four years of working abroad. As I resumed my quest to become a police officer, I felt ready for whatever awaited me. And yet I was totally unprepared for the one danger that was about to trip me up.

A woman.

10

PASSAIC COUNTY

1981

TIBOR and I left Saudi Arabia at about the same time, both headed in the wrong direction. Someone had filled T. with stories of the Wild West, and he took the money he made in Saudi Arabia and invested it in a bar in Boise, Idaho. I returned to North Carolina, bought a house and a car, and took a job with a county sheriff's department there. Before I left for the Middle East, I had fallen head over heels for a beautiful southern belle, but after I returned we quickly realized that it wasn't meant to be. My job with the county wasn't a bad job, but North Carolina seemed to have two speeds: slow and slower. So after about eighteen months I packed up and returned to Paterson. I called a friend I knew at the Paterson Police Department and told her that I was home and looking for a job. She pointed me in the direction of the Passaic County sheriff.

I sat across his desk from him as he read my résumé, which listed my training as a military policeman, my experience teaching Delta Force members and touring with the All-Army martial arts team, my experience working with police in Fayetteville and as a cop in North Carolina, the expertise in international policing, weapons, customs, terrorism, and investigations that I'd gotten in Saudi Arabia. My references—Saudi government officials, American war heroes—were not the kind of references most twenty-five-year-olds present when they apply for jobs.

The sheriff scratched his head. "What are you doing here?" Even though we agreed I was a bit overqualified, I signed on as a correction officer in the Passaic County Jail and started my new job in December. While living abroad, I had allowed myself to forget where I'd been headed when I lived in Paterson. I was quickly reminded in my new job. "Hey, Kerik. How you been? What's happening?" Every day was like a high school reunion. I can't count the number of times I closed a cell door on a former classmate.

I dated a little when I got back but managed to stay sort of detached from the women I met. Then a woman who came to the jail to see her husband every week said she had someone she wanted me to meet. "Is it your sister? Cousin? Does she look like you?"

"No," she said. "She's my best friend and she's absolutely gorgeous."

"You should bring her with you."

"Oh, she would never come here."

"Don't tell her you're coming here. Tell her you're going to lunch somewhere."

Two weeks later she showed up with a beautiful girl. She was tall and long-legged, with a dark Cuban complexion. Her name was Jackie. We were riding to the visiting booths in an elevator with mirrored doors, and when I looked up, I could see her behind me, checking me out and gesturing toward her friend. We started joking around, talking, and I asked her out. We hit it off right away. She was full of life, and there was a strong mutual attraction.

But beneath our attraction to each other there were problems. It wouldn't be long before our strong personalities would begin to clash.

DON was fifteen when I got back from Saudi Arabia and it was flattering to see the way he idolized me. Unfortunately, he hadn't really seen much of me in the last few years, so the Bernie that he idolized was the one he'd grown up with, the smart-mouthed tough-guy truant.

He was a better student and wasn't causing as much trouble as I had—yet. But I was home just a week when I heard echoes of myself in my little brother.

"Don," Mom would say, "take out the garbage."

"Okay, Ma." And he wouldn't move a muscle.

"Don! I said take out the garbage."

"Awright, Ma! I said I would." But he wouldn't budge.

My father would be sitting in the dining room working on a beer. He didn't want to hear any of it. He didn't like arguments or confrontations.

"Don! Take out the damn garbage!"

"Awright, I said!" And still no movement.

So I moved. I popped up, thumped Don once, and the next time Mom asked for his help, my boy was up and running to the garbage. From then on, if I was around I'd give him about ten seconds to do what Mom asked, and if there was no response, I'd intervene.

I worked him hard, almost as hard as I'd worked myself, trying to teach him the discipline I'd learned in the military and the self-reliance I'd developed in Saudi Arabia. I wanted to help Mom, who had put up with so much shit from me, but more than that, I didn't want my little brother repeating my mistakes. And the only route to discipline that I knew was to ride him and never lay off.

Don was hanging out with a couple of real thugs, not just mouthy kids like him but guys with real potential for committing crimes. My cop friends used to pull me aside and warn me that Don was headed for prison if he kept hanging out with them.

So I put him on notice, although to hear Don tell it now, you put someone on notice by sending a letter, not by the means I chose.

One Sunday night, before Jackie and I started seeing each

other, I was on a date with another girl when I got word that Don and these kids were hanging out at a skating rink at a mall in Wayne. I went to the rink, but when I stuck my head in, Don ducked out the back. I came outside and saw him move around the corner of the building. He'd been warned about hanging out with these guys, and he knew this would mean trouble.

I walked purposefully toward him.

"Don't hit me," Don said.

"I'm not gonna hit you," I said.

As I got to him, Don reached down as far as he could, reached down from Florida, as he says, and swung his right fist with every bit of strength he could muster. He landed a perfect punch right to my jaw. My head snapped back a little, and when my eyes returned, Don says, they looked like the eyes of the Incredible Hulk.

He turned and ran into the parking lot of the skating rink. I got in my car and chased him, trapping him in the lot. I could see his feet moving from side to side on the other side of a garbage Dumpster. "Don, come out," I said. "It's over. I'm not gonna hurt you. I love you. You're my brother."

After a few minutes of coaxing and pleading, he came out and walked toward the car. I did everything in my power to control my feelings so he wouldn't see how angry I really was. I opened the car door for him and lifted the seat so he could get into the back of my Camaro. He climbed in. I closed the doors, and the last thing Don remembers was hearing the *click, click* of the electric doors. I turned to face him and climbed through the middle of the two seats. I was furious. A second later, he was out cold.

When we got home and Don came to, he was in a rage. He yelled that he hated me, that he wished I were dead.

The second time he wished me dead was when he was sixteen. He worked part-time at a Honda dealership, emptying the garbage, sweeping the floors, and doing other grunt work. There was a key box on the wall with keys to all the cars, and Don had begun taking cars every once in a while and joyriding with the same friends I'd told him to stop seeing.

I was working second shift at the Passaic County Jail, so I got to my parents' house that night about 11:20. As I walked in, it looked like a wake. Mom and the girls were in the living room staring at the television as if they had blinders on. I walked into the dining room and Pops was at the table having a beer. "What's up?" I asked.

"Nothing," he said.

I walked back to the living room. "Hey, guys, what's up?" No one moved except Terry, who was now watching me out of the corner of her eye. I called her into the bedroom and asked her, "What's going on?"

"Nothing."

Finally she gave it up.

"Donald got arrested," she whispered.

"What?"

"He got arrested."

"Arrested?" I was stunned. "He got arrested?"

"Yeah," she said. "He had to call Mommy and Daddy from jail."

Don and his loser friends had gone joyriding in a stolen car. The police caught them. Mom and Pops picked him up at the jail, and when he got home, Don went to bed early, probably thinking the worst was over. It wasn't.

I jerked him out of bed by the hair, let him put on a pair of sweatpants and a T-shirt, then dragged him outside into the snow in his bare feet. I threw him in my car and we drove down to the police station. I had him personally apologize to the cops who'd had to corral him and his worthless friends.

"You done?" I asked.

"Yeah," he said. I stood there staring at him, and I could picture him and his friends stealing the car. But worse, I could see where he was heading. If I didn't do something he would end up in one of those jail cells that I was patrolling. I was not about to let that happen. I had tried to talk to him, to reason with him. Nothing was working. I let loose a roundhouse kick to his chest, and Don dropped to the floor wincing in pain. I didn't realize it at the time, but I had actually cracked some of his ribs.

Today I know that violence is no way to solve problems, and I feel no pride when Don credits me with stopping him in his tracks and changing the direction of his life. Still, it scares me to imagine where he and his friends were headed.

A couple of years later, when Don was working with me at the Passaic County Jail, I called the housing area where he was working and told him to come down to the receiving area. I told him that I'd just received a call from the Paterson Police Department and they were bringing in someone who had just shot a cop. I told him to stand by and wait for the prisoner's arrival.

A motorcade came down Marshall Street, sirens blaring. One car pulled into the receiving room bay. There were cops—uniform and plainclothes—everywhere. Reporters were trying to make their way through the reception room doors.

The cops reached into the backseat of the car and helped a man out. As his head became visible to everyone on the outside, Don's face turned pale. He was frozen. I nudged him. "Take the prisoner," I said.

"I can't."

"Take the prisoner," I said. "He just shot a fuckin' cop."

Don grabbed the arm of the same kid who only two years earlier was his joyriding best friend from the roller-skating rink, the guy I had wanted him to stay away from.

When the prisoner was booked and processed, I saw Don in the corridor of the jail. Our eyes met. I didn't have to say a word.

"BERN. It's Tibor."

It was great to hear from my old friend. Unfortunately, the bar in Boise hadn't turned out to be such a great investment, and he'd burned through all the money he'd made in Saudi

Arabia. He wanted some numbers for our contacts in Saudi Arabia to see about returning, so I passed the numbers on to him. I told him that work was going pretty well at the Passaic County Jail, and best of all, I had met someone I really liked.

He called me right back. "They're looking for additional people in security there. They asked about you."

"I can't," I said, and I told him about meeting Jackie.

"This job's in Riyadh," he said, "not out in the middle of the desert."

"No," I said.

"They're paying twenty-three hundred a month," he said.

"No," I said.

"Come down to Nashville, just to hear what they have to say."

"I'm not going, Tibor."

At the same time, I had been sensing that the Passaic County sheriff was feeling threatened by me. I had gotten the job in December 1981, and within six weeks I was on the Emergency Response Team. In addition, I had become the training officer for the entire department, teaching self-defense, weapons, repelling, and anything else I could come up with.

People treated me with deference, and I found myself making more decisions and being relied upon to do a lot more at the jail. But I felt the sheriff resented me, so it wouldn't hurt to at least see what else was out there for me.

I told Jackie that I was just going to Nashville to hear about the job. No way would I return to Saudi Arabia. I had finally gotten reacclimated to life in the States. She and I were in the first stages of a relationship, and even though my future with the sheriff seemed sketchy, I was doing well at work. I wasn't about to leave now.

"Don't worry," I told Jackie as I left. "I'll be home in two days."

I got home four months later.

* * *

MY second tour in Saudi Arabia began in October 1982. I was assigned to the King Faisal Specialist Hospital, a beautiful facility at the edge of Riyadh, and a great source of pride for the Saudi government. It may have been the most modern and impressive hospital in the Arab world. Landscaped like a garden—at least by the standards of the dry Arab world—with a huge, colorful fountain in front of the beautiful off-white stone building, there were trees and even a vast lawn, which was said to be the only public grass in all of Riyadh.

The hospital was built next to the palace of King Faisal, who had been murdered by his nephew in 1975. This betrayal of Faisal by his nephew and some members of his security force had caused some members of the Saudi royal family and their confidants to be suspicious of their own people and to look outside the country for security. That was where we came in.

The House of Saud—the ruling family in Saudi Arabia—was not a traditional monarchy. Typically the crown did not move vertically, from father to son, but horizontally, from brother to brother, and so it was Faisal's brother Khalid who became king when Faisal died. Each generation produced more princes and princesses, their children and spouses and their children's children all becoming part of the royal family. By the time I was in Saudi Arabia, there were more than five thousand members of the House of Saud, and royals were spread throughout almost every strata of Saudi life. All of them were wealthy, but the upper level of royals—those close in relation to the king—lived an amazingly opulent life: fleets of luxury cars, huge staffs, private jets, Saudi palaces, and houses all over the world. Many royals also held high positions in the government, and other government ministers were constantly competing for access to the royal family. For this reason, even the most basic political business in Saudi Arabia could be filled with palace intrigue, religious implications, rumors of betrayal, and feuds that went back generations.

I tried to ignore the intrigue and politics and just concentrate on my job—chief of investigations for the hospital. Much of that meant keeping an eye on the American workers who came in contact with the hospital. Of course, Americans living in Saudi Arabia had to abide by Saudi law, which was in fact Islamic law, as dictated by the Koran. These laws could be terribly strict and all-encompassing, and I found myself investigating conduct to which normally I wouldn't give another thought.

For instance, if a Saudi national began dating an American nurse at the hospital, it was a violation of Islamic law. American women were often deported for such transgressions. Sometimes women sneaked into the country to work as prostitutes, and this too would result in deportation. The Saudis were trying to open their country to Western development and expertise while keeping our decadent culture out. Much of my job was to maintain that balance. It was challenging, negotiating such a closed, rigid system and trying to find justice in laws that, to an American, were unjust.

And it was lonely work. Tibor dropped right back into our old Saudi life, traveling to Southeast Asia or to Europe whenever he had time off. But I found that I missed Jackie. We wrote letters and talked on the phone and tried to keep our relationship alive, but finally, I couldn't take it anymore. After four months in Saudi Arabia, I flew home to New Jersey and we were quickly engaged and married. We honeymooned in Spain, and then I returned to Riyadh and Jackie went back to the States. But it was clear that if we were going to make our marriage work, it would have to be on the same continent.

In the spring of 1983 I came home to pick up Jackie and caught my parents in a heated argument. Dad was a functioning alcoholic, going to work every day, seemingly taking care of his family. For him, beer was a place to hide from the disappointments in his life. But his drinking had gotten progressively worse while I was gone, and I didn't think Mom should have to put up with this side of him.

At the house we got into it, and Pops started getting pushy. Usually he wasn't violent at all. But we were standing at the dining room door, and he told me to get out. I opened the door and yelled, "*You* get the fuck out!"

He just stood there looking at me. I was furious. I went to the kitchen, opened the refrigerator, and lined the three six-packs up at the kitchen sink. One at a time, I opened each can and dumped the beer into the sink. Eighteen empty cans stood on the sink and the smell of beer filled the kitchen. I hated his drinking. I didn't like the fact that my mother had to put up with it, and I didn't want the other kids to see what I saw.

I went back into the dining room and Pops was still standing there. It was like I was losing my mind. I screamed at the top of my lungs for him to get out and not to come back. He didn't move but stared at me as if he hadn't heard a word I'd said. So I grabbed him by the arm and pushed him toward the half-open door. I pushed until he was outside the door, and then I slammed it shut. He stood outside in the snow, looking into the house. I went into the bathroom and cried.

That night I got on a plane for Saudi Arabia, wondering if everything would be okay between my parents. When I closed my eyes, I could still see my dad standing out there in the snow, looking lost. I'd been back in Riyadh three or four days when I called my mom and she told me that after my fight with my father, he'd gone to AA and was going to quit drinking. At the time, I didn't believe it. But to my father's great credit, he hasn't had a drink since that day in the winter of 1983. I think a lot about my own will and discipline, but I don't know if I've ever done anything as hard as it must have been for him to just stop like that. I'd like to believe that the argument was the breaking point he needed to make a change.

After he quit drinking, Dad and I grew closer than I ever could have imagined. He began telling me things that he never could when I was a kid, when his emotions were clouded by beer. I was almost thirty years old the first time he told me that he loved me. He hugged me and kissed me on the cheek, and I remember it being awkward. I don't have a single recollection of him kissing me when I was a kid, and when he did it that day, I hugged him back and started to cry. He didn't see me cry, and we didn't say anything, but if there is a lesson to be learned from my father's journey, it is that at any point in your life, no matter how far you've fallen, it's never too late to open your heart.

My relationship with my father wasn't the only one that needed work. It was difficult for Jackie at first, moving to Saudi Arabia, a tough, stubborn American woman in a country where women were second-class citizens, where they couldn't purchase land, couldn't drive, and could only work at jobs where they didn't come in contact with men.

Jackie made the most of living in such a repressive atmosphere. But it wasn't long before the smoldering politics and behind-the-scenes infighting of Saudi Arabia made it a dangerous place for both of us.

NIZAR Fetieh was a cardiologist, director of the King Faisal Hospital and personal physician for much of the royal family. He was also my boss. I reported directly to a man named Edward Burke, who was Dr. Fetieh's right-hand man.

Dr. Fetieh had risen to a position of great power in the Saudi medical community by personally seeing to it that the members of the House of Saud received top-notch care in a safe and discreet environment. Dr. Fetieh's discretion made him the caretaker of a wealth of damaging information, which included the drug and alcohol problems of a few royals—a potentially huge scandal in a country that is supposed to be dry and drug-free.

In the early 1980s, Dr. Fetieh found himself in a bitter war for control of the hospital with the popular minister of health, a man named Ghazi Algosaibi. Many Saudis believed that Dr. Fetieh was part of their corrupt past—protecting and catering to the pampered monarchy. Algosaibi, who hoped to sever the hospital from its past as the private clinic for the royals, represented the growing Saudi middle class. But that simplification missed the truth that boiled beneath all politics in Saudi Arabia: both men were working behind the scenes, lining up powerful allies within the royal family and outside it. It was nearly impossible to untangle the loyalties and motives of those involved, and the rewards that awaited the winner of their battle.

Inevitably, though, the damaging information that Dr. Fetieh had about the royal family turned out to be as dangerous to him as it was to them. Soon Saudi officials were questioning Dr. Fetieh's loyalty to the king, and the Saudi secret police came to the hospital and began conducting an investigation. Rumors swirled about Dr. Fetieh and his American security guards.

They asked me what security services I provided for Dr. Fetieh. Were we tapping phones? Doing surveillance? The allegations were cryptic, and at the same time ludicrous, but even as I tried to ignore them the scandal grew, and intrigue and treachery multiplied everywhere around us. It was nearly impossible to figure out the angles and who might be playing which side. Some people were undoubtedly using the scandal to make their own inroads with the royal family or to consolidate power or to rid themselves of rivals. To be an American caught in the middle of all this was troubling, and I found myself wondering how much longer I could stay.

Even before the scandal, I had begun to think about leaving Saudi Arabia behind. At the hospital I worked with a retired New York City police detective named Eugene Keene, who subscribed to the NYPD internal magazine, *Spring 3100*. When his magazine would arrive, I'd grab it and flip through it and be reminded of my old ambition, to be a New York City cop. Wow, I'd think as I read stories of bravery and self-sacrifice, I could really do this.

One day I was sitting at my desk looking through the magazine when Gene said, "Why don't you just call the New York Department of Personnel, get the application, and when you get home, take the test. You don't have to decide, just take the test."

So I got the phone number and called, and a woman answered. I told her I wanted an application to take the police exam. She asked for my address.

"Well, I live in Saudi Arabia."

"You have to be a U.S. citizen," she said. And then she hung up.

Twelve bucks a minute I was paying for this call and she'd hung up on me.

I called back. "Look, I just talked to a lady about a police application. I'm over here in Saudi Arabia, but don't hang up! I am a U.S. citizen."

"You gotta live in New York State," this woman said, and boom, she hung up too.

Gene suggested that I write to the mayor. So I sat down and wrote to Ed Koch, explaining that I hoped to return to New York and that it was my dream to be an NYPD officer. I listed all my experience and wrote the letter on stationery with the royal Saudi emblem.

I got three applications back from Koch, two from the police commissioner and three from the director of personnel.

That afternoon, when Tibor came in, I handed him one of the applications. "Here. Fill this out."

"NYPD?" he asked. "What are we gonna do there?"

"We're gonna work there," I said.

"How are we gonna take the test?" he asked.

"I don't know. When we go home, we'll take the test." I had to coax him to take the application.

In the meantime the scandal involving Dr. Fetieh was heating up, and he was catching flak for his relationships with Americans.

One man who worked in communications for the hospital was arrested, jailed, and tortured, his back broken. He had no recourse. As Americans working for private companies in Saudi Arabia, we were not supported by the U.S. State Department. We weren't official.

I thought about this one day as the Saudi secret police drove me to a nondescript building somewhere in Riyadh. They put me in a room under a bare lamp at a round table, and a bunch of secret policemen stood around staring at me. Two guys stood at the door, one holding a machine gun. It was as if they'd seen some old Humphrey Bogart movie and decided this was the way to interrogate an American.

"Were you in charge of an investigation of the king for Dr. Fetieh?"

"No," I said, "I don't know what you're talking about." I told them that I worked indirectly for Dr. Fetieh and handled routine hospital business and security and that if they had any questions, they should ask him. I insisted that I hadn't broken any laws.

Then suddenly a scrawny Saudi lieutenant leaned forward. The table was three and a half feet across, and when he finished leaning, our noses were inches apart.

"You know, Mr. Kerik," he said slowly, "you really need to be forthright. You need to tell the truth because your wife is here. This can be a very difficult country for your wife without you."

It took a second for his words to register. When they did, I grabbed him by his headdress, pulled him toward me, and spun him around so he was facing forward, the cloth of his headdress wrapped tightly around his neck. "I will snap your fuckin' head off," I said plainly. "I will kill you in front of all these people if you ever threaten me or my wife again."

The guards pointed their guns at me and yelled, and I finally let the lieutenant go. Several stressful minutes later, they were driving me back to my villa. "You will leave the country," one of the secret police said to me. To this day, I still can't say what was happening behind the scenes and where I fit in the various struggles. All I knew was that I wanted out. Four years of life in Saudi Arabia was enough. Let them sort through their own shit, I thought.

But first I had to actually get out of the country.

They picked Jackie and me up in a black van, the same

kind of vehicle they used to carry people to their beheadings. The windows were covered so we couldn't see out. We
bumped along in the van, hoping that we were indeed going
to the airport and that we had packed our bags for more than
just show.

At the airport, they rifled through our luggage and then
pushed it back at us to repack ourselves. This pissed Jackie
off. She was just twenty-two and very arrogant and not used
to being treated this way. She began flinging her clothes
around and getting louder and louder. Normally I would
have stopped her, but I was furious myself. Finally we
boarded the plane and settled in, next to each other, happy to
be returning to the sanity and security of the United States.

But we were about to find out that life at home would be
no picnic.

11

JOE'S ROOM

1985

HE looked like an ape. The thickest, darkest, jet-black hair sprouted in every direction—and not just from his head. His arms and shoulders were thatched with fine black baby hair. He had sideburns down to his lips.

And he was the most beautiful thing I'd ever seen in my life.

My son was born by C-section on June 11, 1985, at 10:45 in the morning. He was two weeks late, and Jackie and I spent much of that time arguing over what to name him. It was probably the most pleasant of the hundreds of fights we'd had since returning from Saudi Arabia. Jackie wanted to call him Michael Anthony, but I wanted a name from the Bible and settled on Joseph—the favorite son of Jacob, who was sold into slavery by his brothers, only to return as a powerful man who rescued his father and brothers and their families from famine.

I hadn't wanted a boy necessarily. I just wanted a healthy child, boy or girl. But now I kept thinking to myself, This is my son. My son! I could feel him breathing against my chest as they wheeled Jackie into the recovery room. Since my wife was still unconscious, the nurse came into the room and asked me what we were going to name him. I thought for a moment. "Michael . . . no, wait. It will be Joseph Michael Anthony Kerik," I said, unable to look away from his dark, placid eyes, his perfect face. The nurse thought nothing of it. When Jackie came to, one of the nurses walked in and said, "Here's your beautiful son, Joseph." She almost had a heart attack.

"How could you?" she said.

"What? You wanted Michael Anthony and I wanted Joseph. We both got what we wanted."

I was twenty-nine years old. Until that point, my adult life had been one vast construction project—tearing myself down and rebuilding the parts into a better man, into Bernie Kerik the black belt, the soldier, the cop, the husband. I spent years building myself this way—from the *outside in,* from the raw material of muscles and martial arts, army uniform, and stylish European clothes.

And then, in a matter of minutes, as I held my newborn son, I realized that you become a man from the *inside out,* that all my strength, my intense desire to protect and help people, came from within me, not from the military or from my mentors in Saudi Arabia or from a police uniform. And at that moment, every bit of my strength was directed at protecting this tiny, helpless, hairy being. I would give my life for him.

I stared into those dark brown eyes and they stared back into mine and I knew why I'd been put on this earth. Nine years earlier, I'd been too immature to do what I should have done when Yi came to me in Korea and told me she was having a baby. My failure to act responsibly haunts me to this day. I thought about my daughter and hoped and prayed that wherever she was, she had someone there who loved and protected her as much as I would now love and protect Joe.

JACKIE and Joe and I lived in Passaic, right next to Paterson, on the first floor of a two-family house in a nice middle-class neighborhood. Jackie and I had come back to Passaic after leaving Saudi Arabia in July 1984. But behind our new suburban cover was an increasingly difficult marriage. By the time Joe was born, Jackie and I were arguing constantly. She resented the long hours I worked, and wanted nothing to do with my ambition to become a New York City police officer.

On Eugene Keene's advice, Tibor and I had filled out the applications for the NYPD during our last stint in Saudi Arabia. Tibor had come back to the States a month or two after us and resumed his apparent lifelong quest to become one of the ten police officers in Carteret, New Jersey.

I had gotten my old job back at the Passaic County Jail and had been named assistant commander of the SERT, the Sheriff's Emergency Response Team. In fact, my brother, Don, who came to work at the jail, used to jokingly say that I *was* the Emergency Response Team, that the policy was to lock down the block until Bernie Kerik showed up. I also resumed my role as training officer, and I was certified to teach everything from underwater diving to hostage negotiation to counterterrorism. That summer I got Tibor a job at the jail, and in September of 1984, he and I went to Murry Bergtraum High School and took the NYPD entrance exam.

The following spring they let us know that we'd passed, and we had a decision to make. Do we leave good solid jobs with bright futures in an affordable place to go live in one of the most expensive cities in the world and work for less pay at a more dangerous job? Would we get lost in the tens of thousands of police officers in New York, assigned to some subway tunnel somewhere? Whenever I asked anyone for advice, they said I was nuts to consider leaving my good job in Passaic County. The flood of people was moving in the other direction; families worked for years in the city to be able to afford a move out to the suburbs. And here I was, actually considering going the other way.

That's what was constantly on my mind the summer Joe was born. I couldn't decide how to make this decision. I talked to people and read everything I could get my hands on about New York cops. I talked to Jackie and my family about it. But I kept coming back to the same question. How could I leave a good job in which I was so well paid, so respected and valued? The sheriff of Passaic County had even pulled me aside when he heard I was thinking of leaving and told me that if I just stayed patient, I would be rewarded for my hard work. I imagined that he meant I would soon take over as head of the Emergency Response Team.

My reputation at the jail had carried over from high school. Most of the inmates knew me, and to those who didn't, the word would spread: Don't mess with Kerik. When a problem arose, I'd go into the vestibule outside the cells and say, "Okay, crack the gate." Then I'd venture into the dayroom or into the cells, and as likely as not the situation would resolve itself pretty easily. In part because of the success of the SERT, we never had a riot or a serious event involving the inmates. Years later, when I ran Rikers Island, I would realize how exceptional that was.

There were a few inmates who tried to challenge me, or who made veiled threats against me. I remember one serious bank robber, a big guy, six feet, two inches or so, with a reputation for being a stone killer.

When he was admitted to the jail, he was considered a threat to escape, so he was locked down and searched daily. "Crack the gate!" I'd say, and then I'd pull him out, put him on his knees, and search his cell, flipping his bunk and going through his personal belongings looking for weapons.

Then we got a note one day from an informant telling us that this guy had an elaborate plan to kill me and a lieutenant named Scott Chaplain. He had placed two pills inside a condom and inserted it up his rectum. The pill was designed to help alcoholics quit drinking by making them ill when they drank. His plan was to take the pills, then suck on an alcohol swab and make himself sick enough to be taken to the hospital. He knew that if he was transported to the hospital, it would be by Scott and me, and his sister would have someone waiting there to whack us. He and his sister had hired a hit man to do the job. There was only one problem with the plan: the hit man was an undercover New Jersey state trooper.

When we first heard the story, it seemed like something out of a movie, and it didn't sink in until the undercover met with the sister for the payoff. At that point the party was over, and I felt great about pulling this guy out of his cell and whispering in his ear that his sister was in custody. "And one more thing," I said, "I have a search warrant for your ass. You can give it up nicely, or go to the hospital where it will be physically removed." Personally, knowing that he intended to kill me, I would have liked the hospital trip, but in the end it wasn't necessary. He gave it up and the plot was foiled.

It was great when Don came to work with me as a correction officer. He had quit running with thugs and graduated from high school, and I didn't feel the need to watch over him. I was tough on him in different ways now, trying to show him what it took to be the best. I held him to a much higher standard than the other correction officers, but this time Don was up for the challenge, and he worked hard to earn my trust at the jail. Still, he says that he was the most-suspended officer in the history of the jail. I was a stickler for uniforms, and since Don was my brother, I used him as my example. I'd turn Don's tie inside out looking for lint balls, and if I found any, I'd send him home.

Even some of the prisoners would bust his chops. "Hey, Kerik! Your creases are a little crooked. Don't let your brother see that shit."

I also wanted to show him how dangerous the jail could be and that you had to face the danger head-on. His first day on the job, I had him shadow me so I could show him around. Suddenly there was an alarm in one of the dayrooms in maximum security. I responded with Don in tow. The inmates in this area were the worst of the worst, murderers, robbers, and rapists, all awaiting trial.

Someone had been smoking pot in the dayroom, and when the officer on duty tried to find out who it was, the biggest guy in the room challenged and threatened him. The officer then called for assistance, and when other officers arrived, the inmate, whose name was Anthony—six feet, five inches tall, 280 pounds—let it be known that he wasn't leaving the area peacefully. The supervisor on the floor then called for assistance.

When I arrived with Don, I told Anthony to step outside, but he refused. I asked twice more, but he wouldn't budge, so I told him that the next option was to have the K-9 (dogs) go in and get him. He immediately had a change of heart and walked out peacefully. Don and I escorted him to the elevator, walked him in, and I told him to keep his hands on the wall until we arrived on the first floor. As soon as he realized that it was only Don and I in the elevator and the door closed, he turned from the wall swinging. Within ten seconds it was over, and Anthony lay on the floor unconscious. I turned to Don, who was now as white as a sheet. He stared at me with his eyes as wide as silver dollars. I said, "Okay, Don, open the elevator door."

He stood there not moving, and all of a sudden he said, "I feel sick."

I said, "Don, open the fucking elevator."

His hand was shaking so badly that he couldn't press the button. I grabbed his finger, pressed the button, and the door opened.

But most days at the jail were more tedious than they were dangerous, and sometimes they were very sad. One day I walked into the control room on the first floor and looked into the intake area, which is usually empty unless there are inmates being processed. On this day I could see a guy lying on the metal bench, handcuffed and shackled to the wall. Beneath him was a pool of vomit, and you could see that he had shit his pants. I yelled at the officers in the office to have one of the nurses respond, and they said that the man was detoxifying and that the nurse had seen him several times already. I said, "Okay, get a trusty down here and get him cleaned up."

A few minutes later the trusty responded, and I followed him into the intake area. The man was facing the wall, lying on his side. I nudged him and told him to sit up so we could take off the restraints. He slowly rolled over. As our eyes met, I was stunned. I stared at him for a moment, recalling the last time I'd seen him. Ninth grade. I remembered the room. I remembered my mother's look of embarrassment sitting next to me. I remembered what he predicted for me: I'd be nothing but a vegetable.

It was Mr. Johns.

I helped remove the shackles from his hands and feet and walked him into the shower. The trusty cleaned up the mess while I helped Mr. Johns get undressed. After he was showered, I told the officers on duty to watch over him and to get him anything he needed. During his time in the jail, I kept him away from the predators and troublemakers. His words fifteen years earlier had really stung me, and I waited for him to sober up in the hope that he would see what I had become, but by then, Mr. Johns was too far gone.

JERRY Speziale was a fucking nut. That was the first thing I thought as I talked to him about joining the NYPD. I was still having trouble deciding what to do, and a friend at the jail named Jeff Breckenridge said I should call his friend, a former Passaic County correction officer named Jerry, who had decided to quit his job and go to New York City to work as a cop. Four years younger than me, Jerry Speziale had grown up just five miles from Paterson, but we had a lot more than geography in common. He'd been another budding juvenile delinquent who knew every cop in town—in his case, Wayne, New Jersey but who had grown out of it to become a law enforcement officer himself.

My first conversation with Jerry should have convinced me to stay right where I was. He was totally manic—changing subjects every few seconds and barely pausing for breath, talking a hundred miles a minute. He told me all the negative things about being a cop: the low pay, the lack of prestige and respect, the long hours and hard work, the politics. He had worked for the county while I was working abroad, and then in 1983 he'd given it all up to go be a New York City cop. Now he was working in the Four-Six Precinct, the part of the South Bronx known as "the war zone," at a time when crime was high and the cops' morale was low. And yet in between his rants, I could tell just how much he loved it. It was in his blood, like it was in mine. With all the problems that came with being a cop, I asked him, did he ever wish he'd stayed in Passaic County? "Not for a fuckin' minute," he said. Jerry and I clicked right away, and we talked often and became fast friends.

Afterward I asked Breckenridge if his boy was on speed. Nah, he laughed, that's just the way he is. It wouldn't be long before I realized exactly what he meant.

My decision about whether to go to New York was tough, but it was about to get even tougher. In December 1985, I was at home on vacation when the sheriff's secretary called and said he wanted to see me in his office as soon as possible. In my uniform. Uh-oh, I thought. What had I done? I got dressed and went down to the jail, and all the brass were sitting in his outer office quietly.

I went into Sheriff Edwin Englehardt's office, and he explained that an undersheriff was retiring, and he intended to make the warden, John Bonazzi, the new undersheriff. He also wanted to make Curtis Taylor, the commander of the SERT, the second undersheriff.

I knew what this meant. I would finally get to run the SERT myself.

"That's fantastic," I said. "That's great."

"You know what that means, right?"

"Sure. John's gonna have to move his office."

"We're gonna need a warden."

"Yes, sir, that too."

"You're gonna be the warden."

I sat there for a long minute, trying to figure out if I'd just heard what I thought I'd heard. My civil service ranking was essentially that of correction officer. There were maybe a dozen lieutenants, a handful of captains, and a deputy warden ahead of me in line, all of them my superiors. Englehardt was talking about leapfrogging me over a couple of dozen correction officers, some with more than twenty-five years of experience. I had two. How could I be the warden of the jail?

Englehardt told me that I had qualities that transcended rank, qualities that caused others to respond to my leadership and my commitment. In short, the sheriff said, I was a guy people naturally followed, so he'd decided to go ahead and make it official.

I had just turned thirty years old, and here I was responsible for 265 employees, for 1,100 inmates, for the largest county correctional facility in New Jersey—with an annual budget of $7.2 million. At that time, I was the youngest warden ever to run the Passaic County Jail.

If people had tried to talk me out of joining the NYPD before, now they were adamant about it. I was making fifty-two thousand dollars a year—good money in 1986—had a car and a staff and the gold warden's shield. How could I give up all that to walk a foot post on some cruddy street in New York? Even Speziale—whose dream of being a New York City cop mirrored mine—said I'd be crazy to take a 50 percent pay cut to go back to being a rookie.

At that point the New York Police Department wasn't exactly beating my door down anyway. Investigators were assigned to do background investigations on all the candidates who passed the entrance exam, but for some reason, our investigator wasn't moving too quickly.

The combination of this slow process and my success at the jail had just about convinced me that I was better off forgetting my dream of working in the Big Apple. Then I was asked to speak at an antiterrorism conference in Philadelphia. At the conference I met a guy named Donald Hurley, a detective assigned to the NYPD bomb squad who had been injured in an explosion on New Year's Eve in 1981. We had a long conversation, and I told him how everyone said I was crazy for wanting to join the NYPD.

"Listen," he said, "you want to go to the best police department in the world? 'Cause I work for the best police department in the whole world." He shook his head. "So no, I don't think you're crazy at all."

At that conference I also met a guy named David Frazer, who turned out to be an NYPD applicant investigator. He was shocked when I told him that the investigator looking into Tibor and me was dragging his feet. Here I was, training law enforcement agents from all over the country at this conference, and they weren't sure I could be a street cop. He said he'd try to find out what was holding up our files. A few days later he called up, laughing. "What is all this shit in your file? Your fuckin' folders are four inches thick. There's all this foreign writing. What is all this stuff?"

Apparently our résumés had sort of overwhelmed the investigators. They were used to processing guys whose experience was at a Burger King or as a mall security guard, and they were having difficulties checking out our credentials.

Dave Frazer took over our investigations and quickly realized we had more experience than many veteran cops, let alone police academy applicants. So just like that, we were in. Now we just had to decide if we really wanted the job.

ON February 26, 1986, I woke up early with a strange feeling that something was wrong. I looked over at Jackie. It was hard to believe how peaceful she looked. Most days all I got from her was verbal abuse—she berated me and baited me into arguments, mostly over my job. I hate to argue. We had been fighting so much lately that I didn't even want to come home. Instead I'd work late or go to my office at the jail and sit until eleven or midnight or one in the morning. Then I'd call my friend Gary Uher, another correction officer, and have him pick me up and take me for coffee at a little diner until three or four, and then I'd go back to work and get ready for the day. Everything seemed to spark a fight between Jackie and me, and it was plain that we couldn't continue the way we were going.

I got out of bed and looked at the clock. It was 6:30 A.M. and I didn't have to be at work until nine. I went into Joe's room and found him lying in the huge brass crib, gurgling and talking to himself. I lifted him from the crib and sat in a rocker. I held him to my chest as tears streamed down my face. I couldn't do this anymore. I couldn't live with Jackie and watch us make each other miserable any longer. Joe had been the only thing keeping us together, and now I was considering leaving, and yet how could I do that to this little boy? Would he grow up thinking his father had abandoned him? I knew how it felt to be abandoned, and I didn't want that for him. I sat there going over it in my mind, wondering if there was something I was missing, something else I could do, some way to salvage this thing. When I looked down, Joseph had fallen asleep in my arms. I leaned over and kissed him, smelling the baby cologne that Jackie put on him. He looked so soft and secure in his own little world as I placed him in bed next to her. I stood over the bed watching them both sleep, and then I went to take a shower.

The ride to the jail in Paterson normally took about twenty minutes, but at that hour, it only took ten. The officers and shift commander had gotten used to seeing me at any time of day, and I walked right past them to my office and sat down at my desk.

A lieutenant at the jail, Brian Bendle, had left a *New York Post* on my desk. I held it up for a moment to look at the headlines. And that's when I started to get the same uneasy feeling that had kept me from sleeping earlier.

The *Post* headline screamed "2 Dead, 3 Cops Shot in Wild Bronx Shootout."

The hair stood up on the back of my neck as I looked at the picture of Jerry Speziale and his two partners, John Lynn and Crystal Rodriguez. A crack addict had shot a woman to death and shot all three cops during a twenty-minute running gun battle that only ended when the gunman was hit in the head by a shotgun blast from an Emergency Services cop. I flipped through the story, but there were few details. I didn't even know if Jerry was dead or alive.

I had just talked to him the night before and grilled him again about whether or not to come to New York. He was excited because in two days he was going to be transferred to narcotics and begin working toward his detective shield. "If you really want to be a cop," he said, "this is the place you gotta do it." And now he'd been shot while doing the job I was considering giving up everything for.

I reached Jerry at the hospital. He was okay and so were his partners. Crystal Rodriguez's bulletproof vest had essentially kept her from taking a fatal shot to the chest. John Lynn had been shot in the hip, and Jerry had taken one in the arm.

Jerry was completely doped up by the doctors but was still as hyperactive as ever. "The guy shot the fuckin' lady and then the fuckin' bullets are flyin' . . ." I could barely keep up. "Wow," he said at the end of our conversation, "what a great fuckin' job." I laughed. Here was this guy who had just been in a gun battle, who had watched a woman murdered, who saw the suspect's head blown off, who could easily have been killed if the bullet had gone a few inches in another direction, and all he could talk about was how great the job was. And the funny thing was, he may have sounded crazy to most people, but for one of the few times since I've known Jerry Speziale, he made perfect sense to me.

I don't know how many sleepless nights I spent in Joe's room, bent over his brass crib, watching him sleep peacefully, wondering what I should do. Could I still take care of him if I lived somewhere else? If I went to New York, would I lose touch with him? I'd already lost one child in Korea, and I wasn't going to lose this one too.

And yet life between Jackie and me was unbearable. Every night I felt my anger rise as she yelled at me about my work, about being gone all the time, about anything and everything. I had really had enough.

It was the late spring of 1986 when Dave Frazer called and said, "Look, you gotta tell me if you're going." Tibor and I were approaching thirty-two—the age limit for the police academy—and we had to decide.

I called upstairs in the jail where Tibor worked. "Well," he said, "I'll do whatever you do. You wanna go? I'll go. You wanna stay? I'll stay."

I called Speziale, and he said that if I was truly considering it, I couldn't tell Sheriff Englehardt. He had invested a lot in making me the warden of the jail and would do whatever he could to convince me to stay. Jerry advised me to do what he'd done. The day he left for the police academy, Jerry put on his Passaic County uniform and headed off as if it were any other day. He didn't even tell his wife until afterward because he was afraid she'd leave him. He just drove to New York City, was sworn in by the mayor, and returned home one of New York's finest.

On June 11, 1986, we held Joe's first birthday party at a restaurant called Michelle's in Garfield, New Jersey. We had cake and ice cream and everyone smiled as we opened toys and clothes and Joe played with the wrapping paper. Our families were with us, and our friends. But our marriage had deteriorated as far as it could, and Jackie and I kept our distance to avoid arguing. At the end of the party, I picked Joe up and we danced alone in a corner of the dance floor. A song came on—"There'll Be Sad Songs"—and I just stood there, turning in circles and holding my boy. Behind me, I could hear Mom and Jackie and everyone talking, as if everything were fine.

None of them knew that I had finally called David Frazer and told him, "Okay, I'm coming." None of them knew that I planned to move out of my house the next day. None of them knew that in one month I would cross the Hudson River and follow my dream of being a New York City cop. When the music ended, I held Joe to my chest and cried and quietly asked him to forgive me.

12

MIDTOWN SOUTH

1987

"SO who's your hook?"

Tibor stared at the other young PPO—probationary police officer—sitting next to him at the police academy. "Hook? What's a hook?"

"You know," the guy said, "your juice. Who's going to help your career along? You got a friend? A relative? Who do you know?"

For as long as there have been cops, the New York Police Department has run this way, fathers getting sons choice assignments, uncles pulling rank to get their nephews on good foot posts or in cars, friends greasing the skids for friends. The NYPD is a complex society, and the idea of "juice" or "a hook" or "a contract"—a whole system of connections and relatives and favors—is part of that. At its best, the system provides a sense of family in a job that desperately needs it. At its worst, that system of juice and hooks breeds nepotism and creates an environment that the best cops hate because it leads to officers being promoted because of who they are, not what they can do. That's what Tibor and I faced as we came in cold to the police academy in July 1986. We had no uncles, no brothers, no relatives, no friends to get us good assignments and watch out for us.

"I don't know anybody," Tibor admitted.

The recruit nodded knowingly. "You got no hook."

That's when Tibor nodded across the table at me. "See that guy over there? That's my hook."

The recruit looked doubtful. "How is he a hook? He's a PPO like you and me."

Tibor smiled. "Maybe, but that guy's gonna be the police commissioner one day." Even as he said it, Tibor wasn't sure where it came from. It was the first time it had really occurred to him, and yet—he says now—the more he thought about it, the more sense it made. Recently I talked to the cop, now a lieutenant, who asked Tibor about his hook, and we laughed at T.'s ability to read the future. Still, if someone had come to Tibor and me right then, as we sat at the table with the other raw recruits, and said that I would be the commissioner in just fourteen years, we would've arrested him on drug charges.

Mayor Ed Koch had sworn our academy class in during a ceremony at the Brooklyn Technical Institute—Tibor and I surrounded by twenty-two hundred other potential cops, most of them barely more than kids. The New York Police Academy—housed in a green brick building on East 20th between Second and Third Avenues—bills itself as the "West Point" of law enforcement training, but when we attended, it was something of a disappointment to me. There were academic classes in police science, law, and social science, physical education, as well as firearms and tactics training. But for being the biggest and best police academy in the country, it struck me as not challenging enough. Maybe this was because it was the third police academy I'd attended, and I was used to army basic training, the rigors of martial arts, and the rigid requirements of guys like Billy Joe Turner. But I just felt that the academy would have benefited greatly from taking itself more seriously and instituting a more military style.

Of the twenty-two hundred recruits, Tibor and I were the second and third oldest at thirty-two and thirty-one. Most of these kids were twenty. So I guess I could understand the academy being difficult for them academically, or in the area of common sense, but the physical limitations of these guys surprised me. Every other day we were assigned to run inside a gym, and it was painful to see how many of these young guys were sucking wind after running three laps and how many of them had to walk. Tibor and I just shook our heads.

We graduated on December 18, 1986. I sat in a folding chair on the floor of Madison Square Garden in my crisp new uniform and bright white gloves and looked around at my classmates. For many of them this was about finding a good job with benefits and a great pension. For me it was much more. For me the shield of the NYPD represented the best of what a man strives to be—strong and fair, courageous and resilient. I was a police officer in the greatest city in the world. This was who I was born to be.

TIBOR and I lived in Brooklyn, in a tiny two-bedroom apartment on top of a small kitchen on Metropolitan Avenue. Tibor took the bigger bedroom. I slept in the living room, and we used the smaller bedroom as a closet. There was a tiny bathroom and a kitchen just big enough for a small table and two chairs, and that was it. We'd wanted to live in Manhattan but we didn't have a nickel between us, and we needed an apartment right away because we had to have a city address to become city cops. Our first day in the city, I'd grabbed a *Village Voice* and called up the first apartment I saw.

"Is it still vacant?" I asked.

"Yeah," the landlord said. "Seven hundred a month."

"We'll take it," I said.

He sounded suspicious. "Don't you want to see it?"

"Yes, but we'll take it."

I didn't realize just how broke I was. I had been making fifty-two thousand a year as the warden of the Passaic County Jail. I started as a New York City police officer at twenty-seven thousand. A lot of people don't realize it, but cops have to pay for their own uniforms and shoes and guns. The first six months are especially tough, and by the time those extras had been deducted from my pay, my yearly take-home was closer to twenty-five thousand. I had taken a job for half the pay in a city twice as expensive.

I think in the back of my mind, I still hoped that Jackie and I could find some miracle to repair our marriage and that she and Joe would eventually join me in New York, but in reality, we only grew further apart. I gave her every cent I could spare—and many that I couldn't—for Joe's care, and before I knew it I was sinking in debt. On the weekends I'd drive out to Jersey and pick up Joe and bring him back to the city, and he'd sleep next to me in the living room of our tiny apartment. Or we'd hang out with my parents. He'd lost that layer of black baby hair, and he was the cutest and sweetest kid, his big brown eyes so dark they looked black. We had a great time, and I quickly saw that I could be a good father even if I could no longer pretend to be a husband. I couldn't wait for Fridays because I knew that by the end of the night, Joe and I would be together.

But sometimes Jackie wouldn't let me see him. Once, when I went to pick him up, she took the support check from me, then locked the door and would only let me look at him through the window. She wouldn't let me in. That was how I felt then, locked out of his life, stuck outside, staring in. I stood outside her door crying and pleading, but she wouldn't budge. This scene would repeat itself from time to time.

It was the low point of my life. I'd drive over from New York expecting to see Joe for the weekend, but at the last minute Jackie would decide I couldn't see him. So I'd go to my parents' house, sit on the couch, and call her all weekend, hoping she would change her mind. My mom remembers coming in and seeing me sitting on the couch, eyes wet, staring off into space, the phone in my lap. She said it scared her because she'd never seen me beaten before. Eventually my debt topped twenty thousand dollars. I could feel my fu-

ture eroding out from under me. Each week that passed, I'd
pay my bills, give the rest to Jackie, and watch my bank balance fall further behind. Every day I fell a little bit deeper in
debt. It was a smothering feeling, knowing that the money
just wouldn't stretch, no matter what I did. Finally I had to
declare for bankruptcy protection.

Through all of this, Tibor was a great friend. During the
academy, I took classes at 8:00 A.M., while he was on the
second shift, at 4:00 P.M., and when he got off, we'd mess
around Brooklyn or race down to Greenwich Village to hang
around the coffee shops, drink cappuccinos, and people-
watch. Neither of us really liked to drink booze or dance, so
we didn't party or hang out in clubs. For us, it was enough
being two young guys loose in the city.

Like all academy graduates, we were assigned to NSU—
Neighborhood Stabilization Units—where we would get
on-the-job training as patrol officers for six months before
being assigned to our permanent commands. Tibor did his
NSU in Brooklyn South. I went to Brooklyn North, to
Bedford-Stuyvesant, one of the busiest and most racially divided neighborhoods in the city. Most cops spent their six-
month NSU assignment listening, running errands for the
cops, and just staying out of the way. Only the most active
cops make arrests during their time at NSU, and we were
among them, Tibor making a couple of arrests in Brooklyn
South, while I made about a dozen. But then with twenty
years of criminal justice experience between us, Tibor and I
weren't typical rookies. We had more experience and energy than a lot of the cops we were supposed to be learning
from

One day Tibor came home stumped. "Hey," he said,
"where do we want to go to work? We gotta put in for a permanent command." We were almost finished with NSU, and
in a matter of weeks we'd be assigned to patrol some neighborhood.

"I don't know," I said. "I'd love to work in Manhattan. I
mean, that's New York, right? Where else we gonna work?"

That made sense to Tibor. "So which precinct is that?" he asked.

I didn't know. The only thing that popped into my head was Kojak answering the phone: "Manhattan South." So I called a cop I knew and told him that we didn't know what precinct it was, but we wanted to work where Kojak worked.

"Oh," he said, "what you want is Midtown South."

"Midtown South," I told Tibor.

"All right."

What we didn't know was that every cop wants to work in Midtown South. It's one of the most glamorous, busiest, craziest, and most recognizable police precincts in the world. Tibor told a kid from the academy, Bob Flaherty, that he and I wanted to go to Midtown South and that we only wanted to work together. It turned out that Bob's father worked in personnel, and he told his dad about us. A few days later, the permanent command assignments came over the Teletype machines in all the precinct houses.

The young cops gathered around the Teletypes, which churned out the lists of names followed by the numbered precinct houses we'd been assigned to. The precincts rolled past: 102, 75, 17, 94, and then came my name, but there was no number listed after it, just the letters MTS. In Brooklyn South, Tibor stared at the same letters.

I turned and asked a lieutenant, "What's MTS?"

"Midtown South," he said. "Is your dad on the job or something?"

I went down the list. There were seven guys going to Midtown South out of more than two thousand applicants. Somehow, with no hooks, no juice, and no contracts, we had gotten the best assignment in the entire police department.

I was so excited. After work that night I went home and changed my clothes. I called a woman I'd just started seeing, and we went to the Empire State Building and took the elevator to the observation deck. I walked around the edge, taking in the towers of brick and glass, the long strips of asphalt, the land that I was now responsible for. After thirty-one years, I felt like I had arrived.

THE entrance to the Midtown South Precinct House was packed every day like a casting call for a movie—hookers in fishnet stockings milling about with tourists in Bermuda shorts who'd had their cameras stolen, thieves and drug dealers in handcuffs, lawyers and family members, and uniformed cops squeezing past them all to go back out to patrol the streets. A gruff uniformed lieutenant stood behind a huge desk that was as high as visitors' chests, and on the wall next to him was a sign with a big red apple in the middle that summed up life in Midtown South: You Have Just Entered the Busiest Precinct in the Entire World.

The Midtown South Precinct was less than a square mile and was home to only about seventeen thousand people—one of the smallest and least populated precincts in the city. But four million people might walk through it on a given day. Most of the New York that tourists favor is in that precinct—from Penn Station to Madison Square Garden, parts of the theater, garment, and fur districts, the New York Public Library, Macy's, the Empire State Building, and Times Square. If you have a postcard of New York, chances are the picture was taken in the Midtown South Precinct.

We started with orientation. A huge guy—six feet, four inches, 250 pounds—walked in, a fat stub of cigar dangling from his mouth, and introduced himself as Inspector Richard Mayrone. "Okay," he growled, "here's the deal. You don't wear nothing on your uniform that ain't given to you by the police department. And you don't fuckin' take nothing that you don't pay for. If I catch you doing that, I'll kick you in your dick. Any questions?"

And that was Inspector Mayrone's orientation. Not surprisingly, there were no questions. I turned to Tibor and we both smiled and nodded. I liked him. This was the kind of guy we could work for.

My first day in Midtown South I was assigned a foot post, walking near the Empire State Building, on Fifth Avenue between 34th and 38th Streets, a big, busy three-block stretch. They turned me loose, and I stood in my brand-new uniform on the corner of 34th and Fifth, watching the crowds move past. After a few minutes I spotted an older man walking up the block with a cane. I stepped in behind him. There was something in his back pocket, where his wallet should be. He noticed me watching him, and he began walking faster. Pretty soon he wasn't even using the cane anymore, just sort of dragging it behind him. After a while the cane wasn't even touching the ground.

At 37th Street I caught up with him. "Excuse me, sir. Can I talk to you? Are you a policeman? Or a retired policeman?"

"No, sir," he said.

"I was just wondering, see . . . that wouldn't happen to be a gun in your back pocket, would it?"

He just stared at me, shocked. He looked over his shoulder to see if he could see it. "I . . . I got robbed one time."

"I'm sure you did, but, sir, you can't carry a gun in the city without a permit. Do you have a permit for the gun?"

"No, sir."

"All right. You know what, turn around. I gotta get the gun."

He reached for it.

"No, no, no," I said. "Don't worry. I'll get it." I reached in his back pocket and pulled out a small-caliber handgun, wrapped in a sock.

I had him put his hands behind his back and I handcuffed him. He was a pleasant guy, and we had a decent conversation. "You just can't carry a gun like that, sir."

I called for a car to come pick him up, but no one was responding. I stood on the sidewalk with this guy in custody. I called in again. Nothing. I waited another five minutes and called again. "Look, Central, I got a man with *a gun* at Thirty-seven and Five. Could you please send a car to pick us up?" At the mention of a gun, cars came from everywhere, sliding in, cutting each other off. Gun arrests are a priority in New York, but they're somewhat rare. Some cops go a year or two or more without seeing a gun.

The first cop who arrived at my foot post looked dumbfounded at this rookie cop making a gun collar on his first day in the command. "What've you got?"

"Twenty-five automatic."

"Let me see."

"Nah. It's here in this sock."

"Well, let me hold it," the cop said.

"Look, I need to get this guy into the precinct."

"Just let me hold the gun."

"No, you're not fucking holding the gun."

This guy had been on the job five years and had never made a gun collar.

Outside the precinct on West 35th, I jacked out the rounds. I marched my suspect through the front door, past the sign Busiest Precinct in the Entire World, and up to the tall desk, where I saluted the lieutenant.

"What've you got?"

"I got possession of a weapon." I put the gun and the magazine on the counter.

The lieutenant stared at me like he didn't have time for some wiseass. "Where'd you get the gun?"

"I got it off the guy."

"Where was it?"

"It was in a sock in his back pocket."

"Why'd you search him?"

"I didn't search him. I asked him for the gun."

"How'd you know there was a gun if you didn't search him?"

"I could see it in his pocket."

"That guy had this gun wrapped up in a sock in his pocket and you saw it?"

"Yeah."

The lieutenant seemed annoyed. He told me to put the

prisoner in the cells and come back to the desk. When I returned to the desk, he started questioning me all over again. He was sure I was lying and that I had searched the old man illegally and found the gun. When I finished explaining everything all over again, he stomped off to the cells and talked to the suspect. "That officer, how'd he find the gun?"

"I don't know," he said. "He's like Superman. He just knew it was there."

The lieutenant came back out and pulled me aside. "C'mere," he said. "Seriously, how'd you know the gun was in his pocket?"

Now I was getting really frustrated. "Look, I know this is my first day. But trust me. I've been doing this for a long time. It's my job to look for suspicious activity. You watch and you see things. And I saw a gun."

"Wrapped in a sock?"

"Wrapped in a sock."

"In his back pocket?"

"In his back pocket."

I'd end up having the same trouble with the prosecutor, who was positive I had searched the guy illegally. By then, some of the cops were joking about my X-ray vision. I guess when you make a gun collar on your first day, it's something cops don't forget.

Of course I liked the reputation I quickly got, but there's nothing magic about making gun or knife arrests. I just watch people. I see things. Even now I'll be in a crowd and I'll watch waistbands and pockets, watch to see if a guy keeps his hand at his midsection. If I see the imprint of a gun, I'll quickly look at the guy's back pocket. A New York City police shield has two lugs where the pin goes through, and an off-duty or undercover cop will often carry his shield in his back pocket, with those two lugs pointing out so they don't poke him in the ass. So if I see a guy with a gun who also has two small indentations in his back pocket, I figure he's on the job. A big part of policing is just being aware of things like that, just observing and stepping in *before* crimes happen. Guns are a good example. I don't know what would've happened if I hadn't seized that gun. Maybe it never would've been used. But what I'm sure of now is that some other cop never had to bend over and fish that particular gun out of a pool of blood to mark it as evidence.

THEY called us "buffs"—as in crime buffs—the implication being that to us, police work was more than a job and more like a hobby. To the handful of deadweight cops in Midtown South who were threatened by Tibor and me, it might have been a criticism, but it was pretty close to the truth. We came onto the job as aggressive and active as any cops in the precinct, making arrests and writing summonses as fast as we could write the reports.

The brass even took the unusual step of making us partners—something they almost never did with two rookies. Maybe they thought Tibor and I were the only guys who could keep up with each other. For whatever reason, they just turned us loose, and we took to the job like we'd been preparing for it our whole adult lives—which, of course, we had.

Most of the other police officers seemed to respect our military bearing and our desire to be the best. But we could see that we were also pissing off a few—mostly the zeroes who hadn't been pulling their weight in years. I suppose it's always been this way; there are workers and there are slackers. When a recent study showed that 12 percent of cops make 90 percent of the arrests in New York, I wasn't surprised, but I vowed to do something about that. Obviously some cops are in jobs where they don't make arrests, but hiding in those numbers are some burnouts and slackers—cops who spend their day *avoiding* work. In Midtown South we had our share of cops whose biggest action each week came when they cashed their checks. Some of them would even buddy up to us at the end of the month, hoping we'd give them an arrest so they wouldn't look so bad.

There were plenty of good cops in Midtown South. But

there was this thin layer of zeroes on top, many of whom came from cop families and felt that because they were related to someone else on the job, they were entitled to certain things. They expected better posts and sector cars and to be the first ones to go to the plainclothes Anticrime Unit. So to them, buffs like Tibor and me—and a few other aggressive cops in Midtown South—raised the bar and made their arrest totals look even more pitiful.

They counted on the fact that most young cops were intimidated by the job and by these pampered, lazy kids whose idea of being a cop was just to put in their time until their juice kicked in and they were moved to a better job. But Tibor and I weren't intimidated. We started out making twice as many arrests as most of these guys. I had no use for cops who wanted me to slow down so they didn't look bad. Tibor, on the other hand, was always better at getting along with people by charming them. I pretty much just told them to stay out of my way.

One day a cop sidled up to Tibor. "Hey, what's with your buddy?" he asked. "Who does he think he is?"

"Nobody," Tibor said.

"Really?" he asked.

"Yeah," T. said. "Nobody you want to fuck with."

But they did. Someone wrote SUPERCOP in big letters on my locker. I'd see a couple of them huddled off in some corner, talking about me. Or I'd go up to the bathroom on the second floor and see that some coward had painted KERIK IS AN ASSHOLE on the wall of the stall.

I should have let this immaturity slide off my back, but after the year I'd been through, I felt demoralized and disillusioned. I had dreamed for so long of being here, of belonging to this elite police department, and now a few jerks were getting pissed off because I was working *too hard*! I wanted camaraderie and a common goal, and instead I got this bullshit. Somehow this felt like the last straw. Maybe I'd made a mistake.

I was flat broke, still getting over the shame of divorce

and bankruptcy. I had to beg to see my son every weekend, and when I got him, we spent the weekend in an apartment the size of a closet. I began to wonder if this was worth it. I began to wonder if the NYPD was all that I'd imagined it to be, if my lifetime dream was only that. A dream.

I called some of my old contacts in Saudi Arabia and inquired about going back abroad. They told me that there was a job for me. This had been the toughest period of my life, and I found myself seriously considering leaving New York and all of it behind. I suppose the only thing that kept me from leaving was Joe.

Then one day my captain, Tom Fahey, pulled me aside. Fahey is now one of my two press officers and one of my closest advisers. He speaks with a wry and grizzled simplicity, like a good bartender or an old football coach. He said he'd heard that I was thinking of quitting. "Don't go," he said. "You're good at this."

I told him that the assholes in the precinct were really annoying me. I could get along without money or prestige, I said, but I couldn't work with immaturity and cowards who didn't have the courage to sign their names to anonymous letters or to the messages on the shithouse walls.

"I don't think you realize how good you are at this," he said. Fahey convinced me to keep working as hard as I had been. It would pay off, he told me. He also convinced me that I might have been wrong about those lazy cops being in the majority. They weren't the NYPD. Not really. The NYPD was guys like Inspector Mayrone and Captain Fahey, and they knew which guys saw this as a calling, as their duty. Today, most of those guys who harassed Tibor and me are long gone, drummed out for one reason or another. A few of them were even busted for protecting a brothel in the middle of the precinct. But Fahey and Tibor and the other good cops from Midtown South are still going strong.

That day, Captain Fahey told me that I had a great future in the NYPD if I stayed. Still, I don't think either of us ever imagined what the future included. At the end, Fahey patted me on the back and gave me that easy smile. "Hang in there," he said.

"Whatever you say, Cap."

Fourteen years later, I would be the police commissioner and would get the opportunity to return Tom Fahey's confidence, promoting him to assistant chief, one of the top ranks of the NYPD, and making him one of my closest aides.

13

THE DEUCE

1988

WE called it the Deuce. Forty-second Street, midtown Manhattan, New York, New York. If midtown is the heart of Manhattan—theaters and shopping and tourist attractions, glass and concrete high-rises—then 42nd Street is the heart of midtown. Broadway cuts a long, bright diagonal swath the length of Manhattan, and where it crosses 42nd Street and Seventh Avenue is a crash of neon—the block opening up into Times Square, the Crossroads of the World, the loudest, brightest, busiest, and maybe the most expensive piece of real estate in the whole world.

And that's where Tibor and I landed, just months into our careers as police officers. Our foot post was exactly one block long, 42nd Street between Seventh and Eighth Avenues. On some tours, it was all we could do to make it from one end to the other. The Deuce was the trouble factory. On other posts you might do a job or two every tour, but on the Deuce you could easily do twenty or twenty-five jobs. About once a week, someone jumped under a train or stepped off a building. The rest of the time, you had to prioritize your arrests because every time you hauled someone in you had to leave the street for a while. We ran out of cops before we ran out of crimes: armed robberies and thefts, drugs and sexual assaults, con men of all shapes and sizes, teams of muggers preying on tourists. And on every street corner were hookers.

I think now about my birth mother being shipped to New York to work as a prostitute, and I can almost see her in the tide of beaten women moving back and forth along the Deuce. They walked the strip at all hours. It didn't matter how many pimps we rousted, how many cops we posted, how many girls we arrested, there were always new young girls to take their place, girls so young you wondered if they had a choice at all, girls so desperate you couldn't help but wonder about the miserable life that had brought them there. If there is a place where the line between victim and criminal blurs, it was there on 42nd Street. It was there in the eyes of those women.

Still, for cops like Tibor and me, there was no place like the Deuce. If you wanted to be in the thick of the action, there was no other place. It was heaven on shift work. We'd rotate from first platoon—midnight to 8 A.M.—to second—8 A.M. to 4:00 P.M.—to third—4 P.M. to midnight—and back around to first platoon again. I loved being on patrol. I couldn't wait to get to work, and I hated it to end. I didn't even like to stop to eat. Tibor would just be sitting down with a sandwich and I'd be done already, grabbing my hat and saying, "Come on, how long does it take to eat a sandwich? Let's go!"

Once I got past the handful of losers in Midtown South, I found a core group of good cops and we gravitated toward one another, working together whenever we could. One of the first guys I met was Sean Crowley, a bright young kid who looked more like the youngest broker at the firm than the youngest cop on the beat. To this day, Sean is the last guy you'd pick as a cop, and thinking that he looks like a stockbroker isn't too far off, since he also runs his own tax preparation business in his off hours.

Even though we came on the job with Sean, Tibor and I were ten or twelve years older and more experienced, and so he quickly latched onto us as mentors. Later that year we found another eager kid, when a tough, baby-faced rookie named Bobby Picciano asked if he could tag along with Tibor and me. Some of the other older cops didn't want to be bothered by these eager young kids because they were afraid it would interfere with their loafing. But Tibor and I liked having Sean and Bobby Pitch around. They were exactly the guys we wanted backing us up if there was any trouble.

There were also a few veteran cops in Midtown South who had the right attitude, like Gerry Kane, a classic cop's cop who always knew what was going on and who spoke the language of cops in a pitch-perfect Noo Yawk accent: "We jus' put da fuckin' handcuffs on da fuckin' bad guys, eh, Bern?" Gerry was a family man, and he told me that his nervous wife always felt better when he could say, "Hey, don't you worry. I'm with Bernie Kerik tonight."

There was no better place in the world for hardworking cops than the Deuce. Tibor and I ate it up. When I became police commissioner, one of the cops from Midtown South recalled me as a "mayhem magnet" because I always seemed to be in the thick of things. It didn't take the criminals long to get to know us either. I'd just point to a pickpocket or a drug dealer, and he'd nod and start backing down the street. "Hey," he'd ask, "so what time do you get off, Kerik?"

One night Sean and his partner Ray Smith were walking the Deuce around midnight when they saw a guy who'd been busted repeatedly for drug dealing—one of the eighty or so regular dealers who worked that block. He was crouching in a doorway.

"Hey," Sean yelled. "Get out of here."

The mutt just mumbled something.

But when Sean walked back, the dealer was still huddled in that doorway.

"You see this guy, Smitty?" Sean asked his partner. "Didn't I just tell this guy to get out of here?"

"That's what I heard, Sean."

"Yeah," the dealer said, "but let me explain."

"Okay. Explain."

"Mustache was here earlier." A lot of the skells knew me by my thick mustache. "Mustache told me to stay right here until he came back."

Sean looked at his partner, and they both laughed. I had popped this guy on the day tour but didn't have time to book him just then and must've forgotten to come back. Here it was, ten hours later, and this guy was still waiting for me, too scared to move.

A lot of cops would let small stuff go on a beat like the Deuce, thinking they only had time for big jobs. But we felt the opposite way. Tibor and I tried to teach the younger cops that having zero tolerance for any criminal activity would eventually result in a cleaner and safer city. And it was important for another reason to lay paper on the professional criminals—write them up a summons for jaywalking, impeding traffic, or whatever they did wrong. I knew the summons was going in the garbage the minute I left. But then, when we suspected them of a rape or a robbery or a homicide, we had cause to pick them up—the warrant for failing to appear on the jaywalking charge. It was expected that a cop might write twenty summonses or so a month. Tibor and I did that in two days. We wrote everybody up. It wasn't long before the younger guys and the other buffs followed our lead.

But no matter how hard they worked or how much they picked up, even great cops like Sean, Gerry, and Bobby Pitch couldn't figure out how I got so good at taking guns off the street. Ever since my first day on the job I had shown a knack for it. I think part of it was my innate powers of observation, but there was also a trick that I didn't tell anyone about. I'd be walking with one of the other cops, and I'd point out some tough-looking dude. "That guy's got a gun."

They'd stare. "Are you sure?"

"Sure I'm sure."

They'd watch the guy, look at his pockets, at his jacket, and then shrug. "But how do you know?"

"I just know."

They'd seen this so often they eventually had to believe me, and so we'd go over and I'd ask the skell if he had a permit for his gun, and he'd just stare at me, amazed. Sometimes my partner for that day would get the collar, and whoever it was—Gerry or Sean or someone—would find himself on the spot when the prosecuting attorney called to make sure it was a legal search. "How did you know about the gun?" he would ask.

"Well, we just . . . I mean . . . ," Sean would stammer. "I guess we saw it."

"You . . . saw it?"

"Well, I didn't see it myself. . . . I mean, Bernie, well, we were walking and he . . . You know what? Now that you mention it, I have no idea how he saw it."

Gerry Kane's version of these incidents was usually more colorful: "We're humping up the Deuce and ol' Bern sees a couple mutts with a snake and a bag and he yells, 'Okay, who's got the fuckin' gun?' and I'm spinning around, saying, 'What gun? What fuckin' gun?' and he's doing some Pat Morita *Karate Kid* shit, putting these guys against the wall, yellin', 'Put down the snake! Put down the snake!' and then he reaches in this closed bag, and sure enough, he pulls out this .22 revolver all tricked out like a fuckin' .357 Magnum, with stainless steel and a big long barrel, big as a revolver. And I got no idea how he knew there was a gun in that bag."

What the guys didn't know was that I'd watched the block carefully for a few weeks and had come up with a plan. There was a hat store on 42nd that had shiny red metallic bags. Across the street was a store that was called—only on the Deuce—Kung Fu Equipment, Holsters and Fake IDs. So I went to the hat shop and grabbed a bunch of red bags, then I went into the Kung Fu Equipment, Holsters and Fake IDs shop. I got to know a guy who worked there and I asked him if he'd do me a favor. If someone came in to buy sticks or stars or fake ID's, I told him, go ahead and give them the normal white bags. But if they came in looking for a holster, put it in the red bag. After all, there was only one reason to buy a holster.

So I'd see some mope with a red bag, and I'd sidle up to him, as friendly as anything. "So you got a permit for that gun?" Ten minutes later, I don't know who looked more amazed, the guy I was arresting or my partner that day.

Eventually I told Sean and Gerry and Bobby Pitch, and they started doing it too. Someone in the Street Crime Unit heard, and they started doing it. Before I knew it, every third cop in New York was sitting on that store, watching intently for shiny red bags.

THE NYPD gives medals for excellent work—commendations for stopping crimes in progress, exceptional police duty medals for taking a gun off a criminal, medals of valor and honor for putting your life on the line in gun battles. It's a system that rewards officers who go beyond an already demanding job, officers who perform with rare courage and resourcefulness.

I remember one morning in 1987, Tibor and I were walking along the Deuce and we came across a traffic accident. A woman was pinned under the tires of a wrecked taxi. We sprinted over, and I quickly grabbed two guys off the street, and we lifted the cab off her while Tibor pulled her out. She had been loaded in an ambulance when we got a call that there was a bank robbery in progress at 41st and Seventh Avenue, at the Chase Manhattan Bank. We could hear the patrol cars trying to get there, but traffic was at a standstill. Tibor and I took off in opposite directions, to cover both exits. I ran across 42nd to Seventh, then down to 41st and into the bank. People were running away, scattering in every direction, screaming, "He's right there! He's got a bomb!"

A man about fifty years old was coming off the escalator,

carrying a leather bag with wires sticking out of it. I ducked in front of him, grabbed him, threw him to the ground, and handcuffed him. Other cops arrived and were yelling to stay away from the leather bag until the bomb squad could arrive, but I had some training in terrorism and explosives and I could see this was no bomb. I kicked it across the floor and then opened it. Sure enough, it was just some wires wrapped harmlessly around a flare.

That afternoon, we were back walking our foot post when I saw a guy with a bright red bag. "Excuse me," I said, "do you have a permit for that gun?" Of course he didn't, and we arrested him.

I got three medals for that tour—meritorious service for getting the woman out from under the cab, an exceptional police duty for stopping the robbery in progress, and another one for taking the gun off the guy. I didn't think anything of it, but later, Sean Crowley would shake his head and say that a lot of cops could work a year and not get three medals. I'd gotten them in one tour.

I was as happy working patrol as I'd ever been. But I was always looking for something more. I was never satisfied. Here I am in Midtown South—my dream assignment—and I want to move uptown to 42nd Street. I get to the Deuce, and now I want off my foot post. I want a car. Tibor and I are assigned a car, and now I want to get out of the uniform and become an undercover cop in the Anticrime Unit. Luckily, Inspector Mayrone and Captain Fahey were keeping an eye on me, making sure I was happy after my initial disillusionment with the job.

When we'd been there about eight months, Inspector Mayrone walked out of his office as I was processing a gun arrest. I had the suspect standing next to me as I searched his pockets and gave his pedigree information to the desk officer. Mayrone noticed the gun on the desk and said, "Hey, Kerik, where the fuck are you getting all these guns? What are you trying to do, start a revolution or something?"

I just laughed and continued processing the prisoner. Mayrone walked closer to me and asked, "You want to go to anticrime?"

"Yes, sir."

"Okay, put in an application tomorrow." I was ecstatic. Patrol is a reactive job; we showed up at a crime scene well after the crime had been committed. But anticrime was a different ballgame. The job there was to anticipate where a criminal was going to strike, to watch for potential muggings and thefts and try to actually prevent a crime from being committed. On patrol, if you caught a guy in the act of committing a crime, it was through dumb luck. In anticrime, that was the job. We would be on the prowl, watching for the same kinds of patterns I'd seen with the holster shop. But I'd come this far with Tibor and I didn't want to see us separated now. "What about my partner?" I asked.

Mayrone stared at me. "Sure. Okay. Your partner too." So Mayrone went to the lieutenant in charge of the Anticrime Unit and he said, "Lieu, I want to put these two guys in anticrime."

We'd only been there eight months. There were officers who'd been in that precinct for ten years. The lieutenant was aware of the grousing in the precinct. "Okay, Inspector," he told Mayrone. "You're in charge, but I gotta tell you, these guys aren't even off their probationary period yet. People are already pissed at them."

So Mayrone came back to me. "I'll tell you what," he said. "You keep up your activity, and in four months I'll take care of you."

Four months later, just about to the day, when our probation ended, Tibor and I were moved up to anticrime. And we loved our jobs even more. The criminals certainly weren't anchored to just one block, and now we weren't either. Suddenly their advantage was shrinking. We could afford to freelance a little. We weren't just responding after the fact; we were chasing criminals off the street. Throughout midtown, there were teams of predators working in packs of three or four, vultures looking for people to mug. Tibor and I would go looking for these groups and try to nail them. If you were good in anticrime, you could stand on a block like 42nd and Seventh and pick out the criminals before they struck. If you were *great,* you could pick out the victims.

We started seeing the block the way the skells did. Tourists were especially vulnerable. We looked for people with cameras and tour books and shopping bags. We looked for people who looked up. A native New Yorker walks down the street with his eyes looking straight ahead. A tourist can't believe all the tall buildings so he looks up.

We toured our area in sector cars. Midtown had horrible traffic, miles of yellow cabs and black Lincoln Town Cars, the whole mass surging forward a few feet a minute. Tibor and I sat in an unmarked car in that traffic, watching everything. I was the driver. Tibor, a natural athlete who could run fast and forever, was the deer. When trouble came, T. would leap out the door and start running, and I'd find a sidewalk to drive down, and we'd usually arrive right about the same time.

We got very good at anticipating crime. Once Tibor picked up a victim walking near Park Avenue and saw the team following him. T. followed them, and the minute they started to make their move, Tibor stepped out of the shadows with his gun and arrested the entire crew. Later, the assistant district attorney told him that he'd done a great job, but unfortunately, he'd arrested them before they had a chance to actually commit the crime. He couldn't prosecute these guys. We shook our heads. Maybe he didn't get a robbery collar, but we figured the victim was glad that Tibor didn't wait until he'd been stabbed or beaten up to step in.

One of my first days on anticrime, I was driving Sgt. Ralph Chartier and another cop on 42nd Street, midblock, looking east. It was three in the morning and traffic was completely jammed, a crowd of people filling Times Square like Bourbon Street during Mardi Gras. There was a single shot. *Pow!* Then four more came in quick succession. *Pow!*

Pow! Pow! Pow! The crowd went nuts, hundreds of people running down 42nd Street, trying to get away from the shots. Meanwhile, a guy with a gun was running right down the middle of Seventh Avenue, through all this traffic, right down the center lane. My partners jumped out of the car and started chasing him on foot. I was stuck in traffic, so I whipped the car across the oncoming lanes, went up on the sidewalk of 42nd Street, drove all the way to the corner on the sidewalk, then turned down Seventh Avenue.

As I was driving down Seventh, the suspect rounded the corner at 41st, made a left on Broadway, and started running back toward 42nd. He looked backward at the cops chasing him. That's when I pulled in front of him. He banged into my car and threw the gun under a nearby parked car.

As we threw him on the ground and handcuffed him, we could hear over the radio that patrol cars were trying to stop a car fleeing the wrong way up Broadway. When they stopped the car, they could see that the driver had been shot. We found another guy lying dead on the sidewalk, his body draped over the curb like empty clothes. It was a few hours later, when the adrenaline had faded and the reports had been filled out, that I had a realization that can only happen to a cop. This was my first homicide arrest.

As we investigated, we pieced together what had happened. The shooter was walking down the street with his girlfriend when he passed two guys, one in a car, the other leaning against it. They said something about the girl, and a few minutes later the suspect returned with a gun and shot them both. One fell dead on the sidewalk, the other one took off driving, and the shooter ran around the block until he slammed into my car. It was hard to believe that something so trivial could end with one dead, one seriously wounded, and another man going to prison. But that was life on the Deuce.

JOE loved buses. He and I would walk around the city and he'd practically have an out-of-body experience whenever he saw a bus. He was two, maybe three years old and we'd be walking, and all of a sudden Joe would stop, point, and scream as loud as he could—"Bu-u-u-us!" I don't think he'd ever even been on a bus. Underground, it'd be the same thing: the subway train rattling toward us, little Joe bent at the waist, staring into the dark, his eyes unblinking until the train rumbled out of the tunnel. "Tra-a-a-ain!"

As time went on, Jackie and I reached a kind of truce, and I was able to see Joe every weekend. He'd come to the city with me and we'd explore. When he was four, I took him to the twin towers of the World Trade Center. We rode up in the huge elevators, Joe holding my hand and staring at strangers' knees, wondering if the ride would ever end. From the observation deck on the 110th floor we walked around and looked at everything—the bridges, buildings, and boroughs. I held him up and pointed out New Jersey and Pennsylvania. We felt as if we could see forever.

But Joe's favorite place was the Museum of Natural History. Every weekend, that's where he wanted to go. He knew which train and which stop. He knew every dinosaur. People would be standing in front of some skeleton, talking about what kind it was, and this voice would correct them. "That's not a brontosaurus. That's a brachiosaurus." And the people would turn and not see anyone, until they looked down to see Joe's dark, earnest eyes staring up at them. Until he was about five or six, I think he assumed I lived at the Museum of Natural History.

It was still hard sometimes, being across the river from Joe, but we settled into a rhythm, and I lived for the weekends when I could go over to New Jersey and bring him back home with me. I had begun dating a little, and I became involved with a woman who lived in Greenwich Village, a woman seven years older than me, a vice president in a public relations firm. She was sophisticated and smart, and it was great after the fireworks of marriage to be in a solid, mature relationship. She and Joe got along great, and soon I moved in with her.

It had taken a couple of years, but I realized that I was beyond the low point of my divorce and bankruptcy, that my difficult first year in the NYPD had slipped away, and now I was as happy as I'd ever been. I was the cop I'd always wanted to be, and I was also trying to be the best father I could be.

Sometimes Joe even found himself watching me work. Once we were on our way to the Macy's Thanksgiving Day Parade when I saw two guys skulking around a parking lot on 24th Street as if they were trying to hide among the cars. Right behind them came a guy with a gun in his hand—his police shield out. I stopped the car and ran toward them. The plainclothes cop kept his gun on the two suspects.

"They just robbed a lady and cut her throat to get her chain!" The cop and I put the two suspects against the wall and started searching them.

By then, cops were coming from every direction. And watching it all was Joe.

"You okay?" I asked him in the car.

He was completely serene, not afraid at all, staring out the window. "Yeah," he said. I could see he was smiling. "That was cool."

Joe got used to seeing scenes like that one, and later he would tell people at school all about his daddy's job. Once I even got a call from his teacher. "Mr. Kerik, could you tell your son to maybe go easy on the show-and-tell stories. He traumatized half the class yesterday."

But if the late 1980s were something of a rebirth for me personally—happy at work, happy with Joe, happy with a new stable, adult relationship—it felt like a slow death for the city I had grown to love, the city that was now my home. Crime was out of control, the city was broke, and people were divided racially and economically. The city felt like it was constantly on the verge of exploding, and the responsibility for seeing that that didn't happen fell squarely on the shoulders of the NYPD. From one end of the city to the other, we were in a full-scale war with a seemingly endless army of crack cocaine dealers.

And the number of casualties on our side was about to go up.

14

THE HEIGHTS

1989

FOR a few years in the late 1980s, it felt as if the drug dealers had won. New York—even more than the rest of the country—had suffered through years of eroding social values, a liberalized criminal justice system, and a drug problem that was spiraling out of control. Torn by crime and cynicism, mismanaged to the point of fiscal collapse, New York was a city in decay.

In the mid-eighties the highly addictive, easily produced form of cocaine known as crack had been introduced to the United States. Almost immediately crack was the drug of choice, and the gangs and dealers who controlled its sale were wealthier, more audacious, and more violent than the Mafia had ever dreamed of being. The crack trade and the turf wars that accompanied it were unlike anything police had ever faced. The cocaine cartels were international, sophisticated, and violent. At the local level, neighborhoods were raked with gunfire, and innocent children were routinely and callously caught in the middle. Dealers didn't just kill their rivals; they butchered families, shot up neighborhoods, and murdered witnesses and anyone else who got in their way. They introduced Americans to the "Colombian necktie"—slicing victims' throats and pulling their tongues through the wounds. In some neighborhoods, children were taught in school how to duck and cover, and some mothers put their children to bed in bathtubs to protect them from gunfire. In 1961 there were 390 homicides in New York City. Twenty-five years later, in 1986, there were 1,582. And the number went up each year.

The explosion of crack cocaine wasn't just a drug problem. Robberies and thefts and prostitution and muggings all went up; crime in every category skyrocketed as addicts tried desperately to pay for their next rock. It made the job of New York City police officer more dangerous than it had ever been before.

In 1985 one police officer was killed on duty, in a traffic accident. The next year four died—three of them shot to death. In 1987 six were killed, four shot and one beaten to death. And then came 1988, for a lot of cops—for a lot of New York residents—the year in which it became apparent we were losing the drug war. The previous fall, drug dealers had firebombed the house of a man named Arjune, who'd called the police about drug dealing in his neighborhood. Immediately Arjune was put under twenty-four-hour protection. In November a twenty-two-year-old rookie named Eddie Byrne was sitting in his patrol car guarding Arjune's house when drug dealers came up to the car and shot him in the head, execution style. As cops, we couldn't believe it. It felt as if we were under attack.

In April 1988 two more police officers were shot to death—a Housing Authority cop and a Bronx narcotics officer. In August a Brooklyn South narcotics officer was shot to death. And then came October 18, 1988—one of the worst days in the history of the NYPD. Christopher Hoban, twenty-six, was inside a drug dealer's apartment on 105th near Central Park West, making a drug buy, when the dealers shot him in the head. Three hours later a twenty-four-year-old cop in the Three-Four named Michael Buczek was chasing some suspected drug dealers from the lobby of a building in Washington Heights when the fleeing dealers shot him to death.

A year that began with the inconceivable assassination of young Eddie Byrne ended with the senseless drug murders of two cops in one day. The seven deaths of police officers in 1988 sank morale to the lowest point in decades. It was terrible whenever a cop died, but these really hit home for me. Eddie Byrne had done his NSU time in Midtown South with us. He was a great kid—very quiet, committed to learning how to be a good cop—and to imagine him executed like that was sickening. Michael Buczek was from my home county in New Jersey, and while I didn't know him personally, he was a familiar face. One of the drug dealers who killed him, Pablo Almonte Lluberes, escaped to the Dominican Republic and was indicted in absentia on a charge of second-degree murder. New York cops watched with helpless anger as Almonte's brother, a general in the Dominican army, blatantly protected his brother from extradition for years.

And then there was Chris Hoban. A short, skinny kid from Bay Ridge, Brooklyn, with long hair and a baby face, he seemed like a natural for undercover work. His partner was a Japanese-American cop named Mike Jermyn, who hid his feisty toughness with a disarming sense of humor. They had gone into a small second-floor apartment to buy half a gram of cocaine for fifty dollars. It was supposed to be an easy, harmless buy. But when both cops were inside the 11-by-20-foot apartment, the dealers bolted the door. They began yelling that Mike and Chris had to try the drugs first. They thrust the cocaine forward on a playing card. "Sniff! Sniff!" they yelled.

When the young undercover cops refused, one of the dealers walked to a grandfather clock and returned with a .357 Magnum. He pointed it at Hoban's head and began yelling in Spanish. They searched Hoban but didn't find the gun he wore on his ankle. Then when one of the men searched Jermyn, he saw the gun butt in Mike's waistband and began yelling in Spanish, "*Policia! Policia!*" All hell broke loose. Jermyn started to pull his gun, but one of the men hit his arm and knocked the gun to the ground. A third man jumped Jermyn from behind and began choking him, and they fell back toward the door of the apartment. Chris Hoban swept the gun away from his head and threw one of the men into the wall, and that's when Jermyn heard the shots. "Chris!" he yelled. "Chris!" But he got no response. Mike Jermyn burst out of the apartment and down the stairs and found their backup on the street.

Two months after Chris Hoban's death, I found myself in his old unit, Manhattan North Narcotics, working undercover with Mike Jermyn on the same streets where he'd worked with Chris Hoban. It was a tough decision to make. I thought I was too old, too big, and too healthy to pass myself off as a junkie. Who was going to believe that a balding weight lifter was desperate for a fix? But a couple of things convinced me to do it. Like a lot of cops, I really wanted my detective shield, and the fastest route was to be an undercover drug detective. But there was another more important reason. In New York, the drug war wasn't just some hyperbolic slogan. It was a war in which—in 1988 alone—seven cops were lost. And in war, you go where the battle is. You go where you're needed. In December 1988, I was needed in narcotics.

RICHIE Burt was a natural. A short, intense African-American detective, he was great at undercover work, slipping in and out of character easily, keeping his cool in tough situations. We sat in his car as he coached me on my first buy. We were at Hell's Kitchen Park, where we had information that a dealer had set up shop.

Richie leaned across the bench seat of our unmarked car. "See that Spanish guy? In the middle of the park there?" There was a nondescript guy standing all by himself in the middle of the park.

"Yeah."

"He's doing. Go get him."

I sat there for a minute, staring out the car window.

Richie could see that I was nervous. "Just walk up to him, give him ten bucks, and say, 'Gimme two.'"

I watched the dealer out my window. "Two what?"

"Don't worry about what," Richie said. "Just say, 'Gimme two.'"

I turned to face him. "But what am I asking for?"

Richie was exasperated. "Just give him the money and tell him, 'Gimme two!'"

I looked at the guy standing in the park, minding his business. "Are you sure that's the guy? He doesn't look like a dope dealer to me."

"Just go talk to the guy!"

"Okay. Okay." I started to get out, but stopped. "I just wish I knew what I was asking for, that's all."

By that time Richie was losing it. "It's crack, okay? But you can't go up there and say, 'Gimme two *cracks*!' Now go make the fuckin' buy!"

I got out of the car and began walking. A funny thing happens when you go from being a uniformed cop to being an undercover. Even when you're no longer wearing it, your uniform has a very real weight and feel. You get used to the looks you get as a police officer, sometimes looks of respect and thanks, sometimes looks of guilt and hatred. But whatever they're thinking, everyone registers the fact that you're a cop.

Now, all of a sudden, here I was walking the same streets and I couldn't get it out of my head that people knew me, that they could see the uniform, or something in the way I moved, that marked me as a police officer. I'm walking up to this drug dealer in the middle of a busy park, and all I could think was: He knows. He's made me. Was he armed? Would he fight or just refuse to sell to me? My eyes darted around the park. Does he have backup? My mind was racing so fast,

I could barely keep up. And the whole time, I'm telling myself, Try not to look like a cop. Try not to look like a cop.

Finally I reached the dealer in the middle of the park. I had ten bucks in my hand. "How you doin'? Gimme two."

The dealer put his hands out like a magician and then reached up his sleeve. He took out a little plastic bag, removed two vials of crack cocaine, and handed them to me. I gave him the ten bucks.

I walked off, relieved and reaffirmed in my abilities as a cop. I could do this. I was a natural at police work. Perhaps I'd master this kind of police work the same way I had become confident as a patrol officer and working in anticrime. When I got back to the car, Richie was sitting there waiting for me.

"I'm in," I said coolly. "Here's the two." I put the vials of crack in the evidence envelope and called the sergeant so the other units could go into the park and arrest the drug dealer. "Hey, Sarge," I said over the radio. "Confirmed buy. Hell's Kitchen Park."

"All right," he said. "What's the script?" I sat there, staring out of the unmarked car at the faces moving up and down the sidewalk.

"Huh?"

"The description?" the sergeant asked again.

I just sat there.

"Kurik? What'd the guy look like?"

"Uh. Hold on." I looked over at Richie. He looked tired.

"You didn't get a description?" he asked.

"Richie," I said, "I don't have a fuckin' clue." I had been so nervous that someone would make me as a cop, so sure that people know who I was, so intent on delivering my line and not screwing up, that I hadn't even noticed what the drug dealer looked like. I had to get out of the car and go take another peek just so they could move in and arrest the guy. Richie just sat there, shaking his head.

Two years later Richie was working a case at 116th and

Lenox in Harlem. The dealers met him outside and took him inside to buy. I don't have to imagine what was going through Richie's head as he followed them up two flights of stained, littered steps. Inside the apartment, one of the men pulled a gun and demanded Richie's money.

Then he shot Richie in the stomach. That bullet lodged in his spine. "Gimme the fuckin' money!" the dealer said, and he put the gun to Richie's head.

Wounded, Richie reached up and grabbed the gun as it fired. The bullet blew his finger off. The shooter and the other dealer ran away, and Richie lay there, bleeding on the floor. Partially paralyzed, Richie Burt, an outstanding New York City detective, retired early, another casualty of the drug war.

TIBOR and I had both been assigned to the Manhattan North Narcotics Unit, and that's where we began our undercover work, in Harlem and the Heights, neighborhoods besieged by crack gangs, on the same streets where Eddie Byrne, Michael Buczek, and Chris Hoban had all been killed the year before.

Going undercover is much more than just a change in your assignment. For a lot of cops, going undercover changes them forever. It started with my appearance. I was a guy who favored Italian suits and leather shoes, a guy who worked out every day.

And yet within a year I looked so much like a drug dealer, even people who knew me would get nervous when they saw me. I wore six twenty-point diamond earrings, all in a row, from the middle of my ear to the lobe, with a loop at the bottom. I wore a Rolex and a gold ankle bracelet. I never wore socks. I grew a goatee, wore my hair down the middle of my back in a ponytail, and had a full-length black leather coat that by itself would've made the Pope look like a member of the Cali cartel. Tibor grew a ponytail, and his constant scowl made him a dead ringer for Steven Seagal. We had come a long way from our creased and clean-cut army days.

But the physical changes were nothing compared to the psychological impact of becoming an undercover. Our records were purged from the NYPD computer to keep our cover from being blown. We used different names and addresses and jobs. We were other people, out there alone, risking our lives without a net.

We'd say, "Gimme four dimes"—ten-dollar bags. "Gimme two nics"—five-dollar bags. We called the buy a set, like a movie set, and bad guys were actors, named for their distinguishing clothing or features: Red Shoes, Headband, Pimple Face, Tan Coat, Scruffy, and Black Hat. We'd ask for smoke or smack or coke or rock, or for purple tops or black tops—named for the color of the stopper in the vials of crack cocaine.

At first I wanted to arrest everyone myself. Mike Jermyn would laugh because I'd buy the drugs and then just grab the guy. "You're under arrest."

"That's not how you do it," he'd say. "You're gonna blow your cover." We were supposed to be long gone when the bust came down. That was one of the hardest things about narcotics. As an undercover, I never got to see the result of our work. All I saw was the problem, never the solution. And the problem was overwhelming. It was like trying to remove all the sand from a beach one bucket at a time. We'd make a drug buy and another drug buy and another drug buy, and even if we got one dealer off one corner, another dealer moved right in before the cop cars had cleared the scene.

And yet after my initial case of nerves, I think I became a very good undercover. While other cops tried to look like junkies—dirty and strung out—I posed as a major dealer, a guy looking to buy weight—large amounts of cocaine and heroin. I guess it was the same confidence and presence that made people want to follow me that convinced dealers I was The Man—in my long black leather coat and jewelry—who could move a kilo of heroin or crack cocaine. In the two years I worked undercover, I made some huge buys and helped get some major dealers off the street.

But I have to say, I never felt completely comfortable. Of all the law enforcement jobs I've ever had, undercover was the hardest for me. There were two kinds of jobs. B-and-Bs—buy-and-busts—were simple outdoor jobs, like the buy I made with Richie Burt. I'd walk up to a guy, buy a small amount of dope, and that was it. If the dealer was suspicious, he simply wouldn't sell to me, and I left.

The other kind, the inside buy, was more dangerous because we had to go into an apartment building. No shield. No gun. No bulletproof vest. No control. I wore a Kel, a small transmitter that looked like a pager, on my belt, but they were notorious for not working in the canyons between New York apartment buildings, or anywhere indoors, which was really the only place we needed them. Backup would be blocks away, if there was any backup at all. Each undercover was assigned a ghost, a cop to shadow them, but they couldn't do anything once you disappeared behind some battered and graffiti-covered apartment door.

We'd follow the drug dealer down dark, dank hallways, and once inside we were at the mercy of someone who was often paranoid and stoned. We wore the grit and the stench of these places on our clothes and our skin. The dealers might strip us naked, to check for wires or guns. They'd try to force us to use drugs, because our refusal would show that we were cops. I can't count the number of times I sat in some shit-hole apartment hoping my steely eyes and belligerence would convince the skells that I was such a major dealer it was beneath me to sample product.

If an undercover is forced to use drugs—and for some guys, it was the only way to keep from being shot—it's treated by the department as an injury. The cop is taken off duty and put in the hospital. It's one of the worst things that can happen, and we spent much of our time devising a routine to keep from having to use. Sometimes it just didn't matter. If you had a gun in your mouth, you had to use. For me, the trick was never buying low. I always bought high—

spent large amounts of money on large amounts of drugs. If you bought low, you were a junkie, and there was no reason for you not to sample the goods. I played myself as a dealer—buying for resale. I'd tell the dealers I was going back to Jersey and I needed an ounce or two ounces. Sometimes they'd grill me about Jersey. "Which exit is that, to Paterson?"

Other times, some jittery drug dealer would pace around me with a handgun: "Come on, motherfucker. Test the shit!" Several times I had guns to my head. I never knew if I was going to come out of one of those apartments on a stretcher.

It wears on you. I used to take a black marker and palm it in my hand, running it along the dirty walls of tenements and apartment buildings so that when the paramedics came to find me, they'd have a line to follow. It was one thing that always got to me, imagining myself alone on the floor of some rat-infested walk-up, listening to the footsteps as I bled out. Like Serpico. Like Chris Hoban. Sometimes cops raiding a drug house would hit the wrong place, but not when I was involved. There would be a big black line, or if I could get away with it, I'd write BK in big black letters on the door, amid the graffiti. No one ever mistook one of the apartments I was in.

It was hard work for both Tibor and me. On the nights before an outdoor buy we were fine, but when we knew we had to wade into some Washington Heights apartment maze, we'd go to a cop bar called Teachers Too and throw back a couple of drinks to tone us down. I've never been a drinker, but if I put down two drinks, it made it much easier to go into those buildings, knowing that there was a possibility one of us might end up holding our insides together in some dark and dirty hallway.

In Manhattan North, I worked closely with Mike Jermyn and was quickly impressed by his courage and ability. He's a great cop, but I could see that he was haunted by what had happened the night Chris Hoban died, that he replayed it in his mind, trying to figure out if there was something else he could've done. After Mike and I became friends, he would stop by my apartment once every few weeks for a drink. We could talk about life, talk about family, or talk about the job, but eventually the conversation would lead to the night of October 18, 1988, and Chris Hoban, and then he would break down.

When Teddy Roosevelt admonished the graduating class of Groton in 1912 that a real man combines courage with tenderness, and contempt for bullies and oppressors, he was talking about a man such as Mike Jermyn. As tough as he was on the battlefield in the war against drugs, in his heart he was equally tender. I saw that tenderness night after night as I watched him cry for a mother and father who had lost their son and a cop who had lost his partner.

You never get over tragedies like these, and for Mike, whose scars may never heal, returning to work was no easy task. So at first it was hard for him when an undercover went into an apartment to make a buy. He'd pace around and gnash his teeth and say, "Bernie's been in there too long! We gotta go in!"

"It's only been two minutes," one of the other detectives would say. "He's fine."

A minute later, Mike would be pacing again. "Where is he? We gotta go in!"

The brass suggested that maybe Mike might want to transfer out of narcotics after what happened to his partner, but Mike said, "Absolutely not." His partner had made the ultimate sacrifice and saved Mike's life by wrestling with the drug dealer who had the gun. Mike lived just two blocks from the border of the Manhattan North Precinct, and so for him it was like driving an invading army out of his home. He would end up devoting almost his entire career to fighting narcotics.

One night in 1989, I did a buy at an apartment on 161st and Broadway, just down the street from where Michael

Buczek had been shot a year earlier. A bunch of undercovers were spread out doing the whole block. The neighborhood had basically become an outdoor market for Dominican drug dealers, and they tugged at my arms as I moved down the street. "Come on, man." "Come with me." "Come over here." These guys were steerers, drumming up customers to take upstairs where the drugs were actually sold.

I picked two of them. "You and you. I'll go with you."

I followed them up a stoop, past more dealers, and into a dark hallway. We climbed the steps, and I prayed that my backup had seen me go in. We got to an apartment, and one of the street guys knocked on the door. There were two guys inside. I hated to go into an apartment with more than one dealer. It was an invitation to get taken off, to get a blade to the gut or a bullet in the head. I didn't like the way this felt.

The dealers sat me on a chair and frisked me. Then one of them brought in the drugs. They nodded that I was to smoke.

"No," I said. "I don't use that shit. I just want to buy."

"You smoke," he said. "You test."

"No," I said.

"Fuck you." He held a gun at his side and nodded again at the dope.

"Fuck you!" I said back. I could feel my throat tightening. He kept insisting that I try. My mind raced: How long would it take my ghost to find me up here? How much blood would I lose before help arrived?

Outside the apartment there was a lot of commotion, other dealers working. Then, from outside, I heard footsteps, like someone running down the hall. And then *Pow! Pow! Pow! Pow!* Four shots. Right outside the door.

I leaped up. "That's it. I'm getting the fuck out of this apartment."

The dealer could see that he was about to lose a sale. "No, wait," he said. My mind was racing. Right outside the building were other undercovers and backup cops. The shots meant that all bets were off. At any minute this building would be crawling with cops. This was the most dangerous and vulnerable time for an undercover—that moment when you're in the borderland between the cops and the criminals.

I paid the dealer, took two vials of crack, and moved toward the door, wondering if those were sirens I could hear. If the dealer heard the sirens, he'd know that he'd been set up. My back tensed as I moved away, expecting to be shot.

The door to the apartment felt like it weighed two hundred pounds. I swung it open and a body came with it. A dealer had been shot in the hallway, and now he fell into the apartment. I stepped over him and hurried down the hallway, down the steps, and out into the light, breathing heavy and fast. Now that I was outside, I wasn't sure that my Kel worked, but I kept talking quietly and frantically. "Tell these uniforms I'm on the block!" The sirens were right on top of me now, and I could feel the eyes from the apartment building on my back. I also knew what I would look like to the radio cars responding to the report of gunshots.

Lenny Lemer was my backup that day, a tough, cool cop who has continued to be a close friend. "Hey, Len!" I said into my Kel, "make sure everybody knows I'm here." I told him where the body was, and the minute I turned the corner, the block was saturated with cops. I didn't see any cops on Broadway, so I started walking. Two blocks down, I saw Lenny and some others sitting in their car talking.

Lenny asked, "Hey, what's going on up there?" I broke out in a sweat. The Kel hadn't worked. No one had a clue what I'd just been through.

As I think about it, though, the worst part of being undercover wasn't those early jitters or the danger of those buys. It was the cold, cynical resolve that comes over you. After two years, Tibor and I didn't need to drink anymore before an inside buy. It was just business then. Two years on that job leaves you so empty that nothing fazes you. Nothing scares you. You're out of the world, not like the other cops but something in between, in the shadows. People treat you differently, and that's how you feel, as if you live between these two worlds. You see things in those apartments that most people never see.

The idea that you will be in a gunfight becomes so *ordinary* that you don't even worry about it anymore. You begin to expect it.

In my case, that was when the job became really scary.

15

DYCKMAN STREET

1991

HECTOR Santiago was a lean, muscular Puerto Rican kid, as friendly as he was unflappable. A former defensive back on the Brooklyn College football team, Hector came onto the NYPD in 1982 as it was finally diversifying from what had been a traditionally white department. He looked so young he had trouble convincing the old Irish and Italian beat cops that he was actually on the job, until one day a lieutenant noticed Hector and scooped him up for a special drug unit. Just twenty-one years old, Hector found himself buying heroin in Alphabet City, a dangerous section of the Lower East Side. At first he was still too much like a fresh-faced athlete and he had trouble making deals, but eventually he "got over"—as undercovers say—convincing dealers that he was a junkie trying to score smack. As the drug trade began to be dominated by Dominicans and Colombians, it became invaluable to have a young Latino who spoke Spanish and was willing to go into war-zone neighborhoods and put his life on the line. Hector was hardworking, always willing to translate or do whatever was needed, and he became a great undercover and later a great detective.

By the time I came to Manhattan North, Hector had been working in narcotics for more than six years. He'd watched his own personality change as he got deeper and deeper undercover, doing things at first to avoid detection and then, almost by instinct, taking pride in how little he resembled a cop. In 1986 Hector and some other cops were busting a drug house when a dealer named Simon Garcia pulled a .38 and jabbed it into Hector's stomach. Hector shot Garcia in the chest. What happened next reflects those times pretty accurately. Since Garcia was hospitalized, the judge didn't think to remand him to custody while he awaited trial, and Garcia just stood up one day, walked out of the hospital, and fled the country. He is still at large.

In 1990 I ended up working with Hector and some other great cops in the Manhattan North Narcotics Major Case Unit. Our job was to go beyond street level sales to get to the medium-level drug dealers. Our team was made up of a sergeant, six investigators, and two undercovers. We were extremely active. In one year, we served two hundred search warrants. The team worked so well because we had such wonderful people, such great cops. And one of the best was Hector.

For me, Major Case was a choice assignment. After two years of chipping away at drug operations, one dime bag at a time, it was nice to take a full swing. I had recently gotten the gold detective's shield that I'd dreamed about all those years, and I was eager to use my investigative skills.

We worked in Harlem at an office upstairs from the Two-Six. We did the usual buy-and-busts, but it was more like catch-and-release fishing. We'd get a guy, roll him, get his boss, roll that guy, and on and on, working our way up the food chain. Wiretap technology was changing the way we fought drugs, and we made the most of that, tapping phones and sitting translators on the wires. We were even one of the first units to tap cell phones, which had been considered untraceable for years. Slowly we built these cases like pyramids, taking us ever closer to the Colombian cartels that provided the bulk of American cocaine.

One day in early 1991, a confidential informant gave up

the name of a dealer who was supposed to be moving huge quantities of cocaine into four states on the eastern seaboard. She said the man was a Dominican named Junior Gumbs and that he'd grown up on the Upper West Side and still owned businesses there.

But there was one problem. According to our records Junior Gumbs was dead. Two years earlier, a dark Dominican man named J. Gumbs had been shot to death outside a Latin nightclub, so Bronx detectives and federal agents had abandoned their massive narcotics investigation of him. As we asked around, though, we found out something interesting. Junior Gumbs had an older brother who looked just like him. It turned out that it wasn't Junior who'd been murdered. It was his brother.

So while the NYPD and the U.S. Drug Enforcement Administration closed their cases against him, Junior went on dealing more weight than ever, as much as sixty to a hundred kilos a week, laundering the money through his various businesses, which included a sporting goods store on the Upper West Side, a grocery in Washington Heights, and an Italian restaurant called Gianna's in the West Village.

We started surveillance to see if this was indeed Junior Gumbs and if he was really dealing. There was an easygoing, resourceful cop on our team named Donny Trenkle, and one day Donny and I followed Junior into Central Park, where he was playing for a recreation league baseball team that he sponsored. I had a camera, and Junior spotted me taking pictures. When he came over, I told him that I was the staff photographer for a sports magazine. I told him that Donny was my assistant photographer and we were taking a picture of his team for the magazine.

"Oh," Junior said. "If I give you my phone number, can I get a copy?"

"Sure," I said as he wrote out his number and handed it to me.

"Can we get a team shot?"

"Why not." So this major drug dealer got all his buddies

together and they posed while an NYPD detective snapped pictures of them.

For nine months we were all over Junior Gumbs, tapping his phones and putting him under surveillance, putting together a flow chart of his operation. I loved this kind of work, the challenge of an investigation, the struggle to put pieces together. Junior had a number of associates and apartments all over the city where he stashed the drugs. We took photos as he opened new businesses, including a boutique for his wife. They had a garage full of luxury cars: a Lexus, a red Mercedes-Benz, and a BMW. One day we watched as a couple of known Colombian dealers carried boxes filled with sixty-five kilos of cocaine into one of Junior's apartments.

Junior Gumbs lived in an exclusive neighborhood in Leonia, New Jersey, and a few times on the weekends, when I was off duty, I'd go to Jackie's house and pick up Joe and we'd drive out to Junior's neighborhood and case his house, recording who came and went. I knew it was against regulations to bring Joe along on surveillance, but I wanted this guy, though I wasn't going to sacrifice my weekends with my son to get him.

Joe was five or six, and he still remembers sitting next to me, his feet dangling over the edge of the passenger seat. I'd watch the house with binoculars, then hand them to Joe, so he could look at cool stuff around the car. The radio sat between us, and my gun was on the floor at my feet, along with the piss bottle that accompanied every cop on surveillance, so that I wouldn't have to leave to go to the bathroom. We sat there and ate fast food, and I asked Joe how school was going. One time a New Jersey cop pulled up behind us and walked up to my car. "What are you doing?" he asked.

I showed him my shield. "We're on surveillance."

He looked over at Joe, who was staring at his own feet through the binoculars.

"Uh-huh," the cop said. "And who's this?"

I looked over at Joe. "That's my partner."

* * *

THE Junior Gumbs case was exactly what Major Case was all about. We watched and listened and turned informants, and soon we could map out most of Junior's operation. As 1991 went on, we were getting closer and closer to being able to make the entire case against him and his associates.

In November we were sitting on a wire of Junior's phone when he got a call from a guy named Carlos Carrion, a twenty-eight-year-old dealer from Boston who said he was coming in to "pick up five shirts"—five kilos of cocaine—at one of Junior's apartments in the Bronx. On the brisk morning of November 13, 1991, we staked out the apartment. Our plan was to arrest Carrion *after* he picked up the drugs, so that we wouldn't have to arrest Junior yet and could keep using him to get to other people.

We sat on Junior's stash apartment building on the corner of 195th Street and University Avenue in the Bronx, watching cars come and go. We had five cars down there. Hector and I were in separate undercover cars made up to look like livery or gypsy cabs—taxis that aren't licensed by the city and that pick up fares illegally. A policewoman named Wanda Rosado was in the back of Hector's car, posing as his fare. In the lead car—an NYPD patrol car—were Donny Trenkle and Terrence Byrne, dressed as uniformed patrol cops. Our plan was to pull Carrion's car over, making his driver think it was a routine traffic stop and that he could talk his way out. Then we'd swoop in and grab him.

After a few hours of surveillance, a man came out carrying a package and got into a car. We followed him south for fifteen minutes or so, all the way to the Triborough Bridge, where we pulled him over. We were shocked when he showed us a shield. He was a cop. He said the package was books.

People talk about the code among cops, about bleeding blue, and it's true: there is great loyalty among police officers. But we looked at one another and knew we'd have to search this guy. If he was dealing dope, then there was no more code, there was no more loyalty. So we searched his car and we found . . . books.

We all looked at one another. "Shit."

We raced back to the apartment, and then, about 10:00 A.M., a translator called from the wire room and said that Carrion had just called Gumbs and that he was going up to the building with sixty thousand dollars. About 10:40 A.M., a livery cab—a gray 1984 Oldsmobile—pulled up to the building. A Hispanic man got out of the backseat. He was wearing jeans and a three-quarter-length coat, carrying a shoulder bag. He looked around and then went inside. He came out a few minutes later with the bag and climbed into the back of the livery cab. We followed the car south for about fifteen minutes until it crossed the University Heights Bridge into the Inwood neighborhood of North Manhattan. The phony patrol car moved into place. And that's when everything went to hell.

They put on the lights and the car pulled to the curb. Donny got out of the passenger side of the patrol car, but as he began approaching the car, Carrion opened the back passenger side door and climbed out with the bag of cocaine, as if he were just a normal fare going his own way.

"Get back in the car!" Donny yelled, and pulled his gun. Carrion jumped back into the car and it took off. Hector and I had pulled over in front of the gray Oldsmobile, so we took off in pursuit, followed by Donny and Terrence in the patrol car and the other cars in our unit. We screamed along after Carrion and his driver, racing south on Tenth, then west onto Dyckman Street—a wide swath lined by sidewalks and trees and housing projects. We had gone about nine or ten blocks, maybe a mile, when the driver must've realized he wasn't going to lose us. The car slowed to stop, and Carrion jumped out while it was still moving. He was carrying the black bag and a silver Sig Sauer nine-millimeter handgun. But he didn't run away. He walked toward us.

Hector and I were in the lead, and our cars screeched to a stop behind the gray Olds as Carrion approached us. "He's got a gun!" Wanda yelled from Hector's car. "Hector, he's got a gun!" Carrion raised the gun and began firing, as calmly as if he were asking for directions. He stood in front of Hector's car and fired through the windshield. Hector threw his arm up and fell to the side. A bullet lodged dead center in the headrest of his car, right where Hector's head had been. In the backseat, Wanda was hit by shattered glass from the window. Lying against his door, Hector opened it and fell out into the street. From the ground, he could see Carrion's legs as he moved around toward the side of the car to finish him off.

Even as Hector was reaching for his gun, he thought to himself, "I'm done. He's got me."

That's when I opened fire. I had gotten out of my car and pulled my gun. As I watched this guy move around to finish Hector off, I got two shots off. Carrion turned and returned my fire.

By this time Wanda had fired from the backseat, and another one of our guys, Martin McSherry, had pulled up and shot from his car. Carrion fired back, putting one bullet in the right front quarter panel of McSherry's car. A patrol car had coincidentally driven up, and Carrion sprayed them with bullets too. The uniformed cops fired back. Carrion—realizing for the first time what he was up against—turned and ran away, into the low-slung Dyckman Housing Development, firing at us over his shoulder as he ran.

We chased him. Everything moved in slow motion. It was quiet, the leaves jumping at our feet. We sprinted down the sidewalks after him, firing our guns, his rounds flying back at us. It was surreal, as if the whole world had faded away except the *pop-pop-pop* of the guns and the harsh pulls of November air. We chased Carrion down sidewalks deeper into the projects until he came to an alley. Donny and Hector and I were right behind him. We all shot him, and finally he fell. We'd hit him five times, once in the rib cage, twice in the back, and twice in the right leg.

He lay on the ground, his back to us. When we reached

him and rolled him over he was trying to jam another eighteen-round magazine into his gun. But luckily, he was trying to put it in backward. We took his gun and the magazine away and handcuffed him. Another cop on our team, Thomas Barnitt, opened Carrion's bag and found the five kilos along with another gun, a loaded .38.

We stood there catching our breath. "Everyone okay?" Donny asked.

"Actually," Hector said, holding up his right arm, which was dripping with blood, a nickel-size hole in the elbow, "this prick shot me."

WE sat at the hospital while they worked on Hector's arm. They put us in a room to treat us for trauma, and we sat around eating cheeseburgers and drinking milk shakes, making jokes to cut the tension. We were all completely keyed up, the adrenaline still coursing through our systems. Hector was going to be fine. When he'd thrown his arm up, one of Carrion's shots tore through his elbow, and Hector felt the sharp hot pain and knew exactly what it was, and still he'd chased after the drug dealer and helped arrest him. Fifty-eight shots were fired during the gun battle, nineteen by Carrion. He was seriously wounded, but he lived and was charged with attempted murder, assault, and possession of drugs and weapons. We also arrested the driver of the car, Cesar Jimenez, who had tried to claim that he didn't know Carrion.

Hector was out for a few weeks, and when he returned, he was put on wires while his arm healed. His elbow still creaks, and he's losing the feeling in his fingers, but otherwise his recovery was smooth.

In the coming months, our team shut down Junior Gumbs's operation, arrested about a dozen of his associates, and seized his businesses. On the day they finally came for Junior, the brass allowed Hector to go up in the police helicopter as they tailed him from New Jersey to New York. The roofs of the police cars were marked with big X's, and from the air Hector watched as they surrounded him. Junior Gumbs was found guilty of numerous drug charges and sentenced to fifty-eight years.

Donny and Hector and I had been close before the shootout, but now there was an amazing bond between us. We'd meet after work and talk about it. We *needed* to talk about it, to go over it from every angle, to understand what had happened, to joke about it, to thank one another, and maybe to remind one another that we'd made it. And even when we stopped talking about it as much, we still got together. It wasn't until later that I realized how important it was for Donny and Hector and me to have one another during that period.

I think the shoot-out was hardest on Wanda Rosado, who'd fired so bravely to protect Hector. Her hearing suffered from the gun blasts, and she lost weight because of the stress. Like all of us, I think, she was haunted by the vision of that stone killer walking toward her, but I wonder now if she had anyone to talk to about it.

I had grown so close to my team I knew it would be hard to leave. But at the end of 1991, I got an amazing opportunity to go up to the next level of police work.

My old friend Jerry Speziale had made a name for himself as one of the best undercover cops in the NYPD. It was always assumed that black and Latino cops made the best undercovers, but no one worked harder at getting over than Jerry. His manic personality and buggy eyes and his crazy courage allowed him to go anywhere and talk to anyone, and it wasn't long before the brass noticed his unique abilities. In 1989 he was moved to the New York Drug Enforcement Task Force, made up of investigators from the New York State Police and the U.S. Drug Enforcement Administration and detectives from the New York City Police Department. They were even further along in the use of wiretaps than we were, and Jerry may have tapped the very first cell phone. His was probably the best unit of its kind in the world, and

Jerry was its star—a ballsy undercover cop posing as an international drug trafficker. In the fall of 1991 I had helped Jerry on a case he was working, and it was obvious to both of us what a great team we'd make. We had the same intense zeal for our jobs, and our personalities blended together really well. So I applied to join Jerry on the Drug Enforcement Task Force. But before I went anywhere, there were a few loose ends to tie up.

IN December 1991 I found out that I was being transferred to the Drug Enforcement Task Force. I was excited, but I was also nervous about leaving my Major Case colleagues. Hector was recovering from his wound, and we were mopping up the Junior Gumbs case and a couple of others, including a case I'd worked on for months involving a rich guy from Afghanistan who was selling heroin to buy weapons for that country's civil war.

One day we were in our office when the Hello line rang. This was the phone number that we gave out to dealers when we were undercover, a phone we just answered "Hello," instead of "Manhattan North, Major Case."

The guy on the phone asked for Robert Viglione, my drug dealer name.

"This is him," I said.

The guy on the phone was an Israeli who owned a carpet store and dealt drugs on the side. He said the Afghan had told him that I was looking to buy heroin.

We agreed to meet at a bar, where I bought half an ounce. When it checked out, I told him that I wanted more. So we met again, and this time I got two ounces. The next time it was six ounces. When I had his trust, I asked him for a kilo. Cocaine was fairly easy to find in big quantities, but we almost never saw kilos of heroin. If we could pull it off, it would be one of the biggest heroin busts of the year.

Okay, the Israeli said, but it would cost me $175,000.

We went to get the money, but my inspector, Marty Boyle,

was nervous about us carrying that much cash, and he proposed that I fill a bag with paper and then put a smaller amount of money—say $10,000—on top.

"I ain't doing that!" I said. "You don't think he's gonna count the money? Look, you'll get it back. I promise." So Inspector Boyle called downtown and got the approval, and we began to set up the deal. The Israeli dealer wanted to meet on the street. I could see that I would need a car that fit my profile as a major drug dealer. There was a cop in our unit named Vinnie Beckles, who had just bought a BMW, a nice maroon sedan. It was a few years old, but to a bunch of underpaid cops, it was the picture of style. I approached him that morning with my idea as we went over the plan for the bust.

"What, are you fuckin' crazy?" he said. "You ain't using my car for this. I just bought this car."

"Come on, Vin. I'm gonna go up there with a hundred seventy-five thousand and I'm gonna be in, what . . . a fuckin' Volkswagen Bug? Come on, gimme the keys." Actually I had a Honda Civic, but it too would've tipped off the dealer that I didn't have access to that kind of money. No, I needed a BMW.

"Okay," Vinnie said finally.

I drove the Beemer down to 82nd and Broadway and parked, waiting for the dealer. West Side traffic moved all around me, and I sat there trying to find the undercover units that were supposed to be backing me. Often you can spot them, but this time I couldn't see anyone except the backup car behind me. They had to be around, didn't they? It made me a little nervous. I thought about Hector's shooting, just weeks before, and how quickly a deal like this could go bad.

That's when I saw the carpet store owner walking casually toward the car, looking up and down the street. He leaned in the car window.

"You got the stuff?" I asked.

"Yeah. But not with me. I gotta check this out first."

"Sure," I said.

He met my eyes. "You should know. I got a bunch of guys down here with me just in case something happens. Something happens, we're fuckin' gonna shoot it out."

"Sure," I said. As he looked around, I looked around with him. I didn't see anyone lingering nearby, either his guys or mine. "Get in," I said.

He paused and then climbed into the car.

"So where's the stuff?" I asked.

"I got it," he said. "You got the money?"

"Yeah." We sat there staring at each other, and the old doubt crept in. Had he made me as a cop? Or worse, was he planning to rob me of the money, shoot me in this car, and let me die here? This was a lot of money, the kind of money dealers died for every day in New York at that time.

The air was heavy in the car. We were at a standstill, and something had to give. I put my hand out the window and gestured toward the car behind me, where Vinnie was sitting. He walked up to his BMW and climbed into the backseat.

"You got the money?" I asked Vinnie.

Vinnie handed me the brown paper bag with the money in it. I put it between my feet and opened it so the Israeli could see the stacks of bills. Behind the bag, on the floor beneath my car seat, was my .38. As I put the bag on the floor, I must have pushed the gun back.

The heroin dealer leaned forward and looked at the cash. "Okay," he said finally. "Turn your lights on and off once."

I had this quick vision of Vinnie leaning forward from the backseat and pointing out where the lights were, but thankfully, he sat quietly. I flashed the lights once.

Down the street, a man emerged from a Burger King carrying a big shopping bag with a blanket on top. He walked over to the passenger side of the car and handed the carpet store owner the shopping bag. I thought about the dealer's claim that he had men all over the place. Maybe he really did.

When he took the blanket out, I could smell it, the sickly

sweet smell of heroin. It was in small round balls, having recently been smuggled by mules—low-level dealers who swallow condoms full of drugs to get it past customs. The shopping bag was full—more than two pounds of heroin. The dealer put the drugs in my lap. I tried to look calm even as I thought ten steps ahead: How quickly will backup come? Is this guy armed? Does he really have other guys out there? I had lost track of the guy from the Burger King. Was he somewhere with a gun? All the old anxieties of undercover work returned.

Finally I just decided to arrest him. I reached down as if I were going to get the money and felt for my gun. I couldn't find it. My heart started to race. I patted around with my hand and glanced once more out the window, looking for the dealer's men. But there were just tourists and businesspeople and the usual flow of New Yorkers moving up and down the sidewalk. I could feel my blood in my ears. I could feel the dealer staring at me. And I couldn't find my gun.

Fuck it, I thought. Finally I sat up. I couldn't reach far enough to get the gun with this huge bag of heroin in my lap. So I looked over at the carpet store owner, who was beginning to look concerned. "Here," I said, "hold this." I handed him the bag of dope.

I opened my door, climbed out, and reached under the seat. My hand emerged with my gun and I yelled, "I'm a cop! Don't move!"

Poor Vinnie was in the back, worried stiff, staring at the beautiful leather interior of the nicest car he'd ever owned. "Jesus, Bern! Don't shoot him! Don't get blood on my fuckin' car!"

Hector had just come back to work, and he was down the street in a vacant building, a Barnes & Noble bookstore that was under construction. He ran up to the car with several other cops, and they yanked the carpet store owner out of the passenger seat, put him down on the street, and handcuffed him.

In the excitement, some backup patrol cops even pulled Vinnie out of the car and cuffed him. "Watch the car!" Vinnie yelled. "Just watch the car!" Despite the tension, the bust went fine. The inspector got his money back, and Vinnie got his car back.

And for me that was it for Major Case. The very next day I moved up again, to join Jerry Speziale on the Drug Enforcement Task Force. It was bittersweet, leaving Major Case. From my first day on the force, I had managed to draw around me the most amazing, talented, and courageous people, starting with Tibor, of course, who had been my sidekick now for fifteen years; the buffs from Midtown South, Captain Tom Fahey, Bobby Picciano, Sean Crowley, and Gerry Kane; Mike Jermyn and Lenny Lemer from Manhattan North Narcotics, and from Major Case, Donny Trenkle and Hector Santiago. These were guys tested by fire, strong, fearless, and smart cops. As I moved up to the Task Force, I wished there was some way to take all the good ones with me. I thought about how much each of them had taught me, how much they'd inspired me. Even then I thought about just how much we could accomplish if I could get all my guys together. It would be like assembling my own all-star team of cops.

Little did I know that in less than a decade I would do just that.

16

GUATEMALA

1992

EDDIE Beach was a shade under six feet and stocky, with wavy black hair and a voice like a thunderstorm. He was the supervisor of Group 93 of the New York Drug Enforcement Task Force and, at the beginning of 1992, my new boss. We'd just had our first meeting, and when it was over, Jerry Speziale and I left together in my car. We pulled up next to Eddie at a traffic light outside the DEA office where our group worked. Eddie looked over and saw Jerry and me. He stared at us for a minute, then picked up his cell phone and called Jerry's cell.

"I'm looking over at the two of you in the fuckin' car," he said, "and I gotta tell you, it scares me to death."

By the time I came to Group 93 of the NYDETF in December 1991, it was already one of the most productive drug enforcement teams in the history of the United States. But in the next two years, we would go even further. We would literally write the book on how to investigate drug trafficking in the United States.

When Jerry and Eddie were first transferred to Group 93, in 1989, they were convinced that it was as punishment for being too aggressive. They responded by becoming more aggressive. After his transfer, Jerry knew that to really make a dent in the New York drug trade, he'd need a top-notch CI—confidential informant. Most of the time, a drug dealer will become a CI to avoid being prosecuted, but Jerry wanted a bigger fish, the sort of guy who does it for reward money—which can be up to 10 percent of a big cash seizure—and maybe for the thrill.

For months he'd been hearing about a guy named Paul Alexander, a Brazilian Jew and a former agent for Mossad, the Israeli equivalent of the CIA. Paul's name seemed to be everywhere in the highest levels of the world narcotics trade.

"This is the guy I need to get," Jerry told Eddie.

Paul had worked previously as an informant for the DEA, but it turned out that he was blacklisted because of some sort of corruption. Besides, Eddie asked, how would Jerry find him? Guys like Paul live in the shadows; it was their job to be invisible.

So they made a bet—lunch for a week—and Jerry set out to find Paul Alexander. He flew to Miami and left letters everywhere for Paul, with friends and ex-girlfriends, anywhere Paul had ever been. And if he didn't find Paul, it was only because one day in 1991, Paul found him.

"I understand you are looking for me?" said the smooth Latin voice on the other end of the phone. Jerry explained what he wanted: someone to help him use the upper reaches of the Colombian cartels to get at the dealers in New York. For a motivated businessman who was willing to help, there was money to be made, Jerry said. Paul listened quietly and they set up a meeting. Jerry went to the appointed place and watched for Paul, and while he waited, there was a tap on his shoulder.

"You are not ready," Paul told Jerry. He said that he shouldn't have been able to sneak up on Jerry like that. Still, they talked, and maybe it was Jerry's enthusiasm that convinced Paul to work again for the DEA. Then again, maybe he had his own motives.

Our nickname for Paul was Milquetoast. He was small and pale, with a little potbelly and horn-rimmed glasses. He would come to New York and lounge in a five-star hotel in silk robes and five-hundred-dollar slippers. The rest of the time he wore Italian suits. He looked like a jeweler or a banker and carried himself like the wealthiest, most sophisticated guy in the room—which he usually was. The first time I met him he arrived with his wife, a Brazilian model with a waist that couldn't have been twenty-one inches around. I liked Paul right away. Everyone liked him. For two years, Jerry and I would work as closely with him as we ever had with anyone.

Paul's first job was to remake Jerry as a drug dealer. He took him shopping. "You will wear only Armani," Paul said. He taught Jerry what to wear, what to say, how to stand, how to walk, everything. He taught him how to fly a plane, how to pilot a boat, how to build an airstrip. It was a complete education in drug dealing, and Jerry graduated with full honors. Everything Jerry learned about drug dealing and, later, everything that I learned came from Paul.

The DEA has a rule that it won't readmit a blacklisted CI, but Jerry got around that by filling out the paperwork as if Paul were a brand-new informant. Paul went directly to the drug cartels in Colombia and offered his services arranging shipments through Central America and eventually into New York, where the drugs would be divided up and distributed by the cells already in place. Paul told the cartels all about his contact in America, the guy who would meet him in Central America and arrange to have the drugs flown to New York—a crazy American businessman named Geraldo Bartone. Or, as I knew him, Jerry Speziale. Our plan was so simple it still amazes me. Since Jerry would actually smuggle the drugs into New York, we'd know who was in the distribution cells and we could arrest them and seize the drugs. It was an audacious plan, to stop swimming upstream against these drug dealers and start moving downstream, from the top. The drug operations were designed to defeat investigation from the bottom up. Each cell was self-contained and isolated from the others. So a bust usually stopped at the members of that cell, and the main dealers would just cut that part off, like an insect losing a leg. In Group 93, we were going straight for the body to get to the legs.

I was brought into this craziness even before I got transferred to the task force. In August 1991, near the beginning of their relationship, Jerry and Paul smuggled 767 kilos of cocaine out of Colombia through Guatemala and into the United States. Of course, soon after the drugs arrived in New York, the shipment was seized.

Jerry's problem was that if Paul remained on the hook for the lost shipment, the Colombians would simply kill him. Jerry needed to shift the blame away from Paul.

I met with them, and we came up with the idea of getting a newspaper to print a story claiming that the drugs made it all the way to the dealers in New York, so the bust would be the local dealers' responsibility, shifting the blame away from Jerry and Paul. I approached a reporter I knew, but he wouldn't write something he knew to be false.

I called a woman I was dating who worked at a print shop, and approached her about making a phony newspaper page. No problem, she said. So we bought some tabloid-size paper and wrote a phony story that made the bust look like a fluke. The story was set in type and printed on a page that looked just like the New York *Daily News*. Then we took out page 5 of the *Daily News* and inserted our page 5.

"Suspended Registration Leads to Major Cocaine Bust" read the headline on page 5 of our *Daily News*. It reported how the drugs had been in a van with suspended license plates and two detectives had spotted the van through dumb luck. When they searched the van, they found 200 kilos and that led them to a warehouse where the other 567 kilos were stored. We made ten copies of the *Daily News* with this phony story on page 5.

A month after the bust, Paul was summoned to Bogotá, Colombia, for a high-level inquiry about the lost shipment. It was like a court-martial. Paul acted as if he were furious about the seizure. "I won't work with you fuckers any-more!" he yelled, and tossed the newspapers down on the table. The Colombians read about how the dealers had used a van with suspended plates and the detectives had made a lucky bust. The Colombians apparently believed everything they read in the papers, and for the time being, Paul was safe. We thought that if the bust looked almost like an act of God, the Colombians might not punish anyone for the drugs they'd lost. But of course that's not how the cocaine cartels do business.

"WE'RE working at putting you in a group," Lieutenant John Comparetto had said when I was first transferred to the task force and given my federal credentials and a car—a bright yellow seized Corvette that looked like a rocket ship.

"Speziale's group has an opening," I said. "And I've worked with them in the past."

"No," John said. "We're putting another guy in there." But John couldn't take the double-teaming by Jerry and me, and eventually he reconsidered. I suppose it was because Jerry and Paul had reached such an amazing position in the drug-trafficking world that anything that might help them was considered a good idea. Whatever the reason, I was put in Group 93. There were about eight of us in the group, top cops from the state police, the DEA, and the NYPD. It was a great team. Every one of us had a job, and we went about them with professionalism and enthusiasm. Although other guys had been in the team longer than me, Eddie made a decision that because Jerry and I worked so closely together, I would assume the role of co-case agent next to him and oversee the investigation.

At first the DEA brass blew a gasket. They didn't want two NYPD detectives in charge. But Eddie held firm, saying we were the best guys for the job, and that was that. Eddie knew we had the relationship with Paul. And of course, Jerry was Jerry. As for me, I was sort of a natural to run the case. I had become skilled at writing affidavits for search warrants and was, along with Jerry, an expert in the latest in wiretap technology—telephone-record analysis and cloned paging devices. I had vast experience in surveillance and casework, was a good manager, and could coordinate the operation under Eddie's supervision. I was also an experienced undercover who was calm under pressure. And, probably the most important, I was the only person who seemed remotely capable of keeping Speziale from starting an international incident.

By that time Jerry was living a bizarre double life. At home he was Jerry Speziale, Jersey guy with wife, kid, mortgage, and a job in the city. But the rest of the time he was Geraldo Bartone, flying around the world and arranging huge drug deals in the jungles of Central and South America. On his very first trip, Jerry ventured off to Guatemala and checked into a humid, roach-infested motel, waiting to hear from Paul. There was a knock on the door.

"You Jerry?"

"Yeah, I'm Jerry." The guy handed him a bag of guns and walked away.

At every stop, Jerry would meet with some local *jefe* or police official—often as corrupt as the people we were chasing—and explain that he was an undercover U.S. drug agent who needed to find a remote airstrip to refuel a plane that was popping its rivets with cocaine. The locals might ask for a bribe or try to seize the drugs themselves, so Jerry would bluff them or finesse them just long enough to get his plane down, refueled, and off the ground again, and then he'd scramble out of the country himself.

In New York, I stayed in touch with Jerry, kept track of the shipments, and wrote out affidavits for the wiretaps and searches that we'd conduct when Jerry and Paul's cocaine finally arrived. And while Jerry careened around Central America, I was in charge of keeping an eye on him. Eddie Beach even took to calling me Jerry's leash.

Jerry would call from some Central American jungle where he was building a twelve-hundred-meter airstrip to land a Colombian's drug plane. "Look," a local attaché said to him one time, "first we must meet with the major of the narcotics unit"; so Jerry rode out into the jungle in a Suburban, up some mountain road lined with crosses marking all the people who had died driving off the road, until finally they ended up in the middle of nowhere, at some little police station. It was ten in the morning. A grizzled guy with a beard and a bolero came out, with two "aides" who apparently hadn't ever heard of soap. They asked, had Jerry eaten breakfast?

"No," Jerry said.

"Is okay." And the major opened his desk drawer and produced a bottle of Scotch. Then he reached into his pocket and pulled out a dirty napkin. He opened the napkin and handed Jerry some pork rinds. It was like some scene out of a Clint Eastwood spaghetti Western that happened over and over again.

But pork rinds and Scotch were the least of the dangers in the jungle. Jerry was completely out of his element there. Once, a storm created a river where none had been before, and Jerry and his guys had to cross this rodent-infested water and survive for two weeks on bananas, coconuts, and lizards.

He was completely exposed out there. One run-in with rebels or rival drug dealers and Jerry would be dead. Often he had to rely on Central American officials, some of whom may have been in the pocket of the cartels. Jerry had no identification and only the slimmest official clearance for what he was doing. And the U.S. government in these countries was little help. Once, the U.S. embassy in Guatemala refused to provide fuel for refueling the drug plane on a covert airstrip, blaming weekend fuel shortages. Jerry threw a fit.

"That's okay, I'll load the tanks with water and crash the fuckin' plane into the Pacific!" he yelled. "I'll crash it right into the fuckin' embassy!" Finally they relented and supplied him with fuel. I was supposed to keep Jerry in check through all of this, which was something like baby-sitting a hurricane.

And I didn't just watch over Jerry's work. I'd also check on his tough but patient wife, Maggie, and their wonderful daughter, Francesca, who was just a year younger than Joe. The kids spent so much time together that they were best friends. In return, when I was out of town, Jerry would watch over Joe for me on the weekends.

Sometimes just reaching Jerry was tough. For a while we were nervous that someone had picked up our conversations when he was in Costa Rica, so we put a satellite dish up on Jerry's mother-in-law's garage in Jersey, and I'd have to go out there and wait for Jerry to call me late at night on a VHS radio.

In March 1992 Jerry was in Costa Rica with Paul, preparing to land a plane with eight hundred kilos of coke. Paul was on the phone with two Colombian drug brokers—Avelino Devia Galvis and Alonso Tobon—the guys he'd worked with seven months earlier on the previous deal, the 767 kilos that we'd seized and then covered up with the phony newspaper story. As brokers, Galvis and Tobon were in charge of finding dealers in New York. Amazingly, these two guys were actually talking to Paul about doing another deal with him. Then Paul heard a loud noise and the phone went dead. Not long after, armed marines from the U.S. embassy showed up to protect Jerry and Paul.

Jerry called me—frantic. "Jesus, Bern. We're in some fuckin' trouble here." Apparently Galvis and Tobon had been standing outside at a phone booth in Bogotá talking to Paul when a man on a motorcycle rode up and executed them with a machine gun. Jerry was frantic. What did it mean? Had the cartel uncovered our phony news story and assumed Galvis and Tobon were in on it? Were Jerry and Paul next?

We got them home, and Paul contacted his sources. He insisted we were still okay. The cartel had simply decided that its brokers were to blame for hiring the idiot who used a van with suspended plates. It had taken seven months for the cartel to decide, but eventually blame had been assigned—this time squarely on the shoulders of the two brokers. We had learned a hard lesson that we would see repeated over and over. With the cartels, someone is always held responsible.

ONCE Paul and Jerry got the drugs to New York, the rest of Group 93 kicked into action. It was something to see. We had names and phone numbers, and we'd sit up on wires listening to their activity, waiting until the local cells came out of the woodwork to pick up their drugs. Then we'd swoop down and seize the drugs or the money or both. If we arrested a dealer, it was usually just to flip him, to get information and then use him as a confidential informant later. Our investigations spread like a virus. We'd go up on a wire on one dealer and get all the dealers he talked to. We'd flip one mule and have every person he was in contact with. All those people became part of the investigation, and we'd get any person they came in contact with.

At our best, we were two or three steps ahead of the dealers. When that first shipment of 767 kilos came in, a dealer in Queens picked up two hundred keys of it in a van. He drove away and the van suddenly died. He drifted to the side of the road and kept turning the key. The engine would turn over but not quite start. He sat there distracted, working the key, while police officers drove up and quietly arrested him. We had replaced the ignition switch in the van with one that we controlled with a remote radio.

We were on a roll. Between April 1991 and December 1992, we seized 7,768 pounds of cocaine and $2.2 million in U.S. currency and arrested thirty-two people. We were far and away the most active group in any of the DEA's national task forces. We were pulling in something like 90 percent of our region's drugs. While the best groups across the country were measuring their busts in kilos, we measured ours in tons.

And the information we gathered may have been worth even more. There were eight major distribution cells in New York, working for one or more of the three main drug cartels back in Colombia—the Cali, Bogotá, and Medellín cartels. We prepared flow charts that showed the leaders of the cartels, the transportation brokers they used, and the leaders of all the distribution cells they used in New York. It was the most detailed report up to that point of the drug trade in New York.

As exciting as it was for Jerry and Paul to barrel around Central America, the real fuel of our investigation was the wiretaps. That's where I excelled. A lot of cops waited for the assistant district attorney or the U.S. attorney to write search warrants. This would take two weeks at the quickest and two months at the longest. But the dealers dumped their cell phones after four weeks. So I'd write most of our affidavits immediately. I even bought my own personal computer and moved it into the office. I'd write detailed affidavits—sometimes sixty to a hundred pages—run them through David Hennesy or Kevin Suttlehan, two of the brightest prosecutors in the NYC Special Narcotics Prosecutor's Office, and get them signed by a state supreme court judge named Leslie Crocker Snyder in days rather than weeks. We wrote more than two hundred affidavits for wires, and with Jerry and Paul on the ground, we knew more about drug dealing in New York than the dealers did.

It was beautiful. We were smack in the middle, tucking with the players on both sides and getting *them* blamed for all the trouble and chaos. The cartels were paying us up front to deliver their drugs, so we funded our operation with their money. Then, when the dope got to the States, we'd seize the money that the dealers were going to use to buy our drugs. We got paid on both ends. It was like a big game of tag, trying to keep Jerry and Paul safe while we skirted danger among Central and South American officials and terrorized the drug operations in New York. So many of our shipments were getting busted, we had to jab and move, rarely working with the same supplier twice, so that they didn't see the pattern. Jerry and Paul would work with one supplier, then feign anger when drugs and cash were seized from their dealers in New York and vow never to work with such amateurs again. They'd move on and work with someone from one of the other cartels. As Jerry burned bridges down south, we also had to play musical countries, moving from Guatemala to Honduras to Brazil, anywhere that Jerry could scratch together an airstrip.

One of my jobs was to focus the blame on local dealers in New York, to arrange surveillance and wiretaps and then manage the takedowns and seizures when the drugs were in the hands of the local dealers. It was like getting rid of a live grenade. Whoever is holding the drugs when the heat comes down will have to explain.

In 1992 we moved another eight hundred kilos of cocaine into New York and put it in an evidence locker while we essentially took applications from dealers who wanted to sell it. We'd gotten a reputation—or our aliases had—as major drug dealers. We had a phony importing company at the World Trade Center with business cards for Robert Viglione (me) and Geraldo Bartone (Jerry). There we had meetings with drug dealers in the conference room on the fiftieth floor, put cameras and recorders in the lamps, and picked up everything.

Finally three dealers got together and decided to move our eight hundred keys. We'd been following their cell for months, listening to their cell phone conversations, and now they were stepping up to buy the drugs. We listened on their phones as they gathered the money. Two weeks before the deal was supposed to go down, these dealers hired some mules out of Colombia, and we watched one of these guys come out of a house with a bagful of money. As we tailed him, he bought a car. Then he went to another house, where he loaded three big suitcases in the car. That's when we swooped down and arrested him. His name was John Lopez, and in those suitcases he was carrying more than a million dollars—stacks of bills that covered the table like a mountain range of money, until it no longer seemed real.

We gave John Lopez a choice. We could arrest him, or he could give us everything and walk. So he sang. He told us everything. He told us about a Brazilian—Paul—who had brought the drugs in along with some crazy Italian guy—Geraldo—and that they were planning to move eight hundred kilos. The guy sat at the table with no clue that he was actually talking to "Geraldo," who was actually Jerry Speziale, the cop.

Lopez told us that he was working for a major drug dealer named Caliche. We'd been hearing this name all over town, even from Paul, but Caliche remained fairly mysterious at that point. Lopez agreed to work for us as an informant, but when we let him go, he ran back to Bogotá. A few weeks later we received some photos from someone who identified himself as Lopez's cousin from Bogotá. The pictures showed two bodies at a funeral. Lopez and his girlfriend had been executed. Looking at those pictures, we couldn't help but wonder how much longer Paul and Jerry and the group could continue in the drug business. We knew that eventually trouble would come. But we had no idea which direction it would come from and that it was already on its way.

"BERN, I need to talk to you. You and Jerry." It was Eddie, calling from outside the office.

"Why don't you just come up?" I asked.

"I can't," he said. We walked up the street, and there was Eddie sitting in his car. He wouldn't even let us get in the car.

"You don't repeat a word of this," he said. "You got it?"

We looked at each other and then nodded. Eddie said it concerned two New York police detectives working with the DETF, Jeff Beck and Joe Termini, as well as a state trooper on the task force named Robles. We knew them all. They weren't in our group, and they didn't seem to do anything, but we knew them.

"They're dirty," Eddie said.

"Dirty? What are you talking about?"

"They sold heroin to an undercover."

"Bullshit," I said. "Those guys couldn't find fuckin' opium in Hong Kong. They couldn't find a fuckin' aspirin in a pharmacy!"

"Where'd those zeros get heroin?" Jerry asked.

Eddie didn't know. "Look," he said, "this is for real. And it's bad. You need to stay away from it." He explained that a former lieutenant of ours, Jimmy Wood, had told Eddie that these three cops approached an informant about selling smack they'd stolen from the DEA evidence room. "Listen to me," Eddie said. "They got an investigation on these guys and they're trying to get up on the phones."

Jerry and I went back to our desks and sat there staring at each other, amazed that while we were taking drugs off the street, these guys were putting it back.

Jerry and I had to go down to Miami, and we talked about it all the way there on the plane. We were at the hotel, sitting outside by the pool, and we couldn't get over it. I didn't like to tan, so I sat with a towel over my head while Jerry sat out all day, practically basting his body in oil. "How did those fuckin' guys get heroin?" I asked. We were disgusted by what they'd done, but we were mostly confused. Cocaine was fairly easy to find then, but heroin could be tough, especially for zeros like Beck and Termini and Robles.

"Hell," Jerry said, "I can't even remember the last time *we* seized any heroin."

"Nah," I said, "we did half a key, I don't know, four months ago."

I lifted the towel off my head and caught Jerry's eye.

"How much was there?" Jerry asked.

"I don't know. I didn't fill out the voucher."

We both sat up straight. "Joe Termini filled out the voucher!"

"Ralphie!" we both said at the same time. Raphael—or Ralphie, as we called him—was one of our informants, a guy we'd arrested and then turned. A few months earlier, Ralphie had given up a courier who led us to a safe house where we confiscated five hundred grams of heroin along with twelve kilos of cocaine. The courier had escaped and— like so many others—was later murdered by the cartel.

"Yeah, I'm sure," Ralphie said on the phone. "I weighed it myself in the apartment. It was half a key, exactly five hundred grams."

When we got back to New York we pulled the lab sheet, and sure enough, Termini had filled out the voucher, and when it came back from the lab, the analysis report said 320 grams. Those fuckers had stolen 180 grams of heroin. I have no patience for dirty cops. But if it's possible, I have less patience for cops who involve me in their bullshit.

We went back to Eddie Beach, but he didn't want to hear about it. Finally he agreed to take us to see John Maltz, the chief of the task force. John was a great cop and a wonderful guy, but he was a bit eccentric. We'd all heard there was a plate in his head, and John did nothing to discourage that rumor. Every once in a while we'd be talking to him in his office and he'd just fall asleep for no reason. Jerry and I took to bringing poppers and noisemakers to snap when he fell asleep.

Eddie, Jerry, and I sat down across from John. "Chief," Eddie began, "we hear there's an investigation going on in the task force."

"What are you talking about?" John asked.

"There's not an investigation into some dirty cops?" I asked.

"No," the chief said, "not that I've heard. What's it about?"

Eddie looked at Jerry and me. If there really was an investigation into the three cops, then John should know about it. Maybe we'd gotten bad information, because it was clear the chief really didn't know anything.

We stood up and apologized for taking up his time. We started for the door.

"We thought Beck and Termini and Robles were dirty," Eddie said.

"And we thought we knew where the six ounces came from," Jerry said.

John was leaning back in his chair, and he was so startled when he heard the names that he fell all the way back, crashing his head on the shelf behind him. "God damn it! Who told you? Get the fuck back in here! No, go in that room!" He shut us in a room where we sat for almost an hour, staring at one another and wondering what kind of shit we'd just stirred up.

Then the door opened and the uniforms started coming in—more police brass than you see at a parade. Finally in came the chief of NYPD Internal Affairs. I'd never seen this guy in person, only on TV. They all sat down and demanded to know how we'd found out about their secret investigation.

We told them, but I'm not sure they believed us. "It's about six ounces, right? About a hundred eighty grams?"

"How do you know that?" one of them asked.

So we told them about Termini apparently skimming from our seizure. It turned out that Internal Affairs had been investigating this case for three months, trying to figure out where the drugs came from, and we'd just walked in and given it to them. And it was a good thing because, as it turned out, they were looking at us as well.

They swore us to secrecy and turned us loose, but the more I thought about it, the more one aspect of this whole thing started to bug me.

After the shooting, Hector had been transferred into the task force and had landed right in the middle of the group that Beck, Termini, and Robles were in. Right away Hector didn't like Jeff Beck, who was going out of his way to make

Hector his buddy. And the entire unit seemed to lack the commitment and integrity that our group had, that Hector was used to seeing in Manhattan North Major Case. He even volunteered to work with other groups to get away from the lazy guys in his group. Still, I was worried that Hector would accidentally get tangled in the Internal Affairs net. So I pulled him aside.

"Listen, if you breathe a word of this, I'll throw you in fuckin' jail myself. I'm not gonna tell you why, but stay away from Beck and Termini. Got it?"

To his credit, Hector didn't ask why, and he steered clear of the dirty cops.

A few weeks later, Jerry and I were both paged by Eddie Beach and dragged to an unmarked office on the twentieth floor of a building on Church Street. There was a big table in a conference room and everyone was there, the chief of Internal Affairs, the feds, U.S. attorneys. You could've papered the walls with all the degrees in that room.

"We need your help," one of the U.S. attorneys said. They had called Eddie Beach in to help them figure out how to catch Beck, Termini, and Robles. It turned out that the three guys weren't using their office phones or pagers to deal the drugs, and the Internal Affairs guys couldn't catch them in the act. They needed to know which phones to tap. Eddie had told them that Jerry and I were the guys they needed.

I looked around the table. These were the guys who were supposed to investigate dirty cops, yet they couldn't figure out the three least talented guys on our whole task force. It didn't inspire a lot of confidence. So Jerry and I set to work. "Who's got the billing records for the phones? Who's got the office records? Where are the records for the cell phones? Where are their pager numbers?"

We moved to one end of the table and laid everything out, going over stacks of phone records, circling common numbers, cross-referencing and reading numbers aloud.

"Okay, this is a girlfriend because he calls her three times a day. This guy's just a buddy. These are your numbers, right here. Let's get some information on these numbers, and we'll do a reverse dump. Get us a stack of subpoenas."

Pretty soon we were writing out subpoenas and sliding them across the table for these guys to sign and pick up information on a handful of phone numbers. The guys on the other side of the table just stared—open-mouthed. We had done this very thing so many times it was second nature. It wasn't long before a pattern emerged from the pages—calls that were the right frequency, time, and duration for drug deals. But something about the pattern was alarming. It was *our pattern*. These assholes were checking our reports, and if we filed a report that we were going to hit a money drop or seize some drugs, these guys would try to get there first to steal the drugs or the cash for themselves.

"All we gotta do is set these guys up," I said. "They'll do the rest." So the next week, we wrote a phony report that some dealers had stashed two million dollars in a ministorage shed. We talked about it around the office, and when Beck, Termini, and Robles went to get the money out of the shed, they were arrested. On his way to prison to serve a four-year term, Beck told ABC's *20/20* that he was corrupted a little bit at a time by watching the amounts of money that drug dealers tossed around. He said it was hard to see the bad guys driving a Mercedes or a BMW while he drove a "1983 Toyota Corolla with a hundred sixty thousand miles on it and no muffler. It's like . . . why don't I have enough money to do this or why can't I do that?"

During the late 1980s and early 1990s, there was so much money being made in the drug business that a few cops became dirty. People have grown cynical about the loyalty between police officers, about the "blue wall" that keeps officers from testifying against one another, and sometimes cops out of stupidity will try to protect one another. But when a cop is genuinely dirty, we will be relentless in rooting him out. What we do is simply too important to have these guys flouting it. If guys start believing that a Mercedes is the reward for what we do, they're laughing in the face of those of us who do this job because we believe in it. And worst of all, they may as well piss on the graves of Michael Buczek, Chris Hoban, and so many others who made the ultimate sacrifice in their pursuit of justice.

The arrest of Beck, Termini, and Robles closed the door on those dirty cops, but it only made Jerry and me more aware of the deceit and betrayal around us. A person could drown trying to see all the angles and motives. And if we couldn't even trust our own colleagues, could we trust anyone? As we moved into 1993, my second year on the task force, our guard was up. But the next shock would come from a surprising source. Jerry and I were about to learn another lesson in betrayal.

17

MIAMI

1993

THE Colombian said it was imperative that Caliche make his cocaine stash houses look like typical American homes.

"When the daddy comes home at six o'clock, the kids should come out to the door to meet him," said the expert from the Cali drug cartel.

"Yes, sir," said Caliche, the Queens dealer whose name we'd been hearing for months and who ran a massive drug operation out of Long Island in the early 1990s. Caliche and his men rented houses in nice suburban neighborhoods like New Rochelle and Jamaica Estates and put families in them with orders to act like good Americans—or at least 1950s versions of them—to cover the kilos of coke and millions of dollars being stashed in their basements. But as they talked over the phones about how to set up these houses, Caliche and his contacts had no idea that we had tapped their phones and were listening in.

The Colombian told Caliche to get a regular phone and to get cable television so that bills would arrive each month at the house. "They need to have . . . magazines, man—I want five or seven magazines, man. You follow? I want them in English. Even though they don't read them."

"I'm putting that stuff in all of them, sir," Caliche said.

"They all have cable. . . . They all have a phone. They all have magazines, sir."

"There's one magazine we've got to get, Caliche—the *TV Guide*. . . . I think it's almost like the Bible up there. There's one in every house."

"Yes, sir," said Caliche. "Don't worry . . . I do things right, sir."

By late 1992 the domestic priority of our operation was the drug cell run by this mysterious Caliche, whose name we'd first heard from Paul months earlier. Caliche reported directly to leaders of the Cali drug cartel and ran maybe the largest and most brutal drug ring in New York. We'd gotten a leg up on Caliche's organization in August 1992 when we arrested John Lopez with three suitcases full of a million dollars in cash. Lopez gave up names and numbers and agreed to help us, but he went back to Bogotá and was murdered two months later. Even without him on the inside, we were building a huge case against Caliche and his associates, and in the winter of 1992–93, we were hitting the group with quick seizures of cash and drugs that were infuriating Caliche, as well as his bosses back in Colombia.

In December 1992 Jerry Speziale and I seized ten thousand dollars in drug money wrapped in aluminum foil, and less than a month later, the task force took five hundred thousand from one of Caliche's workers. When we heard over a wire that the worker was going to be killed for losing the money, task force members raced to a bar to save him. In January, we took another half million from one of Caliche's men and another twenty-five thousand a few weeks later.

When one of Caliche's men parked a van on Lexington Avenue between 88th and 89th Streets, we pried up the floor of the van and found 123 kilos of cocaine.

Then, on February 22, 1993, we had a team of four cars following a Caliche associate named John, who pulled over in a parking lot in Queens. He got out and called a major Colombian dealer and hit man named David. John said someone might be following him in a black Porsche.

"Where's the money?" David asked.

"In the car," John said.

David ordered him back to the car. But while he was gone, Jerry and I and a couple of other guys had taken a tire iron, popped the trunk, and taken the money—two duffel bagsful. Then Jerry put the locking device back in the trunk, closed it, and we drove away. John came back, didn't see anything wrong, drove the car away, and dropped it off. His contacts called him a short time later. "Hey, bro, where's the money?"

Of course, we had the money. When we had finished counting it, it was $230 short of a million.

The cartel accused John of stealing from them, and two days later we picked up a conversation between David and a hit man whose code name was 007. David told the hit man to "get some bracelets" and find out what John did with the money. That afternoon we followed the hit man to Times Square, where he bought a tape player and some tapes, some masking tape, and several pairs of handcuffs. He drove back to one of the stash houses in Bayside, Queens, and we figured that's where they were holding John.

Caliche spoke with a contact back in Colombia about John's impending torture and interrogation. "Have him turn the recorder on when he asks him. I want him to record it for me," the Colombian said.

"Okay, sir," Caliche said. "Don't worry."

We set up surveillance on the house in Queens, but things were moving quickly, and within minutes the wire room called to tell us that the drug bosses were calling to check on the progress of John's torture.

"How's the roughing up going?" the Colombian boss asked Caliche.

"Fine, man. Just fine."

We had to move right away, before we were ready. Jerry called for backup, and he explained, to the sergeant of the Anticrime Unit that arrived, that a man was being tortured inside that quiet split-level. The sergeant stared at Jerry like he had three heads.

"Um, excuse me, sir, but do you have a warrant?" he asked.

I had to testify in court that afternoon, and when I was done, I put on the lights and siren and raced out to Queens as fast as I could. The tires on my Oldsmobile Cutlass were smoking when I skidded up to our staging area a few blocks away.

"What's goin' on?"

"This guy wants a warrant," Jerry said, pointing to the sergeant.

Just then the wire room called again. The hit men were talking on the phone to David right then, telling him they were going to send John "to heaven."

"You got a sledgehammer?" Jerry asked one of the cops. Jerry hopped in his car, with me following, and we tore off down the street and rolled up on the curb in front of the house. We were trying to stay quiet, but Jerry bumped the siren with his knee as he got out of the car. Later, we could hear the siren on the audiotape the hit men were making.

We busted open the door with the sledgehammer. Two of the hit men raced out the back door. We arrested the other one in the basement, standing next to John, who was handcuffed to a chair. His shirt was sliced open, his chest had been cut, and he'd had a gun at his head for an hour. He was white as a ghost and covered in sweat, but he smiled so sweetly when he saw us, I might have thought he was in love if I didn't know better.

Some other members of the team had chased one of the escaping hit men on foot all the way through the neighborhood and across the Long Island Expressway. Jerry and I jumped in my car and took off the wrong way down the service road of the LIE, dodging and weaving through traffic. We crossed the highway, where our guys had captured the hit man and were holding him down. We handcuffed him.

But we had a problem. Our guys had chased the suspect on foot. There were seven cops, and only one car—mine.

"Let's put him in the trunk," said one of the guys. But I remembered a police captain who was once suspended for that, so we put the bad guy in the backseat with one cop on each side. We had me, Jerry, and another guy in the front, and the remaining guys opened the trunk and sat in the back facing out, enjoying the air as we drove back to the house.

OUR inspector shifted uncomfortably in his chair. "Look, I'm just worried that if you keep this up, you'll get indicted for conspiracy to commit murder."

Jerry and I just stared at each other. We had managed to save the dealer John from torture. In fact, he had given us more information, and we placed him in the witness protection program. We even took a picture of him in a DEA T-shirt, and when we arrested people from Caliche's operation, we showed them the picture, further shifting suspicion away from Jerry and Paul and me by making them think there was a DEA agent in their midst the whole time. Still, a handful of members of the Cali organization had been whacked as a direct result of our busts. Our charts showing the spiderweb of cartels, brokers, and distribution cells included several dealers with the notation "executed" next to their names. We liked to swoop down and take money and drugs without arresting the dealers, so we could continue monitoring their phones. These quick hits also deflected suspicion away from Jerry, Paul, and me. The Colombians would investigate and accuse the dealers of stealing the money themselves. Unfortunately, there wasn't much of an appeals process in the cartels.

Our transcribed wiretaps were full of threats and judgments. "Tell the man that everything is pointing his way and he has to pay for everything," said David in one taped conversation. "If he doesn't have any money to back him up, brother, he's fucked."

But our inspector worried that our hit-and-run tactics

could open us to accusations of complicity in these murders. He asked us to make our money seizures look more like random burglaries or thefts, so maybe street criminals would be blamed. That's how bad crime was in the early 1990s; even the drug dealers didn't feel safe.

During the spring of 1993, we kept hitting the Caliche operation, taking more than a million dollars in four seizures in February and March. Then, on May 7, 1993, we busted the whole group, in a series of raids against the suburban Queens and Long Island houses, with their barbecues and their *TV Guides*. In seven separate seizures that day, we confiscated more than six hundred thousand dollars in drug money and arrested five people, including Caliche, whose real name was Carlos Torres. We picked Torres up about midnight in Queens, as he packed up his apartment to move. He ended up getting thirty-three years and tried to kill himself in jail.

It was nuts. It was raining cocaine and money. With Jerry and Paul working the supply end and the rest of the team working the delivery side, we had more leads than we could investigate. As it was, we were working nonstop. Even if we took an evening or a weekend off, Jerry and I got together with our kids and worked anyway. We worked eighty hours a week and had no time for anything else. I was dating a woman named Damaris, who worked downtown, and I'd pick her up in the morning and drop her off at work on my way in to the office. "Listen," I'd say, "I'll pick you up at five and we'll go eat."

At six I'd call her. "Hey, I'm on surveillance. I'll call you at eight."

At ten I'd call back. "We're tied up on this. I'll call you in the morning."

And the next morning, she'd get a call from Eddie Beach. "Hey, Bernie asked me to call. He had to fly to Miami." There seemed to be no gap at all between investigations.

The night after the Caliche raid, we were all exhausted, having worked all night. I came in that morning and show-

ered and changed my clothes and was about to go home
when I got a phone call from Monica Brozowski, an inter-
preter who listened to the wires. She'd just heard on one of
the wires that a ten-thousand-dollar drop was about to be
made at the corner of 15th Street and Tenth Avenue. The car
would be there alone, the cash in its trunk.

That was only a few blocks away. I ran around the office
looking for someone to come with me, but everyone had
gone home, beat from the long night. Finally I found Lt.
John Comparetto.

"Come on," I said. "I gotta pick up some money. There's a
drop up the block."

John, who'd been jockeying for a desk for some time,
nodded. "Okay, let's get some people together, get a plan
ready—"

"You don't understand," I said. "We gotta go right now."
So John and I drove down to the parking lot, and there was
the car, right where Monica said it would be. I was still under
orders to make these things look like standard thefts, so I
jumped out of our unmarked car and ran to the drop car. I
started it and was about to drive away when I figured I should
make sure the money was in the trunk.

I popped the trunk. The drop hadn't been made yet. So
John and I quickly drove off, past two Colombians carrying
a duffel bag. We hurried back to the office and gathered
some backup, five guys, two of whom I'd never even met before. We raced back to 15th and Tenth and I got out to steal
the car, but a woman behind us started honking her horn, so
I just popped the trunk and grabbed the duffel bags.

But there wasn't ten thousand dollars in the bags. There
was *six hundred thousand*. We were robbing the drug cartels
blind, and it was making them crazy.

A couple of weeks later, Jerry got a call from Miami
DEA, which was also listening in on some of David's drug
business. They'd picked up a conversation with David's
brother Johnny and a woman in New York who offered to
give Johnny information on a couple of New York cops who

were making life tough for them. And then the woman used our names—Kerik and Speziale.

Johnny was a New York dealer, and if he had heard of us, it was as Geraldo Bartone and Robert Viglione. So we might not have been compromised yet. We had the phone company reverse-dump his phone, and we traced the call to a pay phone at the corner of 238th Street and Sedgwick Avenue in the Bronx. I ran the names of everyone who worked in the task force to see if someone on the inside had sold us out. And there it was. Monica Brozowski. She lived just a few blocks away from that pay phone. I was furious. This woman was trying to get us killed. I wanted to confront her, but the bosses said we still didn't have enough proof.

We knew where the proof could be found, but unfortunately, Johnny had dumped his cell phone and we didn't know where he lived. The only thing we did know was that his car had recently been cited for various violations in the One-Ten Precinct, out in Queens. "Hey," Jerry said, "I got an idea."

He and I drove out to the One-Ten and asked the desk lieutenant if we could address the roll call. Jerry stood up and introduced us. "How many guys," he began, "would like a three-day all-expenses-paid vacation to Florida?" They all stared for a minute, as if they thought he was screwing around.

"I'm serious," Jerry said. "Here's the deal: we're looking for this car." Jerry explained that the Miami DEA had an open case on this, and whoever found Johnny's car would have to go down to Florida to testify. "One day of testimony, three days in a nice Miami hotel."

At 3:22 A.M. the Florida vacation paid off. Jerry got a page. A patrol cop had found the car. We sat on it all morning, and at 10:30 A.M., Johnny came walking out of a nearby apartment. We picked him up and said we knew he'd gotten a call from Monica offering to give us up. He admitted it and said she'd offered to give him our names, addresses, and cars for ten thousand dollars. Ironically, Johnny said he didn't meet with her because he was worried about being set up. He agreed to help us.

A few days later he called Monica back and told her that he'd reconsidered and wanted to pay her a thousand dollars for information about the two cops. Sure, she said, she still had information. We couldn't believe it. She would sell us out for a thousand dollars. We sent an undercover cop, who paid her the money. Then Jerry jumped out of the bushes and arrested her. Monica got seven years.

Not surprisingly, Jerry and I were becoming ever more distrustful. The Monica Brozowski case was just one example of the dizzying levels of deceit in the drug business: we used the brother of one of our main targets to arrest our own colleague who had tried to sell us out to the very guy who set her up, a guy who hadn't trusted her because he was afraid she was setting *him* up. For the second time in a year, we'd had to turn our attention away from the drug dealers to catch someone on our side of the law.

And the sad thing was, the betrayals we knew about were nothing compared with the one going on right under our noses.

"DO you know Paolo Ferrara?" the Miami DEA agent asked me.

"No," I said.

"You don't know José Paolo Ferrara?"

"No," I said again.

"You've never talked to him?"

"No," I said again.

Not long after that, our supervisor called Jerry and me in and said the Miami DEA had contacted the DEA's Office of Professional Responsibility (OPR) and NYPD Internal Affairs, and these agencies were investigating us.

We were shocked. Why would they investigate us?

He showed us a picture. "Who is this?"

"It's Paul," I said.

"Then you know him?"

"Sure, it's our stool." It was Paul Alexander, our informant. Probably the best confidential informant in the history of the DEA.

"Miami says this is José Paolo Ferrara, the guy you said you didn't know."

"No, that's Paul," we said.

"There's more," our boss said. "Miami says this guy just moved seventeen hundred keys through Miami into Newark and that you helped him."

As we stared at the picture, we realized that we were in deep shit here. We had denied knowing Paul because we hadn't recognized that name. But it would take the Miami DEA agents five minutes to realize that Paul—or Paolo or whatever he called himself—talked every day on the phone with Jerry and me.

Was Paul dealing behind our backs? Did the Miami DEA agents think we were protecting him? Or that we were involved in his drug dealing?

In December 1992, Paul had been caught with half a million dollars in cash, but he insisted the money was payment from the cartel for the eight hundred–kilo deal we'd done earlier and that he was going to turn it over to us. We believed him. I suppose we didn't want to believe that Paul would double-deal us. He was like another member of our team. After the cases with Monica and Beck, Termini, and Robles, we trusted Paul more than many of the cops we worked with. We trusted Paul with our lives.

So what was the Miami DEA up to, asking us about Paul without telling us exactly what they had on him? Jerry and Eddie and I tried to see it from every angle. We had recently set up another big deal with the Cali cartel, but Costa Rican officials wouldn't let us land there, so Paul had suggested we fly the drugs out of Brazil, his home country. Did Paul want to use Brazil because he could cut a side deal there? Had Paul agreed to cooperate with the Miami DEA to set us up? I look back at how distrustful I had become and it's amazing. We had become so successful that some other agents around the country thought we must be dirty, so we even imagined this whole thing could be a ruse to set us up. Or maybe it was just a case of mistaken identity. Maybe this José Paolo Ferrara would turn out to be someone else entirely.

One day during all of this, Paul called to tell us he was coming to New York. Since he was under investigation now, we should have stayed away from him. Still, it was driving us all crazy, trying to figure out if Paul had some angle we didn't know about. One afternoon Eddie Beach called me in. "Hey, Bern," he said. "We ain't supposed to talk to him . . . but I gotta know."

I started for the door. "I got it."

"You know what to do?"

"I got it."

"Bern—"

"Look, I got it."

He was at a swank hotel in midtown Manhattan. I got there at six the next morning. No one was around. No one knew I was coming. I knocked on his door, and he opened the door in silk underwear and a bathrobe. I grabbed him by the collar and pulled him out into the hallway in case his room was wired. I yanked off the robe and checked it for wires, then made him drop his drawers to check his body for wires. Nothing. I didn't say anything about the Miami investigation, and Paul assured me that everything was still okay. It says something about the business Paul was in that he didn't seem at all surprised to be searched like this. We went on as if everything were normal. And yet we were tied in knots. Was it possible we could still trust Paul?

We got our answer on April 18, 1993. Paul and his wife flew into Miami, where they had a house. They landed and were met by DEA agents who immediately arrested him and charged him with smuggling seventeen hundred kilos of cocaine into Miami, hidden in generators and transformers. Miami officials had been trying to get us to come down for a meeting, but our bosses didn't want us to as long as we were under investigation.

Finally we went down there and met with the DEA agents and U.S. attorneys in the case against Paul. It was pretty tense. They still suspected us of protecting Paul, and we still didn't trust their motives. But as they showed us their evidence, it became clear: Paul was as dirty as Pablo Escobar.

For every load he did with us, Paul was doing two or three behind our backs. He was using other names, not just Ferrara, but Pedro Chamuro, Don Oscar, and Oscar Rothstein. We went to a building he owned in Miami and were amazed to see an entire wall set up with an elaborate phone switching system. There were forty phone numbers on this screen, all connected through this room, cell phones and land lines in Colombia, Brazil, and all over the United States. We'd dial a number for Paul in Brazil, and this relay system would send the call from Brazil to Miami and from Miami to Newark, where Paul would be unloading drugs in a warehouse. We thought he was in Brazil, but it turned out he was right across the river, fifteen miles away in Newark.

In hindsight, I suppose we should have known. Paul had taught us everything we knew about drug dealing, but he probably hadn't taught us everything *he* knew. We explained to the Miami agents that we hadn't known about the name José Paolo Ferrara; we hadn't known about any of his side dealing. When Paul confirmed that we were in the dark, the Miami DEA finally dropped its investigation of us. We were relieved, but we were sad too. Paul had made us stars in the drug world of law enforcement. More than that, we'd grown to like him. I never met anyone as smart as Paul. I think of all the things he could've been if he'd managed to stay straight. That's the thing about the drug trade. It takes the good, bright people and corrupts them with money and power. At his trial, Paul was found guilty and sentenced to twenty-two years in prison. I never saw him again.

AT first we were worried. Paul had been our ticket into the cartels. But as we started our lives without Paul, we realized that we knew as much as anyone. Maybe we'd lost Paul, but we still had wiretaps on phones all over the city. And our massive investigation of the Caliche organization had led us in some very promising directions.

In March 1993 we'd traced a page to one of Caliche's people in a room at the New York Hilton Hotel at 54th Street and Sixth Avenue. There were a couple of middle-aged white guys in the room, not the usual profile of heavy drug dealers. Jerry and some others went over to the hotel, while I called the technical support people and had them put a fish-eye lens in the peephole of the door across the hall so we could keep an eye on them. We sat on the room all night and the next day, and the two guys set up a meeting with Caliche's people.

After the meeting we grabbed the two guys, figuring they had come up to buy dope and would be leaving with a load. Instead they had cash—almost a hundred thousand dollars. It turned out they weren't buyers or sellers; they were boat pilots working for the Cali cartel. We convinced them we had evidence to tie them into a conspiracy with Caliche and they could go to jail for the rest of their lives. "If you help us, you can walk away free as a bird," Jerry said.

One of the men—a former Navy SEAL—agreed to be a confidential informant. But as he talked, we could see that he was holding back. The next morning he called Jerry and admitted that he hadn't told us everything. Jerry and I were in the office, sitting across from each other. He gave me the thumbs-up sign. I quietly picked up the phone to hear what our new CI had to say. "Well," he said, "I got fifteen hundred kilos on a boat in Ecuador."

The boat was a sixty-five-foot steel-lined yacht called *Pegasus,* code-named Second Chance, built especially for drug smuggling by a thirty-two-year-old Colombian named José Ruiz Diaz, the highest-ranking drug dealer we had yet to come in contact with. Diaz worked for the Cali cartel, over-seeing Caliche as well as our new informant. Paul knew him too, but had always been leery about giving up his name. We sent an agent from our group named Terry Hartman to Ecuador, and he had the crew of the *Pegasus* tossed off and then put our own crew on the boat, along with a tracking device. We then monitored the boat's journey from Ecuador to Galveston, Texas, by satellite, and when it arrived in Galveston, we were there to unload it. The drugs—thirty-two hundred pounds of cocaine—were loaded in a trap in the hold, in packages marked with the word *Nike*. The cartels gave every load they sent a phony brand name like that to keep track of it. We had even picked up shipments of cocaine stamped with the words *Reagan* and *Bush*. It took us a whole day to unload the drugs on the *Pegasus,* and as the packages were stacked on one side of the boat, the shifting weight nearly capsized it. It was a huge bust, worth $30 million wholesale and perhaps $250 million on the street.

While we moved the cocaine to New York, we set up a phony meeting with Diaz in Switzerland to pay him for the drugs. Jerry flew there to help local officials arrest him. When Diaz tried to leave the hotel, Jerry panicked, ran to the lobby, and decked him. It would take six months to extradite him to the United States, but when he came, Jerry and I were there to pick him up. Diaz had been running drugs into the United States for more than a decade, doing about *twelve million dollars a week* in drug sales. Just three years earlier I had felt like I was beating my head against a wall as an undercover officer, making one nickel-bag arrest at a time. Now we were taking off tons of cocaine.

Our network of wiretaps was bringing in even more drugs than Paul had. And our operation wasn't limited to New York anymore. Our investigation of Diaz's sailboat led us to a big shipment the boat had dumped in Australia, and we alerted Australian officials, who seized 270 kilos, the largest drug seizure in Australia to that point.

In the United States, we were up on phones in thirteen different cities. When we heard David talk about a big shipment into Houston, we shared our information with agents there, got them up on phones, and within twenty-four hours we had helped the Houston agents seize three tons of cocaine.

For years, local jurisdictions had treated drug investigations as their own private fiefdoms, but we were sharing our technical knowledge and the intelligence we'd gathered, and the results were startling. We made cases in Texas, Alaska, and Los Angeles—where we helped train a talented, eager young DEA agent named George Elliot, who would turn out to be one of the best in the country.

We had become such experts at battling drug traffickers that the DEA flew Jerry and me to Florida, locked us in a room with another agent and a few analysts and lawyers, and had us write a manual on state-of-the-art wiretaps and the legal requirements of running massive drug investigations. The manual took us two weeks to write.

By early 1994 Jerry and I were running on the adrenaline of our investigation. We were on a roll in DETF Group 93, the most successful drug enforcement group in the country. We had seized twenty-two thousand pounds of cocaine, confiscated fifty-six million dollars in drug money, and arrested dozens of people. In January 1994, when I found out I was going to be transferred out of DETF, the only thing I could think was that I was leaving when there was still too much to do.

But Rudy Giuliani had been elected mayor of New York, and he had other plans for me. I found out the day after we extradited José Ruiz Diaz from Switzerland that I was about to begin another phase of my life and take a step forward in my career in law enforcement. It was hard to leave Jerry behind. He grew more manic every year, and as I prepared for the challenges that lay ahead of me, I found myself worried about my friend, left alone in such a treacherous world.

THE CITY

PART THREE

IT WAS A CRUEL CITY, BUT IT WAS A LOVELY ONE,
A SAVAGE CITY, YET IT HAD SUCH TENDERNESS. . . .

—THOMAS WOLFE
The Web and the Rock

18

NEW YORK

JACK Maple is dying. I see it in his face. I hear it in his voice. He is propped up in a bed at Memorial Sloan-Kettering Cancer Center, ravaged by colon cancer and by the chemotherapy that is helpless to stop it. Jack is only forty-eight.

"It's good to see you," he says, and takes my hand. We talk for a minute about the city and about the police department that we both love. I was worried about how he would look, but he looks about the same, just a little more weathered and weak, as if this disease were hollowing out his barrel chest.

Jack Maple is more than a friend. He's a hero. With the exception of Mayor Rudolph Giuliani, Jack Maple did more than any other person in the last decade to pull New York back from the decline of the 1980s and early 1990s.

Jack knows he's near the end. He talks plainly about the arrangements for his funeral—where it will be and who will speak. I suppose I shouldn't be surprised by his strength. Jack Maple will face death the way he faced life: head-on.

I first met Jack when I worked patrol on 42nd Street. He was a lieutenant in the New York City Transit Police Department before its merger into the NYPD and assigned to the subway station beneath Times Square. While we dealt with the craziness above ground, Jack handled the underground version of the Deuce—the dark carnival of muggers, taggers, pickpockets, panhandlers, perverts, con artists, drug dealers, and fare beaters who gave the New York subway system such a terrible reputation. Jack had his own reputation—chasing perps out of the tunnels and into the streets, cruising around the subways dressed as a potential robbery victim, shooting a drug dealer who had busted him in the head with an iron pipe.

Short and stocky, Jack wore bow ties and spats, bowler hats and two-tone shoes. He ate like a king and drank champagne at corner tables in swanky bars like the Oak Room and Elaine's. But behind the colorful exterior was a pure cop, brave, active, and committed to his work. In late 1990 he hooked up with William Bratton to transform the Transit Bureau, developing some of the brash management techniques that they would later apply to the entire city. Jack put up huge detailed maps of the subway system and used them to track crime all over the tunnels, trains, and subway stations with color-coded thumbtacks. Soon the colors began to form patterns, and these patterns became trends, and it became possible to predict what the criminals were doing and where trouble might pop up. Then Jack focused his officers' attention on that problem until it was solved. When he concentrated on reducing gang robberies on the subway, Jack's transit cops managed to cut the number of these attacks from twelve hundred to twelve. In one year.

In 1993 Bratton and Maple left to run the Boston Police Department, but in 1994 they returned to run the NYPD in Mayor Giuliani's new administration. What followed was a historic revolution in criminal justice that I have been fortunate to have a hand in. The vision and the drive for this revolution were Rudolph Giuliani's. And of course, much of the responsibility and leadership came from Bill Bratton. But if you asked me who rolled up his sleeves and did the work, I'd have to say it was Jack Maple.

When he was first appointed deputy commissioner for crime control strategies, Maple butted up against the entrenched culture of the NYPD and its bias against transit police; some city police officers called them "cave cops." Jack also faced down the popular conception that crime increased and fell only for socioeconomic reasons and that law enforcement had virtually no effect on crime rates. Through all of this, Jack concentrated on one goal: accomplishing Giuliani's vision and Bratton's mandate to cut crime. You can talk tough about crime all day, but if you don't come up with plans, it'll never be more than talk. Even before he started, Jack set out to gather information on all aspects of policing, and he called me in early 1994 to debrief me about my theories of drug enforcement. I told him about the things that worked in the DEA task force and how I thought we could better attack drugs at all levels, especially patrol. Under Mayor David Dinkins, patrol officers had gotten away from making drug arrests because police brass worried that they would be prone to corruption. We agreed that it was ludicrous trying to solve one problem—corruption—by creating a worse one—apathy. No, he assured me, uniformed cops would be empowered to make all kinds of arrests, drugs included.

He talked to other cops and commanders, and once he had a good picture of what lay before him, Jack went after New York's crime problem the same way he had cleaned up the subway system.

His big thumbtacked map had evolved into the most important law enforcement tool of the last decade: Comp Stat—Computer Generated Comparative Statistics. Before, crime statistics had come in every six months; Jack wanted them every day. He demanded that the lumbering NYPD react faster and be more technologically advanced and more detailed. He wanted an instant reading on crime in the city, with instant reaction, instant assessment and instant fixes. Every week, he and Bratton assembled 7 A.M. meetings in the NYPD command center—the war room—where commanding officers were held accountable for the crime rates and patterns in their precincts and divisions—like the separate offices of a large corporation. If the crime rate fell or a ring of burglars was stopped, commanders could be rewarded. If crime rose, they were held responsible and could be transferred or demoted or even fired. Combined with the results-oriented management styles of Giuliani and Bratton, Comp Stat powered the New York Police Department's resurgence with the twin engines of accountability and information. In 1994 crime dropped 12 percent, and 16 percent the year after that. In three years homicides were cut in half—falling at three times the national rate. Riding herd over this stampede of good news was the larger-than-life figure of Jack Maple.

I guess that's why it's hard to see the weakened version of Jack lying in front of me, his wife of a few months pacing in the hall outside. I've brought to the hospital with me a couple of Jack's old friends—Tom Fahey and Sonny Archer, a member of my security detail who worked for Jack. Sonny and I have similar backgrounds. His mother abandoned him when he was a baby and his father raised him. When he was a teenager, his father sent him to military school after he got into some trouble acting out. At first Sonny hated the regimented school and tried to run away several times. He was behaving badly and didn't appreciate the fact that his father, Fermin Archer, Sr., was working three jobs just to send him there. One day, after a visit to the school, his father was on his way home when he got into an accident. It was raining, he lost control of the car, and it went off the side of a road and down a very steep ravine. Miraculously, the car went down backward and hit a tree, which prevented him from going off the mountain. Hitting that tree saved his life. It also, in many ways, saved Sonny's life.

"I remember the call that night," Sonny told me once. "The headmaster called and said, 'There's been an accident.' " When Sonny saw the ravine that his father had fallen into, with the trunk of the demolished car in the backseat, he realized just how much his father loved him.

It was the moment that Sonny Archer became a man.

He instantly turned his life around and ended up becoming a great cop. Tall, steady, and quiet, Sonny earned the Combat Cross in 1991 when he gunned down an armed suspect who had shot his partner. And then Jack Maple found him in the transit department and brought him to Comp Stat.

Now Sonny stands next to me in the hospital, watching Jack die. This is tearing Sonny up. He loves his old boss and friend.

After a while Jack seems tired and catches my eye. "Guys," he says, "can I have a minute with the PC?" Sonny and Tom go out into the hallway, and Jack and I are alone.

"Come here," Jack says.

I walk over. He reaches up and grabs me by the shirt, his IV line rattling on his arm. He pulls me close and we say our good-byes. Then he kisses me on the cheek and says into my ear, "You did it. Just like me. Nobody else thought it could be done, but you did it. Nobody can take that away from you."

"No, Jack," I say. "Whatever I've accomplished was on top of what you did. You were the one, Jack."

He leans back in his hospital bed and smiles. I lean over him, kiss him on the forehead, and say, "I love you, Jackie." And I leave the room.

MY executive staff gathers in the eighth-floor command center, the same room where Jack and Bill Bratton first started holding Comp Stat meetings. There are about seventy-five of us in this room, gathered around a huge U-shaped table and a high-tech console that displays the latest maps and charts of crime.

On the agenda today is the one-hundred-day report on one of my highest priorities as police commissioner: the expansion of the Intelligence Division.

For law enforcement agencies, intelligence is simply the gathering and sharing of information. This would seem like a natural activity for any police department, but it's something that the NYPD has struggled with. This is mostly because New York is divided into boroughs that are like separate cities, and information has typically stopped at the border of each borough. It is also because the culture of our department has bred territorialism among the precincts, the boroughs, and the different divisions like narcotics and homicide; officers take pride in their work and want to keep their arrests and investigations for themselves. And it is partly a problem of size, of the glacial speed of changing a department as big as the NYPD.

For decades the only sharing of information between these various units and boroughs was informal: between friends over a coffee or at a funeral or at a racket—a fundraiser for cops. When old cops retired, the knowledge they'd collected went with them. Even with the advent of computers, information didn't seem to flow between units, and the databases for the separate boroughs and divisions weren't even connected.

Unfortunately, the criminals didn't observe the rigid boundaries and categories that the New York Police Department had set up, and so a drug gang in Brooklyn that robbed people in the Bronx to buy crack in Harlem might spawn three separate investigations by detectives who might not know anything about one another and had no way to pool their information to respond more quickly and effectively.

There had always been an Intelligence Division in the NYPD, but it had been greatly decreased following a scandal involving the infiltration of radical groups in the 1970s. When I took over, the Intelligence Division was only a dozen or so officers whose main duties were to provide security for diplomats and dignitaries. The division was good at security, but it didn't answer the larger question of who would be responsible for coordinating the vast amounts of information that should be used to fight crime.

When I worked in the Drug Enforcement Task Force, we realized pretty quickly that intelligence was our best weapon. We used our guns only a handful of times, but we used our computer databases every day. If we got the last four digits of a license plate, within minutes we could have lists of any cars with those four digits and thirty categories of information, from the owners of those cars and their addresses to their associates and friends, their criminal records, and intelligence about all those people. In DETF the collection of information was valued as much as arrests—more in some cases.

My challenge was to show rough-and-tumble police officers the value of sharing information, and to create a system in which officers weren't threatened that another agency would come in and steal their arrests. The information had to flow up the chain of command and back down to the precincts, to every officer who could use it. And the borough and division boundaries weren't the only ones I wanted to break down. I also wanted us to work with federal and state agencies, which meant overcoming generations of mistrust and condescension. And I wanted to do this right now.

I knew I'd need someone bright and analytical, someone who could think abstractly and act quickly. I had just the person. A person I had recently whacked.

In my first week, I had demoted the Bronx borough commander—a veteran cop named Joanne Jaffe. Under her watch, murders in the Bronx had gone up 51 percent in the first eight months of 2000—forty-six more murders than the year before. While I couldn't approve of the results she'd gotten in the Bronx, I knew Assistant Chief Jaffe to be a brilliant police officer with a keen understanding of the way the NYPD operated.

I pulled her aside. "Look, I've got a job for you." I told her all about my vision for the Criminal Intelligence Section, and she was eager for the challenge. I assigned Sgt. Lenny Lemer to work with her because of his experience in the Intelligence Division of the DETF. In May 2001, when Jaffe was ready, we assigned 250 of the most promising officers in the department to this new intelligence division and put a talented deputy inspector named John Cutter in charge. Right away we started seeing results.

In June, an arrest was made in the One-Nine Precinct on an aggravated harassment case—a guy harassing his girlfriend over the phone—and the perp told the arresting officer that he might trade some information on another criminal for a lighter sentence. The other criminal was in another borough. In the past, this information might have died on the vine because it didn't do the arresting officer any good. But in this case it was passed on to the Intel Section. Detectives interviewed the guy and checked out his story. He claimed to know a fugitive who was selling tickets for a tour bus in midtown Manhattan.

The detectives found the bus, and one of them walked over and said the man's name: "Francisco." He seemed stunned to hear it.

Francisco Sepulveda, thirty-one, had been a fugitive since September 1994, when he was allegedly part of a home invasion team that tied the hands and legs of a couple and their seven-year-old daughter while they burglarized the house. They also taped the mouths of the family, and that's how the little girl died, suffocating from the tape over her mouth. For seven years, Francisco Sepulveda had evaded capture, working odd jobs, living under assumed names, and moving whenever he sensed trouble. He was on the FBI's Most Wanted List and among the ten most wanted fugitives in Massachusetts.

"You finally got me," Francisco said when he was collared.

Under the old system, the information about Sepulveda would probably never have made it to another borough. And more than likely, Sepulveda would have simply moved on.

These are the kinds of stories we share at the meeting in the command and control center. The numbers are phenomenal. In its first hundred days, the Intel Section has come up with information that led to the seizure of 113 guns and the execution of 199 search warrants that wouldn't have happened without their work. In addition, the section's information was used to find witnesses and suspects in forty-five homicides and forty-seven shootings. In just three months, this second layer of information gathering—stepping in behind the beat cops and detectives—has begun the hard work of connecting investigations all over New York and creating a safety net to keep intelligence from falling through the cracks.

After the presentation on the section's first hundred days, I praise Joanne Jaffe and the others who have worked with her. It is a perfect example of what I hope to do in my short time as police commissioner—quick development of a program that adds to the good things that have already been done, a program that makes a substantial improvement in the way we fight crime.

Behind the numbers is an even more important story. I think the most vital part of the Intelligence Section might be the inroads we've made with other jurisdictions. The FBI, the DEA, the Immigration and Naturalization Service, Customs, and the Bureau of Alcohol, Tobacco and Firearms have all agreed to be involved, to break down those other borders and share access to the data we've gathered. They've even assigned officers to a Regional Intelligence Section. Anyone who has worked in law enforcement knows how tough it can be to get all those agencies to work together. It is just one aspect of this new program that makes me very proud.

"I talked about criminal intelligence for the past six months," I tell the brass at the meeting. "I put together a great team of people to look at it, to implement it and make it work. I told Deputy Inspector John Cutter, the commanding officer, that this was very important to me. Well, that was a hundred days ago. Today the Intelligence Section is a reality because of the hard work of these people."

I reach into my pocket and pull out an inspector's shield. "John," I say as Cutter stares at me, "on Friday you're gonna be promoted to inspector." If he weren't leaning against a wall, I think he would have fallen over. He just stares at me, stunned.

One of the commanding officers says, "What'd he just say?" Battlefield promotions are extremely rare in the NYPD. There is a whole process for that sort of thing. But Joanne Jaffe and John Cutter have done something extraordinary, building the new Intelligence Section from nothing but an idea, creating a program that builds on the Giuliani style of government—using performance indicators and management accountability to run government like a business. More important, they have broken down traditional walls that separated bureaus and boroughs, state, local, and federal authorities. They have helped me change the very culture of this department.

It's the kind of thing that would make Jack Maple proud.

I'M beat. It's 1:15 A.M. and I've just gone to bed. Within thirty seconds or so, I'm out. I've got to be up at five. I'm dead to the world when the telephone rings in the background. I think I'm dreaming, but it doesn't go away. I roll over and glance at the clock. It's 2:30 A.M.

"Yeah?"

The voice on the line is Bill Allee, my chief of detectives. "We got him, sir," he says. "Fifteen minutes ago we arrested Sean Salley in Miami."

It's been ten weeks since the execution-style murders of the thirty-nine-year-old former actress Jennifer Stahl and her two friends during the drug robbery in the apartment above the Carnegie Deli. The other suspect, Andre Smith, turned himself in two weeks after the shooting, but Sean Salley—the man we suspect was the shooter in the case—has been on the run throughout the Southeast. And we've been one step behind him. Two hundred New York detectives beat the bushes in Virginia, Georgia, Louisiana, and

Florida. Salley took a bus from Newark to Atlanta and then to New Orleans, where he checked into a cheap motel under the name Gayland Bell. He cut off his braids and shaved his beard. He supported himself through odd jobs and by selling the marijuana that he had stolen in New York. After three weeks he moved again, hitchhiking to Miami, Florida, where he moved into a homeless shelter.

He kept to himself at the shelter, praying and doing odd jobs. He told people that he was saving money for a trip to Jamaica. He worked as a short-order cook at the Miami Beach Convention Center and did construction work for a woman who hired men from the shelter. And then one night the *America's Most Wanted* television program featured a piece on the shootings above the Carnegie Deli. And when the program showed a picture of Sean Salley, fifty-one people called in tips, including a shelter employee and the woman who hired men from the shelter to work on her house. They said the same thing: Sean Salley looks a lot like a homeless man named Gayland Bell.

Police waited at the shelter, and about 2:00 A.M. Sean Salley returned. He tried to run again, but a police dog caught him and dragged him down.

I thank Bill Allee for calling. I'm relieved to finally have this guy. The slaughter over the Carnegie Deli—over a few thousand dollars' worth of marijuana—has been the most sensational crime to date in my tenure as commissioner. For me, it's far too reminiscent of the drug murders we had eight or ten years ago. I'll sleep better knowing we've caught him.

"THIS is him." Lenny Lemer drops a thick file on my desk. He has just returned from Ohio, where he and another detective, Bobby Hom, continued to research and meet with detectives working on my mother's murder.

I look down at the file on my desk. I open it and see the cold flat stare of Claude Curtis, the man who was with my mother in 1960 when she and Claude left me at his mother's house. The picture in the file is a mug shot from 1969, clipped to a list of the criminal charges and warrants filed against him during his lifetime. The list covers two pages: vandalism, disorderly conduct, drunkenness, and rape. But Claude Curtis's favorite crime was assault. Between 1960, when my mother lost custody of me, and 1964, when she died, Curtis was arrested four times for assault and battery.

I read the details of Claude Curtis's long criminal history, paying special attention to the assaults. Sometimes he used a knife, but more often he punched people—usually on the left side of their faces. So he was probably right-handed.

My mother's killer was probably right-handed, since the bruises were mostly on the left side of her face and body.

I read about his arrest for rape in 1969. The victim said she was attacked in an alley. After Curtis was arrested, the victim suddenly decided she wouldn't testify. He probably threatened her. When Curtis was booked, he was shown a list of his rights on an information form and "stated he could not read or write."

Curtis's last arrest was in 1980, when the police got a call that he was beating on his girlfriend. The girl was fifteen. Claude was fifty. When they arrived, the girl said Curtis called her "a no-good whore" and punched her on the left side of her face. Then he jerked her blouse, threw her on the hood of her car, and slapped her several times. The police report reads: ". . . all during the assault Curtis was screaming, 'You no good whore, I'm going to kill you.' The victim ran away but Curtis found her and punched her twice more." She told police, "the assault may have occurred because Curtis is upset because (she) will not have sex with him. . . . Curtis has threatened to hurt her in the past and is a constant bother to her."

I set the file down and look up at Lenny. "So what do you think? Is it him?"

Lenny shrugs. "I don't know. Maybe."

I nod. Claude Curtis would be an obvious suspect. And the crime is certainly consistent with his record. But Lenny and I have slowly been putting together a timeline of my mother's life from 1958, when she divorced my father, until her death in 1964, and Claude may have been out of the picture by then. Anyway, by 1964 there were worse guys in my mother's life.

In 1958 Patricia filed for divorce from my dad and for full custody of me. We tracked down the divorce papers my mother filed in Franklin County, Ohio, which ironically allege that *my father* was the negligent one—I guess because he lived four hundred miles away in New Jersey. The settlement called for my father to have full visitation rights, "taking into account the desire of both of the parties to this Agreement to have the child grow into manhood with affection and consideration."

"Grow into manhood with affection and consideration"— that phrase trips me up as I read over the court papers. Whatever they intended, "affection and consideration" weren't in the cards.

In Ohio, Patricia settled in for a while with her family, but they didn't provide much stability or a very good example of how to live without alcohol and drugs. Once she had custody of me, my mother fell back into her old life of booze and men. In the baby book, I am constantly staying with aunts and at the apartments of friends.

In the fall of 1958, she tried to get control of her drinking and entered treatment at a hospital for twelve weeks. During that time I stayed with relatives. Later, at an Alcoholics Anonymous meeting, she met Jack Dean—the "Daddy Jack" she wrote about in my baby book. According to Jack Dean's daughter, her father had been sober for *ten years* when he met Patricia. Jack would be my mother's fourth husband. She was his fourth wife.

IT didn't last long for Patricia and Jack—neither the sobriety nor the marriage. One night not long after they'd met, they showed up at a friend's house completely drunk. Still, they tried to create some sort of family. On Christmas Day, 1958, my mother dutifully noted in the baby book, "your real daddy flew down from N.J. & had Santa Claus bring you a Lionel Elec. Train, guns and holsters set and spurs." She went on to write: "Mommy and Daddy Jack got you a rifle, a wagon set with cowboys and Indians, an airplane and Daddy Jack got you cowboy boots."

But once my father went back to New Jersey, the loving family dissolved. Jack and my mother were off drinking, staying out all night, and leaving me with relatives and friends. Jack's daughter told me they'd get drunk and then get into horrible fights. My mother had a frightening, violent temper and she'd fly into uncontrollable rages. One night Jack came home to discover that my mother had totally destroyed the apartment. She had taken a knife and cut or broken just about everything—curtains, chairs, the couch, the walls, dishes, glasses, the lamps, Jack's clothes, their bed. She destroyed everything except for one small piece of furniture.

"For some reason," Jack's daughter told me, "she stopped when she got to your bed. The apartment was wrecked, except your bed. It was untouched."

After she and Jack split up, my mother found herself with Claude Curtis, and they continued running around in that life of alcohol and violence. Claude's mother lived in Columbus, and they left me there while they boozed it up and my mother turned tricks. That's when my Uncle Bob got fed up and called my father and he began the process of getting me out of Ohio.

My father found me at Claude's mother's house in Columbus sometime around March of 1960, the same month my mother was arrested for prostitution in Mansfield, Ohio, an hour north. My father filed for custody, and while the case moved through the courts, I was put in foster care. I think Claude and my mother may have split up around that time because in 1960 he was arrested twice for assault in Dayton, Ohio—halfway across the state.

Finally, on May 20 of that year, after I spent a few months in foster care, my father was awarded custody. The judge ruled that Patricia was "an improper mother."

With Claude gone and me in New Jersey, my mother drifted even further, going off with men who were even more violent, even more degenerate. She was arrested again for prostitution in 1961 and served two months of a year sentence. She escaped from Columbus Hospital—where she was getting alcohol treatment, perhaps court-ordered—and was arrested again in Cleveland in December of 1962.

She finally hit bottom in 1964, on the east side of Newark, Ohio. At the time, East Newark was a rough, mostly black section of taverns, brothels, and ramshackle houses. The area was so wild it was known as Little Chicago. Men came from all over to drink, buy drugs, and have sex with the hookers. Apparently the police just ignored Little Chicago and left the neighborhood to the pimps, bartenders, and madams. It was there my mother hooked up with a pimp and hustler named William E. Byes, who was—hard as it is to imagine—a big step down from Claude Curtis. Byes ran with an even tougher and more violent guy, an enforcer named Jay W. Allen. Byes and Allen ran a handful of apartments in Newark where they set hookers up to have sex for a buck or two each time, probably taking half of what they made. In one of those apartments, on a cold December morning in 1964, my mother's life ended.

Lenny slides a single piece of paper across my desk. It's a faded newspaper story from *The Advocate,* the Newark, Ohio, newspaper. The 1964 story mistakenly reports that my mother was married to Claude Curtis who was, by some reports, her common-law husband. The article begins by saying that a coroner's inquest "definitely will be held into the death Monday morning of Mrs. Patricia Curtis."

The 34-year-old woman, an autopsy yesterday showed, died of a "fairly large cerebral hemorrhage" . . . foul play was possible because in a person her age death from a hemorrhage of a natural cause would be extremely unusual. . . .

According to police, [William Byes] came home at about 9 a.m. Monday and saw Mrs. Curtis asleep in a bed. A few minutes later she began to have convulsions. Byes called the emergency squad, which took her to the hospital where she was pronounced dead.

. . . the woman had a history of alcoholism and had been treated at Newark Hospital twice in recent weeks for alcoholism.

The police said that she had a black eye when the autopsy was performed. . . . Police said they are still investigating the incident, following up rumors, and looking for witnesses. "We can't have an inquest if there's nobody to testify at it," Police Chief L. L. Hall said.

There was no inquest. No police investigation. No detective was assigned. No family or friends were ever interviewed by the police. The cops apparently had no desire to investigate the murder of a white prostitute who slept with black men. This was the early sixties. And in Little Chicago racism was a way of life. So the case was buried, along with my mother.

Besides her black eye and the cerebral hemorrhage that killed her, my mother had bruises all over her body and face. And yet even in the news story, the police chief seems to be preparing for an investigation that will go nowhere: "We can't have an inquest if there's nobody to testify at it."

A rookie cop could have looked at the bruises and trauma to my mother's body and known that those injuries didn't occur while she was lying in William Byes's bed. No, there is only one explanation. She was brutally murdered.

So why wasn't there an investigation? And if there had been, what would they have found?

The possibilities race through my mind: Byes is an obvious suspect. According to the news story, he claimed to have found her semiconscious in his bed at 9 A.M. So where was he all night? Did he have an alibi? Did the cops even ask? Maybe they believed Byes didn't kill her because he was the one who called for an ambulance. Would he have done that if he had just killed her? Maybe—if he didn't realize that he'd killed her. Maybe he beat her up routinely, but this time he went too far. Or maybe it was his friend Jay W. Allen who killed her. After all, he was known to be more violent than Byes.

And then there is Claude Curtis. I've imagined that by 1964 he was long gone. But the news story states that he and my mother were separated. Maybe the fact that she was working for Byes fueled his anger and caused him to come to Newark looking for her. Maybe he even tried to get her to return to Dayton with him and she wouldn't.

I stare at the stacks of odd documents, police reports, divorce records, and death certificates. I feel empty inside. Lenny and I have said all along that coming up with anything after thirty-seven years would be tough, that solving my mother's murder may be impossible. And yet I can't believe this is all there is. I still have too many questions. There are no answers here . . . only questions. And I need answers.

"I need to go there," I say.

Lenny looks up at me from across my desk. "What?"

"I need to go to Ohio."

19

GRACIE MANSION

1994

I knocked on the door of Ted Buczek's house in Wayne, New Jersey, and he answered, looking nervous. I had read in a newspaper that Ted and his wife, Josephine, were planning a dinner to raise money for a foundation they'd started to honor their son, Michael Buczek, one of the two police officers killed—the other was Chris Hoban—in separate shootings on October 18, 1988. I wanted to do something, and this felt like just the thing. Even though I didn't really know Michael Buczek, his death continued to haunt me, in part because we were from the same county in New Jersey.

But I was also fed up with the cumulative effect of so much bad news in New York. I think many people who lived in the city during the late 1980s and early 1990s had a "last straw" moment like that—a point where they just couldn't put up with the out-of-control crime any longer.

For me the last straw was the senseless murders of those two young cops on the same day in 1988. It was as demoralizing as it was infuriating. The greatest city in the world was in danger of becoming unlivable because we couldn't do the most basic thing a city must do: control crime in the streets.

But I didn't move. I decided to do something about it. And that's how I found myself at the Buczeks' front door in the spring of 1990 explaining that I wanted to help them with the fund-raiser. They invited me in, but I could see they weren't comfortable. It had been only eighteen months since they'd lost their son, and their raw grief filled every inch of their tidy suburban house. Their daughter, Mary Jo, was there, and behind Mr. and Mrs. Buczek hung a framed picture of Michael in his hat and his uniform, smiling, with his head cocked slightly, as if he'd just heard a good joke. Every once in a while they looked up sadly at the picture, as if Michael might contribute to the conversation.

We talked about the dinner—who they had invited, what they hoped to accomplish—but I could sense they still weren't comfortable with me. That's when it dawned on me. I was wearing black leather cowboy boots with a silver metal toe and heel, blue jeans, and a floor-length black leather trench coat. My hair was in a ponytail past my shoulders, and I had a goatee and a cluster of six diamond earrings down the lobe of my left ear with a gold loop at the bottom. I'd come dressed as a drug dealer to the house of a couple whose son had been killed by a drug dealer.

I apologized and explained my job as an undercover, and they immediately relaxed. They were a bit overwhelmed with the idea of starting this foundation and having this dinner, and they were glad for my help. They were the sweetest people. Ted and I became especially close, and I tried to keep him up to date on the hunt for his son's killer and the overall state of affairs in the NYPD.

Since the dinner was only a few weeks away, there wasn't much I could do to help them other than put up a few fliers and posters around precinct station houses, but I promised to help every year, and beginning the next year, I assumed the role of coordinator and eventually chaired the committee for awards that were given to honor cops around the country for acts of bravery and heroism.

That first year, one of the people invited to the dinner was a confident, aggressive former federal prosecutor named Rudolph W. Giuliani. Raised by a working-class Italian family in Brooklyn, Giuliani had worked as a U.S. attorney, a high-powered private attorney, and associate attorney general in Washington, D.C.—the number-three position in the Department of Justice.

In 1983 he became U.S. attorney for the Southern District of New York, and his aggressiveness with all levels of criminals—from Mafia bosses to drug dealers to stock market con artists—became legendary. In just over five years, he had 4,152 convictions—only 25 of which were reversed on appeal.

I was very supportive when Giuliani announced in 1989 that he was running for mayor. Like most cops, I was fed up with the revolving-door court system and the lack of support from City Hall. I'd bust someone in the morning for dealing drugs and see them working the same corner that evening. The only time anyone from City Hall paid attention to cops was when there was a corruption case or an allegation of excessive force. While other politicians paid lip service to being "tough on crime," Giuliani had proved he understood what the best cops understand—that you start by being tough on criminals. But in 1989, the law-and-order Giuliani lost to David Dinkins in the closest election in city history.

The first annual Michael John Buczek Foundation dinner was to be held March 29, 1990, just four months after Giuliani's grueling campaign for mayor. I tried to break it to the Buczeks that while Giuliani was probably a decent guy, he was also a politician, and since he wasn't running for mayor anymore, there was no reason for him to come all the way out to New Jersey to talk to a couple of hundred cops and their families.

"He's not gonna drive sixty miles out of his way to go to a dinner that doesn't benefit him in any way," I said.

Then, about two hours before the dinner, I got a call that Giuliani planned to stop by, but he couldn't stay because he also had to go to a christening in Staten Island around the same time, fifty miles away. I didn't need a map or a clock to realize that he'd never make it.

Some of the other cops at the dinner were excited. I just rolled my eyes. "You people are so stupid," I said. "Do you really believe this guy is going to leave the city, drive for an hour to get here, stay fifteen minutes, and then drive an hour to Staten Island? It ain't happening."

An hour before the dinner, someone tapped me on the shoulder. "Rudy Giuliani is upstairs. He's looking for you."

I was shocked. I went upstairs and met Giuliani. Right away I was struck by the presence of this man: He seemed to soak up the room, to be calming and energetic at the same time. As someone who is constantly told that people want to follow me, I think I understood what people meant the minute I met Giuliani. This was a guy I just wanted to work for. He apologized for not being able to stay longer and asked if he could meet Michael Buczek's family, to pay his respects. He talked with Ted Buczek about his family's grief and the sorry state of the city's criminal justice system. He posed for pictures, including one with a scraggly-looking drug-dealer type with a ponytail and a bunch of earrings. I still have that picture.

I couldn't believe he had come. It was very impressive. This was a guy who believed in cops, who came out to show his support for the sacrifice that one of them had made and for a group of cops and their family members who desperately wanted the city to get better. When he left, I told Ted Buczek to call his office and tell Giuliani to call me if he ever needed anything.

The next year the Michael John Buczek Foundation named him our Man of the Year. This time he stayed for the dinner, and after I introduced him as "the man who should be mayor," Giuliani wowed the seven hundred cops in attendance with his ideas about how to make the city more livable. The first step, he said, was to make the streets safe, and he'd do that by actually letting cops do their jobs. I don't think I've ever heard such applause. Four days later, he met Ted Buczek for breakfast at the Waldorf-Astoria and told him that he was considering running for mayor again and that he would be looking for support. Ted told him we'd be there for him. All he had to do was call. As for me, I had met the first politician who I thought could actually make a difference.

DAVID Dinkins was a disaster as mayor. He had the misfortune to take over as mayor during the peak of the crack epidemic and—following the 1987 stock market crash—at the city's economic low point. But Dinkins's bad luck was made worse by his inability to see New York's problems for what they were and by his own indecisiveness. His answer to every problem was to attack it with the full, unwieldy power of bureaucracy. Nothing got done. If gangs began targeting tourists on the subway, Dinkins's solution was to appoint a blue-ribbon panel to oversee a commission established to study the report of a committee appointed to assess the situation.

Morale among the city's police officers was at an all-time low. We felt the "support" we were getting from Dinkins's City Hall bordered on outright antagonism.

Crime was at its peak in 1990. There were 2,245 homicides that year, up 38 percent in just five years. Scores of children were dying each year from random gunfire, and there were horror stories of tourists being shot dead for a few bucks. A headline in the *New York Post* read "DAVE, DO SOMETHING!"

Dinkins responded by increasing the number of police officers, assigning many of them to his pet project, an expanded community policing program. Community policing—getting officers out of their cars and more involved in neighborhoods—can be a fine idea, but by itself it wasn't going to solve New York's problems. As cops, we wondered, does he actually want us to spend our tours getting cats out of trees and helping old women cross the street while drug gangs continue to terrorize the city? At the same time, we found ourselves hopelessly outgunned. While criminals carried the latest in semiautomatic handguns, the city refused to consider updating our old .38-caliber service revolvers and, in fact, even had us switch to inferior bullets out of a ridiculous fear that ricochets from our gunfire might injure people.

Meanwhile crime, gentrification, and economic pressures were threatening to unravel New York's delicate racial fabric. In black and Hispanic neighborhoods there was a general distrust of the police. Rather than dealing with the handful of problem cops and stand behind the majority who were doing their jobs, Dinkins's actions and words seemed to feed the antagonism.

Finally, on a hot August night in 1991, in the neighborhood of Crown Heights, Brooklyn, the city boiled over. A station wagon driven by security guards for the leader of the neighborhood's Lubavitcher Jews was following a police escort when it sped through a red light and slammed into two black seven-year-olds, killing one of them. In the confusion at the scene, many of the neighborhood's black citizens believed that police and emergency crews were more concerned about the safety of the Lubavitchers than with their children's welfare. Crown Heights erupted in riots: one person killed, a couple of hundred injured, millions of dollars in damage to businesses, homes, and cars. Hamstrung by the mixed signals from their bosses and dulled by a lack of leadership, the police response was slow and ineffective.

After Crown Heights, relations between Dinkins and rank-and-file police officers only got worse. After Hector Santiago was shot during the gunfight on Dyckman Street in 1991, Dinkins called the hospital to talk to him—a common courtesy when an officer is wounded in the line of duty. Angry over the mayor's lack of support for the police, Hector refused to take the call.

The low point for us came in 1992, when a cop named Michael O'Keefe tried to arrest a drug dealer named Kiko Garcia on 162nd Street in Washington Heights, one block from where Michael Buczek had been killed. Garcia resisted, and they fought desperately until Garcia pulled his gun. That's when O'Keefe shot and killed him.

Rumors coursed through the Washington Heights neighborhood. Phony witnesses came forward to say that O'Keefe beat Garcia with his radio, made him beg for mercy, and then shot him at point-blank range. Friends and family insisted that Garcia wasn't a drug dealer. And the media ran with the story.

But I don't blame the newspapers and TV stations. That was the only story they were getting.

The police commissioner and the mayor's office remained strangely silent. They could have released radio transmissions in which O'Keefe desperately called for help. They could have released the fact that Garcia had a gun and had recently violated his probation for a drug offense. They could have released the fact that one of the "witnesses" was a friend of Garcia's who had recently been arrested with guns and ammunition. They could have released a videotape on which Garcia and another man were proudly holding cocaine, and Kiko called himself "king of the street."

In the vacuum that followed, many people believed that Michael O'Keefe had brutally shot an innocent man. Washington Heights erupted in three days of riots in which one person was killed and hundreds of cars were overturned. Amazingly, Mayor Dinkins—apparently still smarting from the Crown Heights riots—responded not by getting the truth out and standing behind his officer but by posing for pictures with Kiko Garcia's family. He promised a full investigation of O'Keefe, offered his condolences, and—in the most disgusting part of the story—had the city pay to fly Garcia's family back to the Dominican Republic and for Garcia's burial there.

An investigation by the city and the FBI would later show that the so-called witnesses weren't in a position to see what they claimed to see and that the evidence completely supported Officer O'Keefe's version of events. This man who had been trashed in the press and by his own mayor was, in fact, a hero.

But it was months before that truth came out. And in the meantime, Dinkins had used the Garcia case and a few isolated corruption scandals to push for a more aggressive civilian review process of complaints about police violence.

When it finally became clear that O'Keefe had been justified in shooting Kiko Garcia, police officers responded with demonstrations and protest signs. And it wasn't just police who were mad.

My friend Ted Buczek was furious. The incident was similar in details and proximity to the one that had ended with Michael's death. Just three years after Michael Buczek's death, here was the mayor abandoning a brave police officer in the same situation and supporting the drug dealer who had tried to kill him. Ironically, O'Keefe even coached in a baseball Little League that was paid for with money from the Michael John Buczek Foundation.

Ted watched what O'Keefe went through, and it was as if his son had died for nothing. I could see how frustrated Ted was, so I sat down with him and helped him compose a letter in which we laid out the Buczek and O'Keefe cases, their amazing similarities. "But Michael Buczek never came home that night in 1988," we wrote. The other difference, we wrote, was that while Dinkins paid to bury a drug dealer, Ted Buczek paid for his own son's burial.

RUDOLPH Giuliani's office called. He was going to run for mayor again in 1993. Would I consider working with him on the campaign?

"Yeah, sure," I said. "Whatever he needs."

Very few people intimidate me. By 1991 I'd been around war heroes, Saudi royalty, drug lords, police heroes, and every level of politician and bureaucrat. But I found myself sweating bullets as I drove to Rudy Giuliani's apartment at six-thirty on a summer Saturday morning. It's funny. He wasn't even the mayor and I was nervous about seeing him.

But once we drove off, it was just Rudy and I—a couple of guys hanging out. He wanted to hear about the cases I'd been involved in and my theories of how to fight crime. We'd get together every once in a while and talk about criminal justice. He wanted to hear about the realities of crime, the situations that we faced every day on the street. He wanted to take the handcuffs off the police officers and put them on the bad guys, where they belonged.

But whatever information I gave him was nothing compared with the education he was giving me. He talked constantly about using business principles to transform government. He talked about groundbreaking research from Harvard, about the theories of people like David Gergen, Jack Welch, and the author David Osborne, whose book *Reinventing Government* was a loose model for the management style he wanted to bring to New York. Gone would be the heavy, inefficient liberal bureaucracy of David Dinkins, to be replaced by models that worked in the business community. This meant finding talented managers and making them completely responsible for every program and initiative. It meant getting up-to-date data from the field and quickly scrapping people and programs that weren't pulling their weight. In short, it meant two words: analysis and accountability. Later I would buy a box of Osborne's books and give them out to my own managers as the first step in working for me.

But without the right kind of leader, all this would have been nothing but some interesting ideas on paper. What Rudy Giuliani was really talking about was a complete change of course after decades of liberal bureaucratic management, a total overhaul, a change in culture, process, and style that might take decades to accomplish. But he didn't have decades. Assuming he could even get elected as a Republican in a Democratic stronghold like New York, he'd have just four tough years. To institute such a radical change in a short time required an amazing individual, someone with unflappable confidence, charisma, and toughness. In

New York–speak, such a feat would require someone with some huge brass balls.

And from the first time I met him, that's what I thought Rudy Giuliani had. He was the most single-minded, brilliant person I'd ever been around. I found myself thinking differently around him, getting the kind of thrill talking about management that I usually got talking about police work. This was not a man who would assign a committee to study the recommendation of a commission appointed to address a problem. This was a man who would listen to a problem and solve it that day. And if the people around him couldn't solve it that day? He'd get new people.

I wanted to do whatever I could to help him, so I brought my strengths to his campaign. In 1991, as he geared up for the 1993 election, I saw that Giuliani had woeful security around him. "Look," I told him, "you're going to spend the next two years in your car. Everything you do or say is going to be in that car. If you can't trust the people you're with, if they don't have your back, then you're done."

I put together a team to drive him around, cops on their off-hours. I made sure they were good cops. The first person I called was Tibor. While I'd gone on to specialize in drug enforcement, Tibor had been transferred to the Intelligence Division, providing security for diplomats and VIPs, so I knew he was a natural fit. He was loyal and someone I could trust. And if I could trust him, I knew Giuliani could trust him as well.

On his first day with Giuliani, they went to dinner, and that night Tibor called me. "Hey, Bern. You were right. This guy is really a good guy."

"I told you," I said. Almost every cop who met him thought the same thing. He was decisive, tough, and honest. He would've made a great cop. To us, it was the ultimate compliment, one you can't give to a lot of politicians.

The next couple of years were busy as I concentrated on my work with the DETF. My weekends I spent in a car with Giuliani, and continued to listen to his ideas and offer my own views of how to solve the problem of crime in New York.

In November 1993, Rudolph W. Giuliani was elected mayor of the city of New York by a wide margin. That night, as he thanked his supporters from the stage of the New York Hilton, I was standing at the edge of the stage when I looked up and saw him beneath the lights and suddenly it hit me. This man I had shot the shit with over coffee, this man I had grown to love and respect as a friend, this man whose wife and children I knew, this man was now mayor of New York City. All the ideas we had discussed, every theory that we thought could transform the city would now be put in place.

I watched happily as he quickly moved Bill Bratton into position as police commissioner and Bratton brought in the like-minded Jack Maple to put their theories of reinventing government into practice. It was a new day for the city and for the NYPD.

As for me, I had every intention of staying with Jerry Speziale in the DETF, but that was about to change.

In March 1994 there was a riot at one of the jails on Rikers Island when inmates turned on correction officers who were trying to break up a fight in the gymnasium. Thirteen inmates and thirteen correction officers were injured, and one of the officers was in critical condition after an inmate hit him in the head with a fifty-pound weight.

Tibor was with the mayor as they drove to the hospital where the correction officers were being treated after the riot. As they looked around, they couldn't tell which were the inmates and which were the officers. That's how sloppy and unprofessional the correction officers were. Meanwhile, none of the managers seemed to know what was going on. As poorly as the police department had been managed in the past, the correction department was even worse. Giuliani was about to hire a new correction commissioner, a man named Anthony Schembri, but based on the scene at the hospital, the situation in correction was even worse than he'd thought.

Back at Gracie Mansion, Tibor did something that surprised even him. "Excuse me, Mr. Mayor," he said. "I may be out of line here, but I got to tell you: Bernie Kerik ran a jail over in New Jersey. And that never would have happened at his jail."

Two days later, I got a call from Jerry Speziale. "Hey, Bern," he said. "Do you know some guy named Schembri?"

"No," I said.

"Well, he's the new correction commissioner, and someone called from his office and wants to know about you."

I didn't know it, but the mayor had offered Schembri my services, and the new correction commissioner had assigned the department's inspector general, Mike Caruso, to check me out. Caruso went through my résumé with a fine-tooth comb. He called the DETF, my present command, and then called cops that I had worked with and that he knew, asking all about me. After his investigation, he went to Schembri's office and asked to see him. He walked in, handed Schembri a file folder with my résumé and other documents. Schembri said, "What's this?"

"That's Kerik's file. Congratulations. You've just hired Rambo."

20

RIKERS ISLAND

1995

INMATES call it the Rock—Rikers Island—a dreary, 415-acre knob of land shaped like a jellybean and covered by miles of twelve-foot fences entangled with coils of razor wire. The island sits smack between Queens and the Bronx in the wide channel of the East River, within throwing distance of the last runway at La Guardia Airport. All day and night the undersides of planes thunder overhead, and the second thing a visitor often notices—after the razor wire—is the harsh smell of jet fuel.

Originally a small private island, Rikers was bought by the city in 1884 from the Riker family for $180,000. For the next fifty years the island was used as a landfill, and tons of refuse were shipped there from the city. So much garbage was buried in the landfill at Rikers that the island grew by almost five times, from 90 acres to 415. Rikers is literally an island of garbage.

It is also the largest penal colony in the world. Rikers is not one jail but ten separate jails. It is a city of inmates and correction officers, a city with one industry—housing society's undesirables. They are packed in old James Cagney–style jailhouses, newer cinderblock boxes, temporary modular structures, even a huge prison barge anchored off Hunts Point in the Bronx. There are facilities for women, juvenile offenders, notorious criminals, inmates with contagious diseases, and the most violent offenders in the New York correction system. The ten jails of Rikers are home to about 120,000 people each year—up to as many as 20,000 at any given time, their average age just twenty-three. About thirteen thousand correction officers and staff members monitor the inmates over three shifts. More than sixty thousand meals are made each day on Rikers, and the jail bakery produces eighty-eight thousand loaves of bread a week.

Every morning a fleet of 440 buses is dispatched to gather up the new guests from the precinct station houses and to take about seventeen hundred inmates to the boroughs for their court dates. Since Rikers is a jail and not a prison system, it houses criminals on a short-term basis while they await trial, sentencing, or release. The average stay is less than two months. Yet when I came to the Department of Correction as the head of investigations in 1994, Rikers had a tougher reputation than the worst maximum-security prison. I drove onto the island, past the gate and checkpoint, past correction officers filing in from the parking lot. A row of trailers lined one shore, each serving as an office for various support units: Emergency Services, investigations, health management, quality assurance. There were boats for the occasional inmate who tried to swim to Queens or La Guardia, but if an inmate did swim for it, the strong current meant that the boats rarely picked up anything more than a bloated carcass.

The jails themselves were self-contained, each one surrounded by hedgerows of chain-link and razor wire. Small windows were set into the buildings, and the inmates yelled at any visitor or any new car—catcalls and threats in which you occasionally made out a few words: "I'm gonna fuckin' kill you, motherfucker!"

At any given time, there were some two thousand members of more than fifty gangs inside Rikers, and they were constantly at war for control of the hallways, the dayrooms, and the yards. But it wasn't just the gang members who fought. Some correction officers felt like prey, constantly watched by inmates just waiting for a chance to take them down, faking fights so that officers would have to wade into the dayrooms or the cell blocks. Most inmates had a weapon hidden somewhere, and the staff considered it a good day when there were only two stabbings. The inmates on Rikers actually took pride in how dangerous it was, as if they had to live up to their reputation as the toughest inmates in the toughest jail in the world.

In fact, behind the sliding steel doors and turnkey locks, some inmates had another name for Rikers. They called it the Belly of the Beast.

JOHN Picciano grew up in an old Italian section of Jackson Heights, Queens, just a block away from the woman he married. He always wanted to be a police officer, and he looked to join the NYPD when he was nineteen. But the age limit was twenty years, six months, so in 1984 he became a correction officer, what he thought would be "the next best thing." He always figured he'd end up crossing over to the police department, but he stayed in the Department of Correction. Short and solidly built, Pitch is bright and quick on his feet. He's a fixer, the kind of guy who instinctively knows how to work a system, how to get things done. But inmates who mistook his friendly intelligence for softness quickly learned that there was a tough guy coiled up in there.

If he expected the Department of Correction to be a close cousin to the police department, what he found was a neglected agency sinking into disarray. There was no pride among correction officers. The general jail population was 90 percent black and Hispanic and the officers reflected that—almost 80 percent were black and Hispanic. Within city government the correction department was treated like a ghetto. Officers were called jail guards and treated as if they were barely better than the inmates. It was a dangerous, thankless job. Morale was so low that every day hundreds of officers "banged in"—took the day off. There was no limit on sick days, and the job was so awful that correction officers averaged twenty-one sick days a year, the highest rate in the city. Since no post could be left unmanned, dozens of officers would have to double or triple up shifts each day, thus lowering morale further and driving up overtime pay to $2.2 million *per week*.

As crime rose in New York in the 1980s, the jail population rose with it, tripling in just ten years. New jails were built, temporary buildings were added, a sixty-million-dollar barge was put in the river, and still there was no place to put the new inmates. They slept on floors and in gymnasiums. Jails meant to hold six hundred inmates held three thousand. After losing a class action lawsuit, Rikers was fined $125 a day for each inmate who didn't have a bed. Some days, to hide the fact that there weren't enough beds, the Rikers staff would shuffle prisoners to holding pens in the city or just load the buses and have them drive around until beds finally opened up.

But the worst aspect of Rikers by far was the level of violence on the island. All day long, the alarms pierced the air and correction officers ran off to another emergency, to break up a fight or pull an inmate away from an officer. Every officer had a story of tangling with inmates; Pitch was beaten up and slashed in the stomach. Most officers figured they'd get it sometime; it was just a question of when. The inmates had nothing to lose because an inmate who attacked an officer was rarely charged with a crime. By contrast, someone who stabs a police officer on the street goes to prison for a decade or more. In 1990 a correction officer try ing to break up a staged fight was stabbed twice in the back with a nail and hit in the head with a telephone. He missed six weeks of work. The inmate's only punishment was to lose some privileges.

"We weren't in charge," Pitch says now. "They were."

A decade of prison reforms and class action lawsuits had

tilted the balance of power toward the inmates and left many officers afraid or unable to do their jobs. Inmates had every amenity. They wore whatever they wanted—$150 basketball shoes, which sometimes got them killed, bandannas and beads in gang colors to differentiate the various gangs: black and yellow for the Latin Kings, multicolored for the Jamaican Posse, black and red for the Bloods. Gang graffiti covered the walls. In fact, Rikers was the best place in the city for recruiting new members. There were gangs representing every ethnicity and neighborhood of the city: Nigerians, Dominicans, Haitians, you name it. They engaged in outright warfare in the halls and yards, and the officers rarely knew which gangs were fighting until they found some inmate bleeding out on the hard tile floor. Thousands of shanks—homemade knives—were hidden throughout the jail, in air ducts, mattresses, books, radiators, and boot heels.

New weapons were smuggled in every day, "slammed" by inmates who shoved razor blades, scalpels, even long knives up their rectums to get them past the metal detectors and strip searches. The most common injury was slashing, swinging a shank to make a long wound, preferably in the victim's face. Inmates got reputations for a good slashing, especially a wound that required 150 or more stitches, something they called "a buck-fifty." One of the most common and dangerous weapons was made by melting two razor blades into a plastic toothbrush handle, set close enough together that the skin was shredded, leaving very little for a surgeon to stitch up and therefore a gaping scar.

Inmates could buy anything in jail: weapons, drugs, food, sex. Inmates and their families smuggled in much of the contraband, but a number of correction officers—convincing themselves they were underpaid and disrespected—gave in to temptation and became part of the island's thriving black market.

For Pitch, the idea that they could ever stop the violence and return control to the correction officers was beyond the realm of possibility. Things in New York didn't move in that direction in the late 1980s and early 1990s. They only deteriorated, just like his beloved neighborhood in Queens, which had become so overrun by criminals that John finally had to move his family to Long Island in 1990.

He probably would've left the correction department too, but his combination of toughness and intelligence led to his promotion to captain in 1988. Still, he was increasingly disillusioned as each year Rikers got worse, the crowding and violence and low morale among correction officers combining to make the island a disaster just waiting to happen.

In 1990 correction officers protested their low pay and lack of support by blocking the bridge that connected the island to the mainland. The protest left the jails shorthanded, and that evening an officer was escorting some inmates when they smeared mashed potatoes over a surveillance camera and then attacked the officer, touching off a riot that left 140 inmates and twenty correction officers injured.

The violence only got worse when, in the early 1990s, the Los Angeles–based Bloods and Crips came into Rikers, sparking a bloody war with the two dominant Latino gangs, the Latin Kings and the Netas. In 1992 the Dinkins administration slashed the DOC budget, and the number of correction officers fell by almost a thousand—at a time when the jail population was increasing from 110,000 to a high of 125,000 inmates. It was a recipe for even more trouble.

In 1994, the year I joined the Department of Correction, *New York* magazine's cover story asked the question "Is Rikers About to Explode?" and the story inside answered with a resounding yes: "practically everyone who knows the place agrees, a full-scale riot is now only one dis, one argument, one short-tempered outburst away."

"WHO the fuck is that guy?" John Picciano asked the first time he heard my name. Longtime officers like Pitch had lived through their share of saviors—criminal justice experts, sociologists, Ph.D.s, tough guys, and "out-of-the-box" thinkers. All of them had wilted under the challenge of Rikers. And now, in early 1994, at the same time he was threatening to lock up every criminal in New York, Mayor Giuliani wanted the budget for the jails further trimmed, and what did he offer in return—some undercover cop who had run a cute little jail in New Jersey. New Jersey, of all places! Pitch and some of his colleagues were unimpressed. "Passaic County is gonna come in here and tell Rikers what to do?" Pitch told a friend the first time he saw me. "I don't think so."

At first I hardly ever went to Rikers. I was in charge of investigations for the entire correction system, and the job kept me at correction headquarters downtown. "Don't worry about this job," said one officer right after I started. "Nothing ever happens." That very day I was racing off to interview an off-duty correction officer who had just shot and killed a guy in Queens. The officer was taking six thousand dollars out of the bank to buy a car when three muggers jumped him. He pulled his gun and killed one of the muggers and wounded a second. Two days later two correction officers—one male and one female—were taking that wounded inmate to the hospital and waiting for a doctor when the inmate grabbed the female officer's gun and shot the other officer in the chest. The inmate shot at the female officer but missed and ran away. She took the gun from her fallen partner and chased the inmate down the hallway while he turned and fired back at her. When the inmate grabbed a child as a hostage, the female officer shot twice and killed the inmate.

Both cases were pretty open-and-shut, but that first week quickly taught me that this was not going to be a slow job.

Giuliani had named Tony Schembri as the correction commissioner, hoping that the likable Schembri would bring the same sort of revolutionary ideas to the DOC that the mayor, Bratton, and Jack Maple were trying to establish in the NYPD. But Schembri's main experience was being police commissioner of the sleepy bedroom town of Rye, New York, where he had thirty-six police officers. He was best

GROUND ZERO
SEPTEMBER 11, 2001

THE NYPD HELICOPTER RIDE
OVER GROUND ZERO

COMING BACK TO 75 BARCLAY STREET ON THE DAY OF PRESIDENT BUSH'S VISIT

THE SEARCH FOR SURVIVORS

ABOVE: TALKING TO CAPTAIN
EDDIE ASWAD AT GROUND ZERO
BELOW: SHEER DEVASTATION

SERGEANT GERRY KANE AND DETECTIVE PETE FRISCIA BROUGHT ME THE FLAG FLOWN AT THE WORLD TRADE CENTER ON SEPTEMBER 11, 2001

AT THE POLICE AND FIRE PRAYER SERVICE AT ST. PATRICK'S CATHEDRAL, WITH CHIEF OF DETECTIVES BILL ALLEE (3RD FROM RIGHT)

FIRE COMMISSIONER THOMAS VON ESSEN,
ME, MAYOR GIULIANI, AND PRESIDENT
BUSH SURVEY THE DAMAGE AT
75 BARCLAY STREET

NYPD EMERGENCY SERVICES
COPS POSTING THE FLAG

NYPD EMERGENCY SERVICES
COPS HARD AT WORK

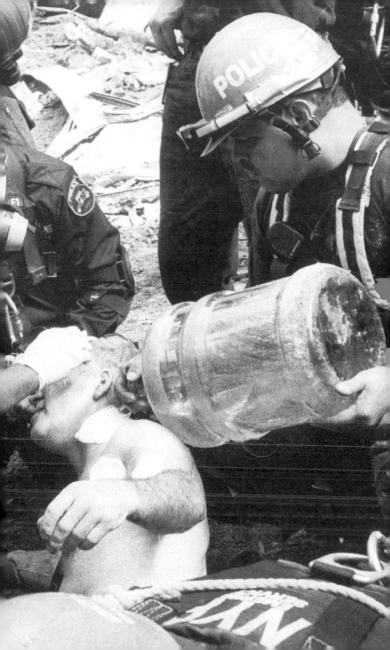

THE LARGEST CRIME SCENE IN U.S. HISTORY. THE EVIDENCE INCLUDES AN ENGINE PART, AN AIRLINE SEAT BELT, AND A TIRE. OPPOSITE, BOTTOM: THE DEVASTATED AMISH MARKET.

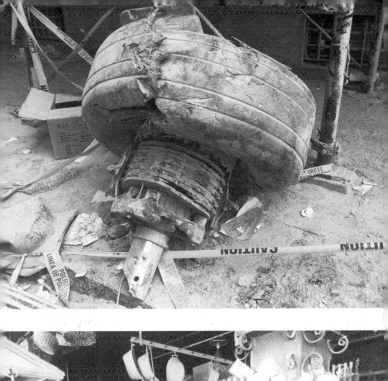

TAKING NOTES DURING ATTORNEY GENERAL JOHN ASHCROFT'S ANNOUNCEMENT OF PROPOSED LEGISLATION TO FIGHT TERRORISM

AT ONE OF MAYOR GIULIANI'S DAILY STAFF MEETINGS

known as the model for the lead character in the television series *The Commish,* and right away he was mildly ridiculed for trying to use his B-level Hollywood connections to impress the inmates and officers of Rikers. But he and I got along well, and he eventually named me his executive assistant and chief of staff.

Everyone agreed that Schembri was a nice guy, but he was in over his head. He refused to listen to his senior officers and staff and appeared to have a self-destructive streak, especially when it came to public relations. He ordered a fourteen-hundred-dollar gun through the department, and when the press made its inquiries, he tried to deny it, but that was difficult when the reporter had a copy of the purchase order. He was living upstate, when by the city charter he was mandated to live in the city. He was constantly saying the wrong thing. Even small things he did were controversial. He was in the paper so much he should have bought stock in the *Post.*

And it wasn't just a problem of perception. Schembri was overwhelmed by the problems of Rikers. In fact, 1994, the first year for both Schembri and Giuliani, may have been the worst year ever on the island.

By January 1995, Giuliani couldn't wait anymore. His experiment in bringing business principles to city government was under way and was just beginning to pay off in other departments, but correction was worse than when he'd started. At 10:30 P.M. on January 23, 1995, he called me at home.

"Hey, Boss," I said. "How you doing?"

"Look," he said, "we need to have a little talk."

"Okay," I said. "I'll come down there in the morning."

"No," he said. "Now."

"Now?" I said. "You want to talk now?"

At Gracie Mansion we sat in a small sitting room sharing a bottle of red wine that Nelson Mandela had given him on a recent visit. The only light came from a small lamp sitting on an end table that separated me, on the couch, from him, in his favorite overstuffed chair. It was good to see him again—it reminded me of the conversations we used to have during the campaign. We talked about his first year, the successes and the things that still needed to be fixed—one of the biggest of which was Rikers.

"I want you to help fix all this stuff," he said.

"I'll do whatever I can, but I don't want the commissioner to think I'm stepping on his toes," I said.

"Schembri's not going to be the commissioner anymore," the mayor said. "He'll be retiring."

"Oh," I said. "Think you could do that when I'm on vacation? I love the guy and wouldn't want to see him hurt."

"That's probably impossible, because tomorrow morning we're going to announce that Michael Jacobson has been named the new commissioner, and you're going to be the new first deputy commissioner."

Jacobson was a great choice; the intelligent and honest commissioner of probation was a well-respected man within government circles. But I wasn't quite as sure about my promotion. "Mayor, I appreciate your confidence in me, I really do. But I ran a jail. One jail. Rikers is like . . . ten jails."

"Just do this," he said. "Do what I'm telling you. I know you can do it."

"But we have a first deputy," I said.

"Well, fire him or something," the mayor said. "Do whatever you want."

The mayor said he wanted to tell his cabinet members what his plans were. They were waiting in the museum downstairs. He told one of the detectives to have them come up to the library where we were sitting. I panicked. I was sure that one of his confidants would talk some sense into him. I could just hear them: "Wait a minute, Mr. Mayor. He's a third-grade detective. He doesn't have the experience to be the number-two guy of an agency that big. You can't do this."

The door opened, and the first one to come through was the deputy mayor, Peter Powers. I stood to say hello and he shook my hand and said, "Congratulations." Then he pulled me over and kissed me on the cheek. He already knew. Next was Randy Mastro, the mayor's chief of staff. He did the same. In this dark sitting room, one by one, the mayor's closest staff members came forward and kissed me. They all knew. I know the mayor is as big a fan of *The Godfather* as I am, and I wonder if he noticed how much becoming part of his team resembled becoming part of a Mafia family.

I was being made.

I was now a part of the Giuliani family, getting the endorsement of the other family members, the other *capos*. We all sat up drinking wine until two-thirty in the morning, celebrating and also bracing ourselves for the work ahead. Then, during the forty-five-minute ride home, I made about forty telephone calls from my car. The first person I called was Jerry Speziale. I called my mom. I called everyone I could think of.

The mayor's people had told me to lie low until they could make all the changes, so the next morning I called Picciano and told him to come pick me up. After his initial doubt about my experience, John and I had become friends, along with his boss, the new chief of department, Eric Taylor. That day John and I went to the heart of Little Italy, to a little corner pizza place. We sat there eating pizza while my pager beeped every few minutes with calls from Schembri. Each call read "9-1-1" on the pager, meaning it was an emergency. But I'd been told to lie low. I kept thinking about Schembri and how upset he must be. As I sat there waiting for City Hall to call, Schembri ran the battery dead on my pager calling me.

Finally, at 2 P.M., I went to City Hall, where the announcement was made. That night I called Schembri and apologized for not being able to return his calls.

"I don't know if you know everything that happened," I said, "but I got called to City Hall. They made me the first deputy commissioner." Trying to be nice, I said, "If you had anything to do with that"—even though I knew he hadn't—"I just wanted to thank you."

"I didn't have anything to do with that," he said crossly. "You'll never be the first deputy. Did you see what they did to me in just ten months? You won't last six months as first dep. Six months, you'll be gone." He slammed the telephone down and we never spoke again.

That night I drove out to Rikers. I'd been out there a few times, but I'd never really paid a lot of attention. I knew the place had problems, but to be completely honest, they were someone else's problems. I had been the chief of staff—essentially an administrative position—working downtown in headquarters. The logistics of transforming a shit hole like Rikers Island hadn't been something I'd given a lot of thought to. But as my car crested the peak of the bridge leading to Rikers, I looked out over the big, gently rising island. At night the lights are everywhere, pointed at the fences and the water, streaming out from all ten jails, glinting off the rolls of razor wire. It looked like a big, frightening city.

I stayed out on the island all night, driving around, touring the different jails, taking everything in. It was disgusting, worse than I'd heard. The floors were filthy, the walls painted with graffiti. The correction officers were sloppily dressed and appeared to have no discipline or morale. There was almost no order or sense to the place. That month alone, there were 130 stabbings and slashings in the jails. The inmates ran the cell blocks, ruling through intimidation and outright threats. I had been so excited to get the promotion, to be "made" into the Giuliani family, I'm not sure I understood just how daunting this challenge would be.

The next morning I had a meeting with the staff, and then I sat down with my new boss. From the outside, Michael Jacobson and I may have looked like polar opposites. I think that's because we *were* polar opposites.

Michael was tiny, his feet barely touching the ground when he sat in his chair. He was as soft-spoken and thoughtful as I was decisive and confident. He was an academic, with a Ph.D. in sociology and a reputation as one of the best administrative and financial people in the entire state of New

York. I was a former soldier, a cop. But if our personalities were vastly different, our understanding of what lay ahead of us was the same. Rikers needed to be cleaner, safer, more secure, and better run. We needed to improve every aspect of the operation, from morale and overtime to investigations and our response to emergencies. We needed to completely overhaul the way the inmates and the officers viewed this place. And we needed to do all of this on a smaller budget than that of the year before. I'm not sure what the hell we were thinking.

A few days later I had lunch with an old friend, a special drug prosecutor named Bridget Brennan. "Don't take this job, Bernie," she said.

"What are you talking about?" I asked. "It's a great job."

"No," she said, "that place will never change. They've had brilliant people in there before. They had the correction commissioner from Cleveland. He was here seven months and he had to quit. Everyone they bring in, it just chews them up. It's been like that for a hundred years."

I could feel the sweat breaking out on my forehead. "I really think between Jacobson and me, we can make a difference out there," I said.

"No," she said. "You don't understand, Bernie. It will ruin your career. That place can't be fixed."

21

THE BING

1996

"WHAT'S your inmate count?"

The warden in front of me shifted his weight. "Well, sir, the jail holds—" he began.

"I know how many inmates your jail holds," I said. "I asked how many are in there."

"I . . . I don't know that."

I looked over at Eric Taylor, the chief of department and the number-three person in correction behind Mike Jacobson and myself. Eric had risen in the ranks before Schembri, and when Mike and I took over, Eric embraced our ideas about leadership. In the months ahead, he'd become a vital part of our efforts to transform the department.

"You don't know the count at your own jail?" I asked. I looked up and down the table, at the handful of wardens at this meeting. There is a warden for every jail on Rikers and for each of the smaller borough jails. My initial week as first deputy commissioner was spent in meetings like this one, with small groups of senior officers in the conference room in the headquarters downtown, gathering the most basic information—like inmate counts, a simple detail this warden apparently didn't have.

I turned to the next warden. "What about you? What's your count?"

"Well, I could call the control room and find out."

I went down the row. Three of the six wardens didn't know how many inmates were in their jails. I wasn't testing them. I really just wanted to know the number. But their ignorance was indicative of the style of management in the DOC and especially on Rikers Island. Too many wardens acted like well-dressed executives who didn't want to get their hands dirty. Too many of these guys had been made warden simply because they put in the time. It was a gift from the city of New York for twenty-five years, nothing more than a gold watch. Some of these guys were completely detached from the day-to-day operations of their jails, as if their own jobs were beneath them.

Later that same day we had a staff meeting with all the wardens and chiefs, and Chief Taylor and I went around the room and asked for inmate counts. Most had figured out that they'd better have such routine information when we met, but two of the wardens who hadn't known the count that morning still didn't know how many inmates were in their jails.

I was stunned. I looked over at Eric again, and he shook his head. This was going to change. I sent the wardens off to get reacquainted with their jails, with one word ringing in their ears: accountability.

Afterward, Eric and I talked about what to do.

"We should suspend them," I said.

"Yeah, but we can't suspend managers," Eric said.

"If a correction officer didn't know the number of inmates in his or her housing area, they'd get suspended in a minute. These guys are being paid a hundred thousand dollars a year to run one fucking jail and they can't even tell me how many inmates are in that jail. What is that?"

"You're right," Eric said, "but there's nothing we can do about it."

I called the personnel director, and he echoed Eric. Punishing a manager was a big bureaucratic mess; essentially all I could do was fire them or demote them.

I thought about it for a while and then called Eric and told him that the two wardens were going to volunteer to give back a day's pay.

There was a long pause. "Volunteer?" Eric asked.

"Yeah. They're gonna give the city back a day's pay. And if they won't do it, tell them we'll draw up retirement papers."

MY first six months on the job, there was tremendous turn-over in the top ranks of the Department of Correction. I made it clear that anyone who didn't want to work, who didn't want to change, had to go. Early retirements were taken; people quit or were fired or demoted. We made the people we needed in the highest positions and whacked those people holding the department back.

The correction commissioner is responsible for overseeing the entire jail system, the first deputy controls the administrative side of the house, and the chief of department oversees the day-to-day operational needs. Mike Jacobson was the financial, analytical, and organizational genius. Eric was a good operations manager yet had never worked in an administration that gave him the support he needed to do his job. I acted as a strategist in putting everything together for the best outcomes, constantly working on a few primary goals: instilling management accountability and changing a culture that had accepted incompetence and tolerated failure.

Besides getting good people in positions of power, our first task was dealing with the immediate threat of a riot at Rikers. A few months after I started, we had a meeting with Mayor Giuliani to talk about it. At the time, it was expected that any day Rikers would, in the words of *New York* magazine's famous headline, "explode." And it wasn't just *New York* magazine. A week didn't go by without one of the papers predicting doom at Rikers. For years the island had been a staple of the front pages. *Newsday:* "Armed Rule by

Inmates." The *Daily News:* "Brutal Gangs Roam Rikers."
The *Post:* "Powder Keg at Rikers." From 1988 to 1993, the
correction department I'm sure led the New York tabloids in
negative editorials.

If the island erupted—*when* the island erupted—the
mayor's staff wanted to know, should there be contingency
plans involving other agencies? "Can you control Rikers?"
he asked. "What do you need from us?"

In the past, the answers would have been "No" and
"Everything." The DOC's Emergency Services Unit had con-
sisted of eighteen officers, who only worked day shifts, when
the jail was at its calmest. During one disturbance the ESU
officers couldn't even find the tear gas, and when they did,
some of them didn't know how to use it, which was probably
fine because some of the canisters were out of date anyway.

But Mike and I had talked the mayor into increasing the
funding, allowing the ESU to employ 150 members who
would work around the clock and to improve their training,
preparation, and equipment. I had been over every scenario
with Eric and the chiefs and wardens, and we knew that with
the beefed-up ESU we could take care of anything that came
up, even a major riot. So when the mayor asked, I didn't hesitate. "Sir, we don't need anything."

But a few months later I got a page late one Saturday
night. The NYPD Emergency Services Unit was at the
Brooklyn House of Detention, trying to get a mentally disturbed inmate out of his cell to go to the hospital. I was sure
I misunderstood the page. I called the DOC operations desk.
"Are you sure it's the *police* Emergency Services that's doing this? Where is our ESU?"

"They're off tonight," said the person on the other end of
the phone.

"What do you mean, 'off'?"

"They're not working tonight, sir."

I called Eric Taylor and had him reach out to the chief of
security. A few minutes later he called me back. It was true.
We had been led to believe that the ESU was staffed twenty-

four hours straight, but there were still two holes in the schedule, two nights when the entire Emergency Services Unit was off duty. One of the holes was Saturday nights.

I bugged out. At midnight I summoned all the bureau chiefs—the level of management just below Eric and just above the wardens, and had them come out to Rikers. The chief of security stepped forward and took full responsibility for the problem. He had allowed the ESU's coverage to lapse a couple of days a week, from 7 P.M. to midnight, in order to save money and make his budget. And he hadn't told anyone.

I reminded him of the recent meeting at Gracie Mansion. "Weren't you sitting right next to me? Weren't you sitting there when I said we were ready for anything?"

"Yes, sir."

"And during that meeting, you knew that I was lying to the mayor?"

"Yes, sir, I guess I did."

I nodded. "Okay. Everyone get out of here."

The next day I talked to Eric. While it was commendable that the security chief had taken full responsibility, he had knowingly deceived us. And he had knowingly allowed me to deceive the mayor. What if a massive riot had broken out some Saturday night at 8 P.M.? It's only a mile across that bridge from Rikers to Queens.

We had no choice. We had to replace the security chief. Although I have a reputation as a tough manager, firing someone is not something I take lightly nor is it something I get any enjoyment out of. The chief of security was a proud man who was well liked and had worked for years for the Department of Correction. I liked him very much. And there were other considerations, the kinds of political realities that may only exist in New York City. The security chief was the highest-ranking Italian in the department. Like every other ethnic group, the Italians have a fraternal organization that closely monitors the top ranks of the NYPD and the DOC to make sure Italians are well represented.

At the time, John Picciano was Eric Taylor's confidential

aide. I told Pitch to reach out to the head of the Italian fraternal group and let them know what was coming and why. Then we called the security chief in.

Eric began by explaining that what had happened was unacceptable and could not be tolerated. The chief of security wasn't hearing a word of it. "Look," I said, "you took responsibility for what happened and that's good. But you gotta go. You lied to us. You deceived us. It's that simple." He was terribly upset and pleaded for a demotion, for anything short of having to leave. "No," I said. "I'll do anything I can to help you, but you have to go." I don't believe that people who fail in one area should be moved elsewhere for another possible failure. They become dissidents and malcontents and eventually turn into a cancer within the agency. At the same time, you've got to treat them with respect and dignity, and when you do, they know it. The chief of security retired, moved on in his life, and today we remain close friends.

EVERYONE expected a catastrophic riot to break out sometime on Rikers. The only question was when it would happen. We were constantly on the lookout. It was like waiting for an earthquake in California, waiting for the Big One. The minute we got intelligence that the inmates were becoming restless, I'd load up the streets with Emergency Services vehicles and send out the ESU teams in full body armor to march and do drills, to test-drive the armored vehicles and run the dogs. When the inmates came out into the yard for recreation, they'd see this army training, and we'd avoid a disturbance, at least for that day.

But that wasn't going to solve the problem for long on Rikers. I knew the only way to address the underlying problem was to return control of the jail to the correction officers. And the first step in controlling the jail was decreasing the violence. By 1995 Rikers was averaging more than a hundred slashings or stabbings a month. It was a war zone. We had drawers full of Polaroid pictures of inmates with long gaping scars down their backs, across their chests, and covering their faces.

The gangs were to blame for most of it. Gangs at Rikers had been allowed to run the jails in much the same way they ran the streets outside. They ran the drug trade, extorted money and goods from other inmates and their families on the outside, traded sexual favors, and controlled the contraband that flowed in and out of the jail. They started wars and ordered and pulled off stabbings with alarming ease. While representing only 12 percent of the jail population, gangs were responsible for a majority of the assaults and other crimes inside Rikers.

The first step was to deal with the *appearance* that the gangs owned Rikers. This had a large psychological effect on them and on us. We painted over graffiti the minute it appeared, and punished inmates for tagging the walls. We put in new lights and fans and constantly scrubbed the floors and walls, transforming dark, grimy hallways into clean, bright corridors. I believe strongly that appearance improves performance, and I demanded that wardens keep their jails clean and well lit. Word quickly spread from officer to officer that I had better not find a burned-out lightbulb on their tour.

Changing the appearance of the inmates proved to be a bit harder. When we tried to eliminate gang colors, we ran into a fight from the Legal Aid Society, which said inmates had a right to dress the way they wanted. But eventually we got a court order to eliminate gang paraphernalia—the bandannas and the beads that gang members used to identify each other. When we started giving out clothes and shoes to inmates, we eliminated two more problems: the occasional attempted murder for a pair of expensive basketball shoes and the smuggling of weapons and other contraband in the soles and heels of boots.

But the biggest step in taking back the island might have been the Gang Intelligence Unit, an elite thirty-six-person unit that we set up to investigate crimes and keep tabs on gang activity within the jail system. There had been almost no investigative component within the correction department and certainly no one actively collecting information on the gangs within the jail system. Investigations had been totally reactive; there was no investigation until it was too late, until the shank had already been put in someone's back. But the new Gang Intel Unit gathered intelligence nonstop and kept a computer database—called the "Super Base"—which kept track of each of the twelve thousand gang members who passed through the jail system: their affiliation, criminal records, associates, even tattoos. If the Latin Kings were fighting for turf with the Five Percenters, I expected Gang Intel to be able to tell me all about it.

Before, crimes inside Rikers were handled by limiting privileges, but the Gang Intel Unit began making scores of arrests and charging inmates with crimes that could easily double or triple the time they would spend behind bars. Quickly we went from a handful of arrests each month to more than a hundred, and the inmates began to get the message that violence would not be tolerated. Slowly, almost imperceptibly, the numbers began to fall.

OF course, it wasn't just inmates who were in danger at Rikers. Some of the worst situations occurred when officers went into cells to get inmates. To "extract" an inmate, five officers would go into a cell, with one captain waiting at the door. They'd bring the inmate out and then handcuff him. If the inmate resisted, they'd have to wrestle and fight with their fists, and that's where many of the injuries—to both inmates and correction officers—occurred. And even if the inmate came out peacefully, he might be concealing a shank, which he'd swing at officers or at other inmates. It was crazy. Our officers were averaging twenty-five to thirty-five serious uses of force a month against inmates—which was dangerous for all of us. As I watched this happen over and over, I broke down the procedure into its parts to see what we could improve. For instance, why wasn't the inmate handcuffed before he was brought out of his cell?

If you spent any time on Rikers, you got used to hearing the same sad chorus whenever you suggested something new: "We've always done it this way" or "We just don't do it like that."

"Well, let's start," I said. So officers began cuffing inmates before they left the cells. But even with this necessary change, the inmates' hands were cuffed in front of them so that even with the shackles on, they could swing at someone or pull out a shank and slice someone.

"Why don't we cuff 'em behind their backs?" I asked.

"We've always done it this way."

Usually it took five or six questions to get beyond this excuse to the real reason. In this case, jail activists feared that if inmates fell with their hands cuffed behind their backs, they wouldn't be able to catch themselves and could get hurt. So I told the wardens to cuff inmates behind their backs and then post an officer in front of each inmate. That officer's responsibility was to keep the inmate from falling.

By far the most dangerous moment, for both officers and inmates, was that initial moment when they went in to extract uncooperative inmates. "If an inmate resists," I asked, "why don't you incapacitate him first, then bring him out?" The most obvious way to incapacitate inmates was with chemical agents: mace or pepper spray.

"We just don't do it that way."

"Why not?"

"Legal Aid gets pissed when we use mace."

For more than twenty years the Legal Aid Society had pushed for jail reform at Rikers, filing countless lawsuits on behalf of inmates. Some were necessary. But many of the "reforms" made life *more* dangerous for both inmates and officers. For instance, when mace or pepper spray is used, an inmate may be temporarily uncomfortable or in pain, but within a few minutes he's fine. There are no lasting effects, and no one else is put in danger. Using mace or pepper spray actually decreases injuries and improves morale.

But when the brass attempted to arm some officers on Rikers with mace during a pilot program in the late 1980s, a few officers misused it and the program was dumped. Amazingly, with all the problems at Rikers, mace had never been used again. Rather than figuring out why the pilot program failed or dealing with the officers who misused the mace, the bosses just dropped the whole project. That was Rikers for you.

"Okay," I told Eric Taylor, "let's give some of the officers mace, and if they misuse it this time, we'll just fire them."

The culture of "We've always done it this way" and "We just don't do it like that" was so ingrained at Rikers that there was resistance at first. Under the old style of management, getting mace to the officers could've taken months, maybe years. But we didn't have years. Rikers was in constant danger of boiling over. So at Thanksgiving, 1995, I told my staff that I wanted a pilot project on mace begun by December 10. We needed a place to start, someplace where violence was a constant threat. There was only one real choice.

The Bing.

The Central Punitive Segregation Unit—or the Bing, as we called it—was like something out of a horror movie. It was home to the worst of the worst: hundreds of cold murderers, rapists, and hard cases who would slice your throat for a cigarette. Many of them had been caught for serious offenses and were headed for long prison terms. They felt as though they had nothing to lose and had no reason to follow the rules. The Bing was filled with such lost causes.

Any inmate who attacked another inmate or a correction officer ended up in the Bing, alone in a seventy-two-square-foot cell, double- or triple-locked behind thick steel doors, with only a slot for the food trays to be passed in and out. As officers walked down the bright halls, there was no telling what might come flying out of those slots—not just food and trays, but urine, spit, and semen. Inmates were locked in the Bing for twenty-one to twenty-three hours a day, and the close quarters and isolation made them even more dangerous.

The Bing was created in 1988 as a way to segregate the most dangerous and uncooperative inmates. For correction officers, CPSU was such a tough job that they were given their choice of assignments in exchange for volunteering to work an eighteen-month stint in the Bing.

Even with the extra security precautions, the Bing had more incidents of violence—especially against correction officers—than any other area of Rikers. If there was one place on the island where mace was needed right now, it was the Bing. But we had to proceed cautiously to avoid the mistakes of the past. We began the program by training the officers in the correct way to use sprays and in following a strict procedure that began with verbal warnings and only used mace as a last resort. The project was a success, and soon we were training officers all over the island in the proper use of mace.

I don't think Mike Jacobson, Eric Taylor, or I took a breath that first year. Every day there was some new challenge, some new program to set up, some crisis to fight. When you're up to your neck, you don't realize you're making progress. And we weren't just battling the problems; we were swimming upstream against decades of doing things the wrong way. Still, we began to see some improvement. Between 1990 and 1994 the number of stabbings and slashings in New York City jails had run between 1,000 and 1,500 a year. In 1995, our first year in charge, there were 1,093. But in 1996, when our programs and innovations really took hold, the number dropped to 407. We had cut violence by 60 percent in one year, and if you went back to the historical high, in 1990, inmate attacks had fallen by almost 75 percent.

But the number was less important than the way it was achieved. After thirty years in which it was just assumed that everything had to get worse, we had shown that if you put enough effort and intelligence into it, if you put the sheer force of will behind it, even Rikers Island could get better.

I was working around the clock. Correction officers expected to see me on a surprise 3:00 A.M. tour, the window whirring down and my face leaning out of the car. "Why is that light burned out?"

Eighty-hour weeks were standard, and some days it seemed as if my whole life were contained in the charts and graphs that slowly began to reveal a turnaround in the Department of Correction. Without realizing it, I suppose, I allowed my private life to fade into the background. But every spare minute I spent with Joe, and that was fine with me. We settled into a great rhythm, spending every weekend together. Just like when I'd been a cop, I wanted Joe to understand what I did and the importance of committing yourself to your work, so he sometimes accompanied me on weekend trips to Rikers Island.

Usually Joe spent Christmas with his mother, and I had to make do with seeing him two nights earlier, on December 23. We'd go out to dinner, go down to Rockefeller Center to see the tree, and the next morning we'd open presents. But I kept bugging Jackie to let me have him for a real Christmas, and one year she relented. We had dinner on Christmas Eve and opened presents later that night. In the morning, I got up at 6 A.M. to be at Rikers for roll call. I felt that if my correction officers were going to have to work the holiday, to be away from their families, their boss needed to show that he understood their sacrifice by doing the same thing. So I worked Thanksgiving morning, and after the ball dropped in Times Square on New Year's Eve, I could be found inside Rikers, thanking my guys for their commitment.

That Christmas I was so excited to have Joe with me that I brought him to Rikers. At the CPSU, he got to sit in the control center—a big glass bubble in the center of a spiderweb of secure hallways—and press the buttons that opened the doors and allowed inmates to move from one hallway to the other. We stopped by each of the jails and visited with the correction officers, and then we went to my parents' house for Christmas dinner. He still talks about that Christmas.

In 1994 I had moved to Riverdale, in the northernmost

part of the Bronx, just this side of suburban Westchester County on the Hudson River. From there it was easier to get in and out of New Jersey to see Joe. And it was also nice to be close to the center of the city.

Always being on call and managing a department in crisis didn't always mesh with having a normal, quiet, residential life. For one thing, I was always missing dental appointments. I'd make an appointment and then just fail to show up. Or I'd call and cancel because of work. My dentist's office manager was a woman named Hala Matli. She hated me. Actually, we despised each other. Something would come up and I'd have to cancel an appointment and she'd get obnoxious with me about it. It was a running battle between us, me skipping appointments, her pointing out how inconsiderate I was being.

So we both might have been a bit surprised when, in mid-1996, I asked her out. After we got past our initial hostility, I saw a beautiful fair-skinned woman who was bright and sweet—as long as you didn't blow off your dental appointments.

Hala's family was from Syria, and they'd brought her here when she was fourteen. They were an extremely rigid Orthodox Christian family, steeped in traditions that they'd brought from Syria, and I didn't realize what a big deal it was when she invited me to the christening of her nephew.

We'd been seeing each other about six months, but Hala hadn't told most of her family. After all, I was divorced. I had a child from that marriage. I didn't belong to her church. And as if all that weren't bad enough, I was American. I suppose I didn't look very good on paper.

The restaurant where the reception was held was filled with 250 of Hala's friends and family. Hala's immediate family were sitting at a dais in the front of the room, and I was put in the middle of the room at a table that sat ten, but with me were only three other people, none of whom I knew. I sat down, and soon I began to realize that everyone was watching me. If I scratched my nose, four hundred eyes would turn toward me to see what I was doing. I got up to go to the men's room and felt like I was walking around nude.

Finally Hala's mother came over. "Bernie," she said, "would you mind meeting some of the family?"

"Of course not," I said. At that, Hala's uncle and aunt moved in and sat next to me, one on my right, the other on my left. There was no small talk, just straight to the inquisition: Where did you meet her? How many times have you gone out? What are your intentions?

I had just finished that round of questioning when another uncle appeared: What do you do for a living? Where do you live? One by one, these relatives played a game of Syrian musical chairs on either side of me. It was grueling. The New York Police Department could learn a few things about interrogation from these people.

"You're the correction commissioner?" one uncle asked.

"Actually, I'm the first deputy."

"Aren't you a little young?" Still not satisfied, this particular uncle went to Hala's mother. "How do we *know* he's the first deputy commissioner?"

Hala's mother considered the question. "Well, I see him on TV with the mayor." That was good enough for the uncle.

But I appreciated her family's zeal in checking me out. One of the things I realized that I loved about Hala was that traditional side and her commitment to family. Unlike other women I'd been with, she was so demure and patient, so supportive of my career, that time with her began to feel like a refuge from the hassles of work.

One night I told Hala that I had to go to a political event with the mayor, but before that we would go to the Water's Edge, a lovely restaurant on the Queens side of the East River, for dinner. We ordered our appetizers and dinner and sat talking, enjoying the Manhattan skyline. Then I looked over at the doorway to the kitchen and made eye contact with my executive assistant, a veteran correction officer named Jorge Ocasio. I gave him a slight nod, and with that Jorge took a diamond ring from his pocket, put it on a bed of flowers on a silver platter, then put the silver top on the platter. He handed the tray to the waiter and pointed to me.

"See that table?" Jorge said. "You go from here to that table, and if you make a right turn or a left turn, I'll shoot you."

When the waiter arrived with the platter, Hala spread her napkin in her lap and leaned forward. The waiter pulled the top off the platter, and there was the ring, sparkling in the bed of flowers.

"Will you marry me?"

Her eyes lit up and a smile spread across her face. "Yes," she said.

We were married on November 1, 1998, and at the beginning of the summer Hala and I traveled to Majorca, Spain, on vacation with friends. The whole ten days we were gone I spent on the telephone with Pitch about Rikers. Violence was at an all-time low, but we were trying to make it lower, so my vacation kept me just as busy as I would have been had I stayed home. But I wasn't too busy to see that something was wrong with Hala. She wasn't acting like herself. I wasn't sure if it was me or her, so I just let her be.

When we returned, we walked into our apartment with our luggage and put it down, and she ran into the bathroom. She was in there for nearly thirty minutes. Then the door opened, and she walked out with a huge smile on her face and handed me something that looked like a thermometer.

"What's this?" I said.

Looking as surprised as I was, she said, "We're going to have a baby."

Celine Christina Kerik was born on March 3, 2000, at 6:18 P.M. Not since my son, Joseph, was born had I felt the emotions I did on that day. My life has been blessed with successes and accomplishments as well as heartache and pain, yet on that day my life felt complete. She is and will always be Daddy's little girl.

22

THE ROCK

1998

JERRY Speziale stopped sleeping. Most nights he didn't get more than two hours anyway, but by February 1996 he was so edgy and strung out on work that for three whole days, he went nonstop. It wasn't surprising. In the two years since I'd left DETF, Jerry had become a one-man task force. First he lost Paul, our confidential informant, and then he lost me, his leash. Now it was just Jerry doing all of our jobs—posing as a high-level drug dealer, organizing airlifts into Central America, and monitoring the dealers in New York. He had become probably the most successful drug agent in America, but the anxiety of not being able to trust anyone, the same anxiety I'd sampled in my two and a half years with DETF, was taking its toll. Jerry lived in constant fear of being double-crossed. Every day he got further out there and harder for his bosses to control. When I talked to him, I could hear a paranoid edge in his voice. As well as hardly sleeping, he was occasionally swilling vodka to calm his nerves before undercover meetings.

Then one day in February 1996, I got a call from my old boss in DETF, Eddie Beach. He wanted to know if I'd heard from Jerry. He said that Jerry was following a truck up from North Carolina when he began acting very strangely.

Jerry had gotten a tip that millions of dollars in drug money were stashed in a truckload of canned tomatoes. Sleepless and paranoid, he followed the truck up the eastern seaboard and finally seized it when it got to New York. He X-rayed the cans but couldn't find the money, so he got a team together and they began opening cans of tomatoes, rooting through them with their hands. For hours they slopped around in tomatoes in the parking lot of DEA headquarters until it was clear there was no money in the cans.

When his tomato-soaked colleagues began busting Jerry's balls about the mistake, he looked nervous. And then he just walked away.

An hour later Eddie Beach paged me out at Rikers.

"What do you mean he disappeared?" I asked. "Did you check at home?"

"Bern," Eddie said. "His car is in the parking lot. His gun is here, everything. I'm telling you, he just disappeared."

I rushed to the DEA offices. Jerry's bosses were frantic, certain that drug dealers had finally come in and snatched him. He was gone all night, but it became clear after talking to his wife that he'd disappeared on his own. Jerry had finally snapped, convinced that people in his own office had turned against him and had somehow replaced the cans of money with real cans of tomatoes.

On the second day, we all gathered at Jerry's house, where the DEA agents were tapping his home phone in case he called his wife. "Listen," I said, "you're wasting your time. If he doesn't want you to find him, then you won't find him. He's like a ghost. Do you really think you're going to trace his phone calls? We wrote the book on this shit, remember?"

I had driven to Jerry's house with one of the correction captains, a guy named Richie Palmer. "You know what," I said to Richie, "I got an idea." I paged Jerry with one of the numeric codes we used when Jerry was in Guatemala. I was the only other person who knew that code.

Twenty seconds later, my cell phone rang. "Hey, motherfucker!" Jerry yelled. "Don't try to set me up! I know what you're doing! I know!"

"Where are you, Jerry?"

"It don't matter where I am. I know what you're doing, Bern. And that's forty-five seconds." He hung up.

I paged him three or four times, and each time he called back but hung up after forty seconds or so, just in case we were trying to tap the call. The last time I talked to him, he yelled, "And you tell Terry Hartman to stay the fuck away from my house! And to stop petting my fucking dog!"

I ran into the house, where the DEA agents were nervously pacing around. "Terry," I said, "where were you petting the dog?"

"On the front porch."

I looked out the front window. "Guess what. We got company. Jerry's here."

But even though he could see us, we still couldn't find him. I got him back on the phone, and this time I didn't try to talk him out of the conspiracy he'd imagined. "You're absolutely right," I said. "Jerry, they are trying to set you up. You know what you need to do. Turn yourself in. Turn yourself in with a lawyer. That's the only way you'll be safe."

That afternoon the DEA set up surveillance on Jerry's lawyer's house. Pretty soon his lawyer walked out, got in her car, and drove to the Tick Tock Diner on Route 3 in Clifton, New Jersey. DEA agents were right behind her. I could hear the whole thing on the radio as I drove back to New York with Richie Palmer. As we drove past the Tick Tock Diner, Richie spun his head back.

"Hey, aren't you gonna pull in at that diner?" Richie asked.

"He ain't in the diner." I looked at my watch. "She might not even be in the diner anymore." Sure enough, when DEA agents went in, neither Jerry nor his lawyer was in the restaurant. He'd gotten her out and into another car without anyone seeing.

Thankfully, the lawyer talked Jerry into going to a clinic

to get help, because we might never have caught him otherwise. The diagnosis was sleep deprivation and a kind of post-traumatic stress disorder. In layman's terms, he bugged out from too much work and not enough sleep. After the tomato can incident, Jerry had just walked away from the DEA offices, caught a cab to New Jersey, walked through the swamp of the Meadowlands, dug a foxhole, covered himself with leaves, and gone to sleep.

When Jerry was healthy again he returned to DETF, but he was confined to a desk. Soon after that, he retired, citing the many physical injuries he had sustained on the job over the previous eighteen years. He was finally done fighting the drug cartels.

But they weren't done with Jerry.

He'd been retired for about six months when he got a call from a lawyer who wanted to meet with him in Manhattan but wouldn't say why. It turned out the lawyer was from Colombia. He wanted Jerry to come to work for the cartels, to use his knowledge of American drug enforcement techniques to help the cartels avoid prosecution. They offered to set up two offices for him and to pay him $250,000 a year. Jerry listened and then politely explained that he wasn't for sale.

JERRY'S anxiety attack made me realize just how far I'd come in the two years since I worked with him. In 1994 I couldn't have imagined anything better than the adrenaline of our international drug investigations. But two years of running the Department of Correction—of trying to turn around a floundering eight-hundred-million-dollar-a-year agency—had given me a deeper sense of accomplishment than anything I'd ever done. And after a year as the first deputy commissioner, it was thrilling to see the results of the work we were putting in, to see cleaner, safer corridors and correction officers who were beginning to take some pride in their jobs. But just *improving* the DOC wasn't enough. I wanted excellence to become a part of the system.

The NYPD was just beginning to be transformed by Jack Maple's innovative Comp Stat program, and by the end of 1995 I'd convinced Michael Jacobson that we ought to try a similar program—a system of performance indicators and management expectations that would allow us to accurately measure our successes and to hold employees at all ranks accountable for our failures. It was essentially taking the business principles that Rudolph Giuliani preached and applying them to our jails. Philosophically, it wasn't very different from the approach we'd already taken, but it was important to make our style of management standard procedure—a road map for correction officers and bosses to follow, a system of analysis and responsibility that would live on long after Jacobson and I left.

I called the program TEAMS—the Total Efficiency Accountability Management System. Since jail security and inmate violence were our most pressing needs, we started with those statistics. But rather than just listing numbers of slashings and stabbings, the collection and analysis included the location, the time, the weapon used, and whether or not there was a documented arrest for the event. Each day we could look down the rows and try to find patterns. Were there more attacks at the end of one shift? Was one jail having more problems than others? We quickly expanded the TEAMS performance indicators from about thirty-five to ninety—everything from overtime pay to maintenance factors.

Besides collecting and analyzing data, we started holding monthly meetings much like Comp Stat where we went over the numbers. Before TEAMS, each jail and each department was run as a personal fiefdom, but now all the wardens and chiefs and deputies—eighty to a hundred top managers—sat down together once a month to look for patterns, not just in their own facilities but throughout the system. These meetings were not for the faint of heart. Wardens were called upon to defend their performance, and if I saw a spike in slashings in your jail, then you had better know why.

In the beginning, many of the managers were terrified of standing in front of their colleagues and answering rapid-fire questions about their performance. So I'd deliver a short speech each month. "The purpose of this is not to beat up people, or to judge your public-speaking abilities. No one is interested in embarrassing anyone. But," I'd say at the end, "if you're asked a question . . . have an answer."

Soon the TEAMS meetings were bringing out the best of the best in our managers, inspiring them to come up with innovative ways to solve their problems and to share those programs that worked with other wardens.

After going over the numbers, TEAMS meetings might veer in any number of directions. At one point we had a spike in the number of down cells—cells that we couldn't use for inmates, usually for one of four reasons: the electronic door wasn't functioning, the toilet overflowed, the lights didn't work, or the sink was broken. Rikers was constantly battling overcrowding, and we needed those cells back on line as soon as possible.

Using TEAMS, we dismantled the process we used to fix down cells. It turned out that the Capital Improvements Unit had evolved into four separate entities, one for toilets, one for sinks, one for lights, and one for doors. These specialized groups of plumbers and electricians barely communicated with each other. There was no chain of command between them. When I asked why, they said they'd always done it that way.

"This is the most ridiculous thing I've ever heard," I said at the TEAMS meeting. "Here's what we're gonna do. You're all gonna get together with the department head. I want a chain of command. I want some communication. I want this fixed, and I want a report on my desk in by Monday. Understand?" By Monday, the problem was solved.

One of the wildest TEAMS meetings resulted from an elaborate scheme hatched by two inmates who smuggled a .22-caliber handgun into the jail. At the TEAMS meeting, a warden and the three deputy wardens were called up to the podium to explain how a gun got into their jail. Other managers squirmed in their seats as I raked them with question after question. But I didn't ask about the gun. I asked about garbage.

Every week work crews went out to what was called "the foot" of Rikers, an area on the Queens side of the Rikers Island Bridge, where a guard post and parking lot were located and where the public had its closest access to the jails. The work crews would cut the grass, clean up the security booths, and pick up garbage in the parking lot and along the public areas of the river.

"So how do we dispose of this garbage that we gather across the bridge?" I asked.

The warden swallowed and began to answer. "Well, we bring the big black plastic bags back onto the island and then . . ."

"Stop!" I said. "Hold on! Right there. Are you telling me that we go a mile out of our way to pick up this garbage, and then we turn around and bring these unsecured bags of garbage right back onto the island?"

"Uh, yes, sir."

That was how the gun had gotten onto Rikers. It turned out that someone on the outside was paid to put a .22 in some garbage on the ground. The inmate on the work crew walked over, grabbed the gun, and dropped it into his black garbage bag. Then he went around picking up more garbage until the whole crew was done. They piled back onto a truck and headed back onto the island—with their bags of garbage.

The inmates had to pass through a magnetometer, but the trash didn't. The garbage was then taken to the loading dock of the jail, and from there the gun made its way into the bowels of the jail, where an inmate passed it along to the guy who'd originally paid for this service. And then it was used to shoot another inmate.

We spent the entire TEAMS meeting discussing garbage pickup, making sure there were no other lapses like this.

"And why do we do it this way?" I asked.

"Well, we've always—"

I held my hand up. "Don't say it . . . I know . . . we've always done it that way."

MIKE Jacobson had always been something of an odd fit: a brilliant, gentle man at the helm of the largest and most dangerous and chaotic jail system in the country. But it worked very well, in part because my hands-on management style allowed him to concentrate his analytical genius on the big picture of fixing Rikers. But toward the end of 1997, Mike sat down with Mayor Giuliani and told him that he was returning to the academic world, to teach at the John Jay College of Criminal Justice.

"So who are we gonna put at Correction?" Mayor Giuliani asked.

"It has to be Bernie," Mike said. "If it's anyone, it has to be Bernie."

"You think he can handle it?" Mayor Giuliani asked.

Mike smiled. "Mayor, just let me tell you what I know. Overtime goes up? I see a blip on some report? I tell Bernie, 'Hey, overtime's going up.' He says, 'Yeah? Okay.' The next morning I come in and there are six or eight of those big burly wardens and bureau chiefs all dressed up in uniform, looking sharp, standing at his door. An hour later, they come out of Bernie's office, their ties are off and they're sweating.

"Now I don't know what he does in there. I'm not sure I want to know. And you know what, Mayor? You don't want to know either. But whatever Bernie does, right after that meeting, overtime plummets."

In my first two years at DOC, I had been given a complete education from one of the best teachers in the world. Mike gave me a crash course in setting up programs, budgets, and finances—about the paper version of the concrete and steel jails that we ran. I've never met a person who could coax so much information from a column of numbers.

I suppose I spent my whole life looking for a certain kind of mentor—karate instructors, soldiers, cops. For years I thought the way to become a man was to surround myself with the biggest, boldest, and strongest. If someone had told me that I would learn from an unassuming college professor that an adding machine could be a tool far more powerful than a handgun, I would have laughed. But by late 1997, I would put my ability to understand, manage, and maintain a budget up against anyone's. I learned how to translate ideas into the numbers and policies that could make those ideas come alive. And I learned this from Michael Jacobson.

Throughout my life, I've found myself pausing and wondering, "How did I get here?" Two days before Christmas, in 1997, I stood at City Hall wondering: How does a kid from a shattered home, a high school dropout, a simple cop, wind up running an agency with an annual budget of more than eight hundred million dollars? Is this supposed to be happening? How does this kid find himself in charge of a workforce of thirteen thousand civilian and uniformed people, responsible for a total of sixteen jails, fifteen holding facilities, and four prison hospital wards—and for 125,000 inmates each year? People have a tendency to give me all the credit for what I've done and how far I've climbed, but the truth is that I could never have pulled it off myself, without all the people who reached down to give me a hand and over time acted as mentors.

On December 23, 1997, one of those people, Rudolph Giuliani, announced the retirement of another one of those people, Mike Jacobson. And then he announced the name of the new commissioner of the New York City Department of Correction. "When you make appointments of people to very, very difficult jobs like this one, there's always a bit of uncertainty, because you never know how it's going to work out," the mayor said.

"In Bernie's case, I already know how it's going to work out."

IF anyone expected me to slow down, they didn't know me very well. I lived and breathed the mayor's theory that you fix big problems by fixing all the small problems that make it up—the so-called quality-of-life issues. I had made progress at Rikers by believing that no detail was too small for my attention, and I certainly wasn't going to change now.

Back when the job was closer to that of a warden, the correction commissioner lived on Rikers Island, in a house in the middle of the island. But for years before Mike Jacobson and I took over, the commissioners rarely even visited the island, spending most of their time in the downtown headquarters. However, the house still stands and today is being renovated as a command and control center for the department. The commissioner's office, which was rarely used, I had renovated, not only to serve as an office but also as a signal that I meant to spend just as much time on the island as I had as first deputy—maybe more.

When Eric Taylor retired as chief of department, I snatched up John Picciano, first as my confidential assistant and then as my chief of staff. I'd been impressed by John's loyalty in addition to his intelligence and toughness and his ability to get things done. It wasn't long before he was getting the 3 A.M. telephone calls. "Pitch. I'm at Rikers. Get four-way stop signs on this corner to prevent accidents. And why are correction officers in Emergency Services slipping and sliding down this heavily sloped parking lot? Get some steps on this fucking hill!"

How good is John Picciano? The next morning there were four stop signs, and two days later, there was a staircase built into the side of the hill.

Like a lot of veteran correction employees, John was amazed at the improvement in the culture of the department. He and Tom Antenen, my deputy commissioner of public information, often told stories of how bad morale within the department had been. Much of that was due to the sorry state of the jails during the 1970s, 1980s, and early 1990s. What was there to be proud of? It was a dangerous, thankless job.

But even when we began transforming the DOC, there was no way most people would ever know what tremendous public servants these officers were. Unlike cops and firefighters, they had almost no interaction with the public; there were no news stories of correction officers saving people or putting their lives on the line. Of course, they did this—every day— but it was behind chain-link and razor wire, on an island that New Yorkers only saw if they were criminals themselves.

You can't fake morale. You can't send a memo telling people to be proud of themselves. Over the years, I took hundreds of steps to improve morale. Many were small. I changed the uniforms, to make the officers appear more crisp and to instill a paramilitary pride. The mayor was constantly posing in a fireman's cap or an NYPD cap. I made sure he did the same thing with a correction cap. I put a sign at the edge of the island that read Rikers Island: Home of the Boldest Correction Officers in the World. It had long been the slogan of the department—just as the police are called the "finest" and the firefighters the "bravest"; but the "boldest" had been something of a joke before.

Law-abiding New Yorkers never saw correction officers at work, but they did see correction department buses all over the city, bringing inmates to and from court. In 1995, our buses were disgusting: filthy old school buses, battered and dinged, the bumpers hanging off, the decals coming off, the metal gratings rusted over the windows. I couldn't imagine some father who worked for correction driving with his kid and pointing to one of those buses and saying, "That's where Daddy works."

So we took the simple step of painting the buses. I chose the color and the lettering myself—right down to the font and type size—sleek blue and white buses with "New York's Boldest" painted on the sides. But even after they were painted, the buses were filthy. At a TEAMS meeting, I demanded to know why. After all, we had our own car wash, staffed by inmates. I drove down there and saw the inmates washing the cars of the wardens and bureau chiefs. So if the wardens' cars could get washed, why couldn't we get our damned buses washed?

It turned out that the car wash ran on weekdays, when the buses were out collecting inmates and taking them to court. On weekends, when the whole fleet of buses just sat there, the car wash was unmanned. I asked if this seemed stupid to anyone else.

"We've always done it that way," someone said.

"We have fifteen thousand inmates on this island and we can't get our buses washed?" I ordered that from then on, the wardens were to wash their cars at their own jails, and on weekends and during the evenings we would wash the buses. And then I retooled the car wash with better hoses and machines for washing buses.

But safety would always be the biggest morale issue at Rikers, and that was where we had the most success. Who wanted to go to work thinking that he might be stabbed that day? Or that he might die at work? Adding mace and improving the way we handcuffed inmates had been great steps, but we weren't done. We added stun shields to the officers' arsenal—big Plexiglas shields threaded with wires that sent six-second bursts of 50,000 volts of electricity to violent inmates. Like mace, the stun shields briefly incapacitated inmates without causing any serious damage.

For the most dangerous inmates, I ordered tube mitts, handcuffs with long tubes to cover their hands, so that when they were transported from their cells, they couldn't swing shanks anymore. Gang Intel was having huge success all the time investigating violent offenders. Arrests went from five or six a month in the early nineties to more than a hundred a month by 1999.

We also quadrupled the number of random searches of cells and dormitories—from two thousand a month to eight thousand, and as the searches went up, the number of weapons that we confiscated fell, from ninety-three hundred in 1997 to a little more than five thousand two years later.

To keep weapons from being smuggled in, we brought in what was called a BOSS chair—a Body Orifice Scanning System. When inmates sat on it, a metal-detecting magnetic scanner built into the chair searched their bodies for hidden razor blades, knives, and other weapons. With each innovation we made another dent in the violence at Rikers, and each time people thought the numbers couldn't continue to fall, they did. There were 115 stabbings in Rikers in August 1995, just months after we took over. In August 1998, three years later, there were 7. Overall, we cut violence by *93 percent* in less than five years. And just to ensure that officers were as safe as we could make them, I worked with Norman Seabrook, the president of the Correction Officers' Benevolent Association, to get the officers stab/slash–resistant vests that could be worn under their uniforms.

In that kind of environment, success feeds on itself: lowering violence improved morale, which meant fewer sick days, which meant less overtime, which meant that more money could be spent improving security, which meant lower violence, and on and on. From the time Mike Jacobson and I started, we cut sick leave—in an agency once known as the sick leave department—by 31 percent and cut the dreaded overtime budget by 44 percent. To deal with the crowding, we pushed to streamline the system, cutting the inmates' average stay from fifty-eight days to thirty-seven. By 1999, supervisors who used to tremble at TEAMS meetings couldn't wait to share their success stories.

These staggering numbers aside, officers realized now that their bosses respected them and cared about them. Before we arrived, when officers were stabbed or beaten, the brass rarely visited them in the hospital. There was certainly no policy for someone from administration to go to the hospital or go help that officer's family.

"Let me get this straight," I said when I first encountered this. "You have a guy who works for you who just got pummeled doing his job, and he's sitting in a hospital room by himself? How come no one went to get his wife? How come no one picked up his kids at school? How come no supervisors are at the hospital checking on this guy?"

So I set up a team to help the officer and his family, and to make sure it worked, I went to the hospital myself. In fact, I was usually the first one at the hospital. In 1999, when I appointed Bill Fraser as chief of department, he set up a plan to break the city into quadrants for his four bureau chiefs to cover, so that if an officer went to any hospital in the city, or there was to be a response from the executive staff, they could beat me to the event or hospital. It didn't work. I was still the first one there.

With John Picciano as my point man, I also worked hard to improve relationships with the unions and ethnic organizations. We opened our office to them and dealt with them in honest and straightforward ways. A former warden and longtime David Dinkins supporter named Ali Al-Rahman was the leader of the Guardians Association, the fraternal group for black correction officers. He came to me once, upset that a number of black women had failed the weapons test at the training academy. We realized that the women had been tested with the newer, heavier nine-millimeter Glock handguns, without having a chance to strengthen their arms. So I gave them another chance to take the test and they passed. He and the head of the Hispanic fraternal group told the *Daily News* that I was the best commissioner they'd seen in dealing with the concerns of minority officers. It was all about being firm but fair.

Every day a different officer would approach me and shake my hand: "Thank you for making the jails safer." Inmates who had been in Rikers years earlier were amazed by the change. Praise began to come from the outside too. Newspaper and magazine reporters began showing up, asking questions about the amazing transformation of the correction department. In years past, Rikers never made the news unless it was about a riot, an escape, or its horrible conditions. Headlines that four years ago had screamed about the "Powder Keg at Rikers" and "Armed Rule by Inmates" now read "Why the Jails Didn't Explode," "A Safer World Behind Bars," and "An Iron Hand at Rikers Island Drastically Reduces Violence."

Soon, people from other jail and prison systems around the world were visiting us, watching the way we did things, borrowing our ideas. Our TEAMS program was one of twenty-five finalists among sixteen hundred different programs considered by Harvard's JFK School of Government for its prestigious Innovations in American Government Award.

Things were going so well, it never occurred to me that I'd want to do anything else. Then, in the spring of 2000, I heard a strange rumor. Mayor Giuliani's second police chief, Howard Safir, was leaving. And on the short list of replacements was a surprising name.

Mine.

23

ONE POLICE PLAZA

2000

THEY called it the New York Miracle. While I was working to transform Rikers Island and the rest of the correction department, Rudy Giuliani was restoring order to the city, most notably through the police department's efforts to control crime. Under William Bratton's leadership and Jack Maple's innovative Comp Stat program, crime was reduced considerably during Mayor Giuliani's first term, and by 1996 the number of murders had fallen to 983 from a high of 2,245 in 1990. Across the board, the results were incredible. From the brink of collapse, New York had emerged a richer, safer, and healthier city than it had been in decades.

Bratton left in 1996, after a very public squabble with Giuliani over taking credit for the improved crime figures. Maple went with him out of loyalty, and when Giuliani passed up First Deputy Commissioner John Timoney, he left too. The mayor's choice to replace Bratton, Fire Commissioner Howard Safir, was immediately less popular among the rank-and-file officers, and many people predicted that crime would return to pre-Giuliani levels under Safir. But the numbers continued to fall, and in 1998 there were only 633 murders, the lowest number since 1963.

While crime remained under control, the NYPD was coming under attack from other directions. In August 1997 a Haitian immigrant named Abner Louima was arrested and taken to the Seven-O precinct house in Brooklyn by an enraged cop named Justin Volpe, who thought that Louima had punched him during a street brawl. At the precinct house, Volpe took Louima into the bathroom and tortured him, brutally beating and sodomizing him with a broomstick, while at least one other cop watched. Volpe was convicted of civil rights charges and sentenced to thirty years in prison; three other cops received lesser sentences for watching or not stopping the horrible abuse.

That case still haunted the city when, on February 4, 1999, four plainclothes cops spotted a twenty-two-year-old West African immigrant named Amadou Diallo standing on a corner in the Bronx, looking up and down the block suspiciously. The cops said later they thought he looked like a serial rape suspect they were seeking. As they moved toward him, Diallo stepped into a vestibule. One of the cops held out his badge and said, "Police. Can I have a word with you, please?"

But Diallo—maybe thinking the plainclothes cops were muggers or simply nervous to be approached by the police—moved backward and started reaching for something. The officers told him to show his hands, but he backed into the vestibule, turned, and held something black out toward them.

"Gun! He's got a gun!" yelled one of the cops. At once they opened fire. Somehow they thought Diallo was wearing a bulletproof vest, and they just kept firing until he hit the ground. The echo and rush of their own shots may have keyed them up even more, and when one of the officers fell backward, the others reacted by firing into the vestibule, believing that their partner had been shot. In all, they fired forty-one shots into that vestibule. Nineteen of them hit Diallo, killing him instantly.

When the officers reached the fallen man, one of them reached down and was shocked to find only a black wallet in his hand. Amadou Diallo was unarmed.

"Where's the fucking gun?" the cop yelled. "Where's the fucking gun?"

One of the cops testified later that as it dawned on him what they'd done, he held Diallo, rubbed the bleeding man's face and cried, "Don't die! Please don't die!"

It was a terrible tragedy, and coupled with the Louima case and a few other allegations of racial bias and police brutality, it gave the NYPD the reputation of a department out of control, wracked by racism and violence. The same aggressive policing that had turned the city around was now described as harassment. Activists said that Giuliani's tough-on-crime tactics were patently unfair and directed against racial minorities. In the wake of Diallo's death, there were months of protests, and cops got used to people waving wallets and yelling "Murderer!" The protests continued a year later when the four officers were acquitted of second-degree murder after an emotional trial in Albany, and in the spring of 2000, when police shot and killed another young black man, Patrick Dorismond.

Accompanying the decline in the NYPD's image was a drastic drop in officer morale. Cops were stung by criticism from neighborhoods that they'd risked their lives protecting. They worried that their every action would be second-guessed. Inside the department and on the street, support for Howard Safir began to erode. The commissioner was criticized for going to Los Angeles for a police chief convention two days after Diallo was shot. A month later when he accepted a free trip to the Oscars from a New York businessman, the newspapers called him "Hollywood Howard" and pushed the perception that he was spending his time in lavish hotels around the country while the city smoldered. Community leaders demanded he resign. Citing "lack of leadership, lack of integrity," the main union for police officers, the Patrolmen's Benevolent Association, gave Safir a vote of no confidence—the first such vote in 105 years.

Throughout 1999 and 2000, rumors circulated that Safir was preparing to resign. At one point, a *Newsday* columnist named Leonard Leavitt wrote about the most likely candidates to succeed him: Joe Dunne and Bernard Kerik. And for the first time in years, I found myself daydreaming.

"YOU gotta tell him you want the job," Tibor said one day. He still worked on Mayor Giuliani's security detail, and he said I should talk to the mayor immediately.

"I'm not gonna tell him I want a job that isn't even open," I said.

"Look," Tibor said, "I know him. You gotta tell him that you can do this, that you want the position."

"Bullshit," I said.

But the next time the rumor of Safir's exit appeared in the newspaper, I called City Hall to see if the mayor had a minute.

His secretary, Beth Petrone, was very short with me. She said he was busy.

"He's busy?" I asked.

"Listen," she said, "you cannot leave." A number of commissioners were leaving, and the mayor's secretary assumed that was why I had called.

"Oh, no," I assured her. "I'm not leaving."

"Okay," she said. "How about two-thirty?"

He was reading something when I came in, and he gestured to the chair across from his desk. "What can I do for you?"

"Well, sir, you asked me to go to the Department of Correction and I wasn't sure I wanted to go," I said. "I was happy being a cop. But I went, and I think I've shown my abilities as a manager."

"Yes," he said. "You have."

"I don't want to be stepping out of bounds or anything,

but there are all these rumors about Howard Safir leaving," I said. "Well, I hope he doesn't, but if he does, I just wanted you to know . . . I would like to be considered for that job."

He looked up at me. "You would," he said simply. "Between you and me . . . you would." Neither of us said another word about it.

For the next six months Safir continued in his job, and I just assumed it was all rumors and he wasn't going anywhere. So I concentrated on improving our own little miracle on Rikers Island until August 7, when Safir announced that he was leaving. Within minutes I was flooded with phone calls. Apparently I was on a very short list of candidates for the job.

The next eleven days were the most hectic and stressful of my life, until I began writing this book. Every job I had gotten to that point had come as a surprise, as a result of my success at lower levels, and I had never really had to compete or campaign for a post. But this job was different. This job I really wanted. I wanted to return to my first love—the NYPD—to improve on the work Giuliani had begun and to patch the holes in community relations and morale. I desperately wanted the chance to blend my management skills with my instincts and insight as a cop.

But my work was cut out for me. The *Daily News* reported on the day Safir resigned, "NYPD Chief of Department Joseph Dunne . . . the city's number 1 uniformed cop, emerged yesterday as a likely successor to departing Police Commissioner Howard Safir." I was mentioned in the same story as "a long-shot possibility."

Still, I was in the game. Safir resigned on a Monday, and on Tuesday night I got a call from someone in the mayor's office, who gave me the address of a small, nondescript office, away from the glare of the media. "Tomorrow morning at eleven A.M. . . . Go to the twentieth floor. . . . Have someone drop you off. . . . But come by yourself."

I wasn't sure if it was an interview or a ransom drop.

In the office was the mayor's full cabinet, eight people

sitting around a U-shaped table, with a chair in the middle of the other side for me to sit in. I sat, and after some pleasantries, they began peppering me with questions: "What would you do if you became police commissioner?" "What would you do about morale?"

I thought it went well, but for days afterward there was nothing but conjecture. It was excruciating. I paced the floor of my office with John Picciano, Eddie Aswad, and Tom Antenen, trying to figure out what it meant that the decision was taking so long. The rumors about Safir leaving had been out there for months; surely the mayor had been preparing for this. We stopped cold whenever the phone rang—and of course, it rang all the time. Reporters, cops, and friends called to ask if I knew anything or to offer support or to give me the latest rumor they'd heard.

Most of them were very kind, but I have to think they didn't give me much of a chance. The whole time my own brother, Don, assured me that I'd get the job, even though he believed in his heart that Joe Dunne had a much better chance.

And why not? Joe was a great cop, a thirty-one-year veteran who was intelligent, honest, and popular among rank-and-file cops. He'd had great results lowering crime when he ran a precinct house in Brooklyn. He was also the muscle under Safir who got things done.

Still, I believed that my résumé stacked up against anyone's and my experience in management and running a troubled agency gave me some advantages.

For days, we waited to hear anything. One hour I was up, the next I was down. And after talking to Joe Dunne, I knew he was going through the exact same thing. Newspaper and TV reporters seemed to tilt one way and then the other, but usually toward Dunne.

Then, on Friday, August 11, five days into this torture, the *New York Times* ran a story under the headline "City Hall Split on Who Should Take Over 1 Police Plaza." There must've been a gaping leak in the mayor's office because the story read like minutes from one of his staff meetings. It had two of the mayor's aides strongly supporting Dunne—for his knowledge and experience as a cop—and two strongly supporting me—for my ability as a reformer, to make changes and shake things up.

"The split is so wide," the story read, "that the administration yesterday gave off signs that it was flailing about, with key advisors throwing out new or even unlikely names." The two camps were so adamant, they were in danger of casting both Dunne and me aside to look for a third candidate that they could agree on.

That day, I got a call. "The mayor would like to have breakfast with you."

I knew the mayor well enough to know that the recommendation of his staff only went so far. In the end, it would be his decision. This was the real interview.

I stayed up all that night with Tibor, John Picciano, Lenny Lemer, Mike Caruso, the Department of Correction inspector general, and Chauncy Parker, a former Manhattan DA, U.S. attorney, and longtime friend, going over numbers and management principles and theories, existing narcotics initiatives, staffing levels and budget items, every nuance of *Reinventing Government* I could think of. I crammed like a first-year medical student.

Saturday morning at 9 A.M., I sat down across from the mayor and I knew I was ready. It felt great, discussing my plans for continuing the reduction in crime, improving morale, and healing the relationship with communities around the city.

"Mayor, everything you've done in this city is based around performance measures and indicators," I said. "And one of the most important perspectives of policing in this city is community affairs and community relations. Yet Bill Bratton and Howard Safir didn't create performance indicators to measure how we're doing in communities."

"And we can do that?" he asked.

"You bet we can." And I laid out the things we were doing

in correction, like the monthly civility tests in which we tested a hundred officers a month to weed out the arrogance and rudeness that contribute to the distance between cops and people of color.

At one point the mayor asked whom I would choose as a first deputy, assuming I was made commissioner, if the choice were between Joe Dunne and another police official. "Joe Dunne the men will follow," I said.

Three hours later I climbed into John Picciano's truck and nodded. "I got it."

"You're kidding!" he said. "He told you that?"

"No," I said, "but Joe Dunne can't do better than I did." I could feel it.

But my confidence was short-lived. That night there was a shootout in Gravesend, Brooklyn, and it turned out that the shooter had been a correction officer almost twenty years before. Why does it have to be a correction officer? I thought. I was fuming.

In the meantime, Joe Dunne was the one at the scene, holding the press conference, out in the media spotlight, looking like the police commissioner.

"I can't believe I'm going to lose this thing because of some guy who was a fucking correction officer in 1982!" I yelled to Pitch at one point.

But this was New York, and an hour later the stories were spinning again. The momentum flip flopped so many times, you couldn't keep track of who was in the lead. And still, from the mayor's office, nothing.

Rumors were everywhere. Every ten minutes someone would call to tell me Safir was begging the mayor not to make me. Then we heard that Safir's last day was supposed to be August 20 and I would only be named commissioner after Safir left because he was so strongly opposed to me. But most experts agreed: the smart money was still on Dunne.

On August 18, Howard Safir's last day—eleven days after this horrible beauty contest began—the mayor said that he'd reached a decision and would announce it the next day. Stung by the leaks in the *New York Times* a week earlier, Giuliani shut his staff out completely. It is literally impossible to keep a secret in New York—at least it was until that day.

The *Daily News* story the next morning reflected what most people were thinking: "Dunne appeared to be the clear favorite, according to sources at Police Headquarters and City Hall." The story went on to say that:

> Police officials were surprised the decision on a replacement took so long, because it had been an open secret for months that Safir and his first deputy were leaving.
>
> Asked how he made his choice, Giuliani said, "It all of a sudden occurred to me this was the right person and that it would work."

I got a call from Tony Carbonetti, the mayor's chief of staff, that afternoon. "Commissioner, where are you going to be tonight at eight o'clock?"

"Tony? Where would you like me to be tonight at eight o'clock?"

"Could you be home at eight o'clock? The mayor would like to talk to you."

"Tony, is it good or bad?"

Click.

At 8:00 P.M. my house was full of my closest friends and colleagues—people who had shared the battlefield with me every step along the way: Eddie Aswad, Pitch, Tibor, my brother, Don, Mike Caruso, Lenny Lemer, Jerry Speziale and his wife and daughter. And of course, my wife, Hala, and our five-month-old baby daughter, Celine. I had no clue whether it was going to be good or bad. All I knew was that all these people were making me nuts. I was just about to throw everyone out when, at ten minutes after eight, the phone rang.

"Hello."

"Bern?"

"Who's this?"

"Tommy Santino." A detective friend from the Intelligence Division.

"I can't fuckin' talk right now, Tommy!" Then I hung up on him.

Coincidentally, the mayor was on CNN, being interviewed on Larry King about something unrelated, and we all sat in the living room, hanging on his every word. When he left, we all stared at the phone, but still it didn't ring. The pressure of eleven days of this shit was getting to me. Joe was with his mom, so I sat on his bedroom floor, a towel pulled over my head, waiting. At ten-thirty the phone rang.

"Hello."

"Hey, Bern, it's Tommy Santino."

"God damn it, Tommy! Not now!" I was shot. Drenched in sweat.

Then, at 10:50 P.M. the phone rang. Hala was outside Joe's room, so I called her in to stand with me.

"Bernie?" the mayor said. "It's Rudy. I just want you to know, I just hung up the phone from Joe Dunne." And there was a delay of a few seconds that felt like two hours. Like he was calling on a cheap cell phone from the moon. And all I could think was, Do you call the winner first or second?

"I've asked Joe to become the first deputy commissioner," he said. Another pause from the moon. "And I'd like you to accept the appointment of the city's fortieth police commissioner."

My eyes brimmed with tears and my knees buckled. In front of me, Hala's hands were out to the sides and she was mouthing the word "What?" over and over.

"Hello," the mayor said. "Are you there?"

"Yes, sir."

"Okay," he said. "Let me tell you why I made this decision." One thing I admire about Rudolph Giuliani is how direct he usually is, but on this night he was a fourteen-year-old girl on the telephone. He just could not shut up.

"Uh-huh," I said. "Yes, sir." And Hala just stared at me, trying to read my face, wondering if my tears were a good thing or a bad thing.

Out in the living room, everyone had collapsed, dying of suspense, while Tibor tried to read the signs from the years he'd spent with the mayor. "No, it's bad," he said. "He'd never give him the job over the phone."

Finally, I pushed Hala away and gave her a thumbs-up sign so she would get out of my face and leave me alone. She opened the door and ran out into the living room and gave the thumbs-up. While the mayor finished talking, I could hear the guys whooping in the living room. Hala came back in, kissed me on the cheek softly, and said, "Congratulations." I walked out of the room just in time to see Jerry popping the cork from a bottle of champagne.

I quieted them down and then called Joe Dunne. He was devastated, as I would have been, but he took the news graciously. I told him that I had recommended to the mayor that if I got the job I wanted him to be the first deputy. I said that I was grateful he was staying on and we were going to do great work together.

Tom Antenen had promised the reporters he worked closely with that as soon as *I* told him, he would let them know. But the mayor had asked us to keep it secret, to keep it out of the press that night. So Tom—ever mindful of his ethics and his relationship with reporters—had requested that someone else call him, so he could honestly say I hadn't told him who got the job. In the excitement, I called Tom. But after he answered I remembered and handed the phone to Pitch.

"Thumbs-up," Pitch said.

At 2:00 A.M. I was free to start telling friends and family. As soon as the clock hit two, I called Jackie's house and asked her to wake up Joe. "Hey," I said. "I got it."

"That's great, Dad."

I called my parents and then spent the next couple of hours calling everyone I could think of. Finally I dozed off. As my mind faded into black, I was there again, alone in that dark room, I called for my mother. As my cries went unanswered, I began to panic. I began to sweat. I woke up and looked at the clock. It was a quarter to six.

It was useless. I had gotten all the rest I was going to get.

On the way to the press conference at City Hall, the news guys on the radio were still saying that Dunne was the favorite. It was amazing. Never in the history of New York had a story been kept as quiet as this. It wasn't until a few minutes before the ceremony started that word began to leak out.

We sat on the stage in the Blue Room of City Hall, my friends and family mixing with the reporters, cops, and officials. "Bernie has the thing so important as police commissioner," Mayor Giuliani said, "having served as a police officer, understanding the difficulties and split-second decisions an officer has to make. . . . He brings a quality of leadership." Then Safir handed me the century-old commissioner's shield, solid gold with five platinum stars and the seal of the city, the same shield that Theodore Roosevelt carried. The cameras flashed, and I looked out at all the faces—expectant and proud. I don't think people who strive, who are driven to prove themselves, pause very often to appreciate where they are, but I can honestly say, that was the proudest moment of my life.

MY first day was a blur. I had vowed to visit the officers, to go directly to the communities. "You'll see a lot of me," I said. From the press conference I went straight to an Honor Legion picnic in Brooklyn, for the families of officers who had died in the line of duty, and then to Midtown South, my old precinct, where I spoke to the patrolmen gathered at roll call. "Everybody in this room has the same opportunity," I told the officers. "The same opportunity that I had." I raced all over the city that Saturday, to neighborhoods and precinct houses. At 11:00 P.M., I ended up in the Five-O

Precinct, the one in my neighborhood of the Bronx, to speak at another roll call. A photographer from the *New York Post* was there and he handed me something. It was the front page from the next day's *Post*. My picture took up half the page, next to the words, "New top cop vows to listen and learn: YOU'LL SEE A LOT OF ME." It was startling, as if I knew now that this was real, that I was actually the police commissioner.

I was up the next morning, Sunday, at 5 A.M., and off again, doing another roll call. Later that morning I went down to One Police Plaza, my car driven quietly through the checkpoint, past the post officer and down into the base-ment, where I was brought up on a private elevator to the fourteenth floor, escorted on all sides, uniformed officers and civilians smiling and nodding or jumping out of my way as we strode down the narrow hallways. It was strange to see the looks on all those faces as I passed. I felt like a general on his way to the front.

Beyond the cubicles and the small offices, a plain door opened into an enormous but simple office, completely bare, nothing on the walls but one portrait, nothing in the room except an enormous desk. But it was not just any desk. It was Teddy Roosevelt's desk, sitting in the middle of this room with nothing on it but a sterling silver pen and ink set, and behind it, the one portrait hanging on the wall was that of Roosevelt himself.

"Commissioner?"

I stared, open-mouthed.

"Commissioner?"

"Yes."

Someone explained that the silver pen and inkwell had been given to the police commissioner for the capture of a notorious terrorist. In 1879.

"This is your phone," said another person. "There are thirty-six lines. Behind here is a private line for your wife and immediate family. The red telephone next to it is a hot-line to the mayor at City Hall, and that," pointing to a large box-type telephone with a key activator, "is a secure line in the event that you have to talk to the mayor or the president."

I stood there wondering why I'd need a secure line to speak to the president of the Patrolmen's Benevolent Association. Then it hit me. It wasn't for that president. It was for *the* president. "Oh," I said. "Sure." But I was thinking something else: How the hell did I get here?

Throughout Mayor Giuliani's deliberations, the criticism of me had focused on my résumé. As a cop I'd never made it beyond third-grade detective, a relatively low rank. My critics hammered away at that fact. Even though I was correction commissioner, one of the highest appointments in the city, the head of the black officers' fraternal organization and others referred to me as "Detective Kerik."

The other knock was that I didn't have a college degree—a requirement for the higher ranks in the police department. In my spare time I had been seeking a degree in labor relations from Empire State College, but I put most of my time into my work and was still a few credits away. My supporters argued that it didn't matter. I was also the first correction commissioner in decades not to have a college degree, and yet the halls of Rikers were littered with Ph.D.s who had failed trying to turn the jails around. The only pertinent facts were what I had accomplished—my abilities and my experience—not how many credits I had.

There are few cultures as closed and as incestuous as the NYPD. There is a whole language, a code of honor and loyalty. Outsiders are rarely embraced by the NYPD, and even though I'd been a cop, I took over the department at the end of August 2000 as a classic outsider, a person from another agency vowing to come in and make changes.

So one of the first things I did was to gather my command staff in the auditorium at police headquarters—450 people who held the rank of captain or higher. I explained that I had three objectives: improving and maintaining the historic drop in crime; improving morale among police officers; and easing tensions between cops and minority neighborhoods. I told them we had a rare opportunity, a chance to make the police department better and more responsive, to show people once again that the NYPD is a department of heroes. "That's where I'm going with the department in the next sixteen months," I said. "I promise to be tough, but I also promise to be fair. For those who are loyal and productive, you will be rewarded. For those who can't do what needs to be done, or who won't do what needs to be done, you may have to look seriously at your career."

It was dead still in the room, 450 pairs of eyes on me. I looked down in the audience and saw a chief who'd been overheard on the day of my appointment saying to some people near him, "He'll come and go like the rest of them. He won't last because none of us are going to work for a third-grade detective."

I remembered the Department of Correction, the disloyalty and the culture and how long it took to change. This time I didn't have that long. "Oh yeah, and for those of you who don't think you can work with a third-grade detective . . .

"Get over it."

24

TETERBORO AIRPORT

2001

LUIS "Louie" Lopez was a gifted undercover cop in Manhattan South Narcotics. We'd see each other in court and talk from time to time, and I got to know him better after he filed a request for assignment to the Drug Enforcement Task Force. One afternoon in March 1993, Lenny Lemer and I were sitting in the DETF office when we saw several cops running out the door with their bulletproof vests and gun belts.

"What happened?" Lenny asked.

"Louie Lopez from Manhattan South has been shot."

That day Louie had bought four pounds of marijuana from a T-shirt shop in Greenwich Village that also sold guns and drugs. When the field team was ready to move in, Louie returned with them. As an undercover he knew he shouldn't go back with the field team, but he also thought that since the suspects knew him already, they would open the door for him and it would be safer for his team. He wasn't wearing a vest when he approached the door, opened it, and yelled "Police!" The men inside began firing. Louie was hit twice in the chest.

He fell back onto his partner, a brave, quick-witted cop named Gary Combs. Gary grabbed him and dragged him out of the room, firing into the room to cover their retreat.

That day, Lenny and I jumped into my car and drove to Bellevue Hospital. There was a light snowfall and the streets were slick and wet. Mayor Dinkins was at the hospital, along with dozens of cops. We were approaching the end of the hospital corridor when we heard the screams. Horrific screams. I had heard those screams before, the night that Mike Buczek and Chris Hoban were killed.

The doctors had just delivered the bad news to Gary and the other members of his team. I grabbed Lenny by the arm. Neither of us said a word. We turned around and walked out. Louie Lopez was dead.

Louie's death was one of those things you never forget. At the time, I didn't know his partner, Gary Combs, but seven years later, in August 2000, Gary sat in the police commissioner's conference room at police headquarters with ten other cops, some of the best in the NYPD. They had been chosen as members of my security detail. For the next sixteen months they would shadow my every move and not just provide protection to my family and me but serve as my right hand, as extensions of the police commissioner.

"You're here because you're among the best," I told them. I explained that if they were looking for an easy ride, the best thing to do, personal and professional obligations aside, was to go back to their commands. I told them that the hours would be long and that I expected only the highest standards from those who worked in my office. I talked about some of my goals on crime reduction and boosting morale and community relations and told them that they would be instrumental in achieving those goals.

"On a personal note," I said, "if you work for me, you will wear white shirts and dark suits. Your shirts can't look like they were ironed with a hot rock. They need to be starched. Dark suits are not dark tan, dark green, or dark purple. They are dark blue or black. I don't want your shoes looking like they were shined with a Hershey bar. They should be highly shined at all times. Now, if you don't think you can live up to those standards, it's in your best interest to turn around and go back where you came from."

After my speech a couple of the cops asked to go back to their units, so we replaced them, and slowly my team took shape. More than half my detail was made up of great cops I'd worked with throughout my career, including Mike Jermyn from Manhattan North Narcotics and Hector Santiago and Donny Trenkle from Narcotics Major Case. I also picked up Bobby Picciano and Sean Crowley, both of them older and wiser, having more than lived up to the promise they showed as young cops on the Deuce. Sean had recently been promoted to captain and would serve as commander of the detail. Bobby Pitch was a Medal of Valor winner who had also earned the Combat Cross for a shoot-out in Times Square in which he was hit in the leg. And I chose Lynne Silver-Meriwether, a talented detective I'd worked with in Manhattan North.

The others I knew only by reputation. Craig Taylor, Mike Sanchez, and Vincent Gericitano were referred to me because of their intelligence, courage, and selflessness. I found Sonny Archer—who had been discovered by Jack Maple—working at Comp Stat.

The team was perfect, filled with cops who had shown integrity, courage, and honor. One newspaper called them "Bernie's Battalion." Another, responding to my detail's mandated sharpness, called them "The Fashion Police."

Many of the cops on my detail have a quality that has nothing to do with rank or with the countless medals they've received. Cops like Gary Combs and Mike Jermyn have experienced profound loss and displayed profound courage in their careers. It is a blessing to be surrounded by cops who remind me of the selflessness and bravery that cops are capable of achieving.

While I was putting together the detail, I was also putting together my staff and management team, to help run this massive agency of fifty-five thousand people and a $3.2 billion yearly budget. I was very fortunate to have Joe Dunne agree to be my first deputy and Joe Esposito, my chief of department. Their talent and integrity are tremendous even without factoring in the sixty-five years of experience they brought to the job.

To fill some of the other top spots I looked to the people who came up with me. I named Tibor a deputy commissioner for administration and Tom Fahey one of my press officers. From correction, I brought Tom Antenen to work with Fahey; L'Tonya Meeks and Eddie Aswad, two of the most loyal people I've ever met; and the tireless John Picciano as my chief of staff. In my first few days at One Police Plaza, there was a fresh-faced young guy named Chris Rising hanging around the office, and I eventually asked someone what he did.

"He's a speechwriter."

"I don't need a speechwriter," I said. "What do I need a speechwriter for?"

But I quickly found that five times a day I was in some situation where I needed research for a briefing, counsel on a legal matter, or advice on a community issue. Chris immediately showed why he came with the office. He was a great strategist, writer, and researcher, and as if that weren't enough, it turned out that he was a lawyer too. Within six weeks he was an integral part of my team—the special adviser and counsel for my office.

As I started making assignments at the top, some people had to leave. I replaced the chief of patrol, to give a fresh perspective to that office. And I replaced the assistant chief in the Bronx, where murders were up 51 percent. All told, that first month I promoted, demoted, or transferred fifty high-ranking NYPD officials.

As I looked at the amazing group of people that I'd gathered, it almost seemed as if I had met them along the way for just this purpose. Our task was overwhelming. We had just sixteen months to try to improve the culture of the NYPD. Yet I couldn't imagine a group of soldiers that I would rather lead into this battle.

* * *

THE most pressing matter was the deep rift between the NYPD and the city's minority neighborhoods. I didn't sleep the first month on the job. I went nonstop. I should have been ordained for the amount of time I spent in church. From Holy Name of Jesus Catholic Church on the Upper West Side to the Great Bright Light Missionary Baptist Church in east Brooklyn, I went from churches to temples to mosques, and from community group to community group, pledging to be more open and responsive. We sent out a five-page letter to all the houses of worship and community groups and held open forums at the Police Museum for precinct councils, community boards, and the clergy. We held six such meetings of 150 to 200 people at a time with the top leaders in the community. The response was wonderful, and in a short time I could feel the frost melting between police headquarters and community leaders.

Some people complained that this early barrage of meetings and outreach was simply attacking the *perception* that the NYPD treated minorities unfairly.

To those critics, I say . . . you're damn right. The truth is that a huge part of the problem *was* perception, the long shadow cast by the horrible Louima and Diallo cases. Very few people knew that while the NYPD was being branded as a violent agency, police shootings of civilians were actually going down—forty-one in 1990, thirty in 1996, nineteen in 1998, and eleven in 1999, the year Diallo was killed. Civilian complaints fell during the same period. While the reputation was getting worse, the department was getting better.

Saying that the NYPD's problem was one of perception does not minimize the fact that there was nevertheless a problem. But before I could make inroads with the substantive issues between police and black and Latino neighborhoods, I needed to create an atmosphere in which both sides could be heard and understood. So I ordered Street Crime Unit cops to attend community meetings in their neighborhoods. To fight the insidious arrogance and condescension that can often be mistaken for racism among cops, I instructed beat cops and commanders to be more polite and responsive. I demanded that station houses be more businesslike and that officers greet people respectfully as they enter the buildings. And I tried to lead by example, going to more community meetings than anyone.

Another misconception in New York was that the police engaged in widespread racial profiling—stopping and frisking people simply because of the color of their skin, without legal justification. The fact is that NYPD cops go where the crime is. And the sad, simple truth is that crime is highest in poor neighborhoods. Because crime rates are higher, those neighborhoods deserve—and get—the most police attention. Statistically in New York City, the poorest neighborhoods have a higher percentage of blacks and Hispanics. Most *victims* in those neighborhoods are black and Hispanic, and the suspects *they describe* are also most often black and Hispanic. The people stopped by cops should match up with the people described as suspects by the victims, and when you look at the numbers, that's what you see. I studied the data and this is what I found: From 1998 to 2000, violent crime victims described the suspect as black 61 percent of the time, and 49 percent of the people stopped and frisked were black. Hispanics were identified as suspects 28 percent of the time and stopped 33 percent of the time. Suspects were identified as white 8 percent of the time, but white people were stopped 15 percent of the time. These numbers tell me that New York City cops are stopping the people they are being told to stop, by the victims themselves. In the spring of 2001 I released these statistics on the NYPD's website. More than a few newspaper columnists and editorial boards took note and I was pleased to see the facts finally getting as much attention as the rhetoric.

But perception wasn't the only thing I needed to change. I implemented a new stop-and-frisk policy, which made cops more accountable by having them fill out a two-page questionnaire explaining why the person was searched. Before, cops often just wrote something like "suspicious behavior." Now they had a checklist for the kinds of behavior that could be grounds for stopping someone—everything from "bloodstains" to "furtive movements"—and cops had to record their reasons. In addition to providing a better means of analyzing patterns for possible misconduct or failures in training, these forms also require cops to give the person frisked an explanation for the stop. If cops take the time to provide an explanation, or do something as simple as asking the radio dispatcher to repeat the suspect's description so that the suspect can hear it, they can diffuse hostility and prevent resentment.

As we had done with TEAMS in the Department of Correction, my staff and I worked hard to make everything measurable, to make officers and commanders more accountable for their dealings with the public. Cops believed that community relations couldn't be measured. I think we showed in correction that you could measure anything.

I assigned one of my best people to the task—a brilliant woman, Maureen Casey, the deputy commissioner of policy and planning. We standardized the forms and procedures for all community issues and complaints and began gleaning numbers on the public effectiveness of cops, especially commanders. During the late 1990s, crime was beaten down using the Comp Stat formula, but now we applied the more extensive TEAMS system of analysis and accountability to community issues. Then we told precinct commanders that these numbers would be studied as carefully as crime stats and they were to file reports on issues in their precincts. They would also be required to attend monthly Precinct Community Council meetings and to sit down with local clergy and community groups. Amazingly, New York police commanders had never been trained in how to deal with community issues. We wanted them to defuse crises, but we hadn't trained them for it. So we gathered cops who had a knack for dealing with the public, and we put together a training program from their best practices.

The results of all these efforts were immediate and promising. Longtime critics of the police department called our efforts "a good first step" and "a promising beginning." Among professional New York activists, that was about as close to actual praise as we were likely to get. Editorial writers who had been bashing the NYPD for two years lauded our efforts: "the abyss between the NYPD and the city's minority community may be narrowing. . . . [Q]uietly, during the past five months, Police Commissioner Bernard Kerik has been building goodwill with local leaders."

The first major challenge to the improved relations arrived in May 2000, when NYPD investigators agreed with a New York State jury and the U.S. Department of Justice that the cops who shot Amadou Diallo hadn't broken any state laws or violated any federal civil rights statutes. Now it was up to me to decide what to do with them. There was a great deal of pressure from activists and police union leaders and everyone in between. A lot was at stake—the careers of these police officers and the trust of racial minorities throughout the city. The same *Daily News* editorial that praised me for building goodwill also asked, "if he decides not to discipline the four cops who shot Diallo, will his supporters bail out?"

In some ways, the decision was an obvious one. The officers had to make a split-second judgment call—shoot or don't shoot. They made that decision holding the honest—but mistaken—belief that their lives were in imminent danger. The results were tragic. But since they hadn't broken any laws or even any departmental regulations, they couldn't be fired. So the question became, could they return to the streets and do their jobs objectively? Would they hesitate when they shouldn't because of what had happened? Would they be accepted in the communities after twenty-seven months of unrelenting criticism? And the most important question of all, did I want these guys back on the street with guns? The obvious answer was no. So I grounded them, put them on desk duty and took away their guns and their shields. As I expected, I caught hell from both sides, but I think the majority of people agreed that it was a fair decision and the right thing to do. Even the usually hard to please *New York Times* noted in an editorial that "Police Commissioner Bernard Kerik made the right call. . . ." Trust me, in this job you don't get very many of those.

FROM the outside, the Amadou Diallo case was all about civil rights. But inside the NYPD, where cops were tired of being portrayed as racist and violent, it was also a morale issue. The overwhelming majority of cops are good people who have to endure the scorn that should be reserved for the handful of bad cops.

For an agency on a six-year run of unprecedented success in lowering crime rates, the NYPD was suffering from horrible morale when I arrived. Cops felt unappreciated by the public, unsupported by their bosses, and under suspicion from all sides. And of course cops always feel underpaid. Luckily, most people don't become police officers for the money. I'm not sure anyone who wanted to become a cop to get rich would be smart enough to pass the test anyway. Like all public servants, cops will always lag behind a hot economy—the kind that New York had in the 1990s. And as someone who took a 50 percent pay cut just to be a cop, I suppose I'm not terribly sympathetic to the issue of pay.

But if I couldn't do anything about police officers feeling underpaid, I could do something about their feeling unsupported.

As I toured precinct houses, I couldn't believe the sorry condition of much of the equipment and the buildings. Bathrooms didn't work. Furniture was shabby and dirty. The first week, we got a call from Pat Lynch, the head of the Patrolmen's Benevolent Association, complaining that the couch in his old precinct, the Nine-O in Brooklyn, was falling apart, the springs coming through the cushions. I went there and saw for myself that he wasn't exaggerating. I talked to Pitch the next day. "Do this," I said. Replacing a couch is a small budget item, but it's the kind of thing that can have a big impact.

But the worst problem we encountered was the shortage of patrol cars. We had five thousand cars for forty-one thousand officers—at least two thousand cars less than we should have had to do the most basic police work. One Brooklyn North detective squad had just one car. One cop attempting to serve a warrant had to go there and back on a city bus.

Everywhere I went it was the same story. And when I asked my deputy commissioner of management and budget why we weren't buying new cars, he kept coming up with excuses.

"So how many spare cars do we have?" I asked.

"None."

I just stared at him. "We have a three-point-two-billion-dollar budget and no spare cars? I may be stupid, but I'm not that stupid." For the next couple of weeks I drove around the city looking in lots that I'd noticed in my years living and working in the city. These lots are everywhere, tucked behind precinct houses and city buildings. The truth of public agencies like the NYPD is that people hoard. They stockpile things like cars just to keep them under their control. In a week I found 380 cars.

We had a meeting and I mentioned what I'd found. "What about these three hundred and eighty cars?"

"Oh, those are for special events. Like if the president comes, then we have some nice shiny cars that aren't all dented up."

While cops delivered warrants on city buses, we had 380 perfectly good cars sitting in parking lots in case the president got an urge for a slice of New York pizza. It was fucking crazy. So I put 120 of those cars away for special events and sent the other 260 cars out in the field, including two cars to the Brooklyn North squad.

The final straw came when I was told that there was no money in the budget for an emergency appropriation of thirty thousand dollars to replace the thirty-year-old telephone system for the fourteenth floor of One Police Plaza, a phone system installed when the building was built. We had a $3.2 billion budget and we couldn't find thirty thousand dollars?

A few days later I told Joe Dunne I was sending someone to interview for the job in management and budget. Joe asked if I was going to get rid of the guy in that job.

"I already did," I said.

With new financial people in place, and with the mayor's support, I started buying cars and getting them on the street. It was simple. We needed more cars. Yet sometimes, if direction doesn't come from the very top, if it isn't the express command of the police commissioner, then it isn't going to happen. Well, it got done. We put two thousand cars on the streets in less than twelve months.

Management for me is a combination of unblinking leadership, common sense, and finding the right people for the right jobs. If I have a secret, it's in the people who surround me. I get the best. I get the best bean counter. I get the best lawyer. I get the best computer guy. I ask them what their opinion is. And then I make the decision. When I started, I'd come into a meeting and some poor guy would set up his Power Point presentation and his projectors and pie charts on stands, he'd get ten slides into his presentation, and I'd say, "Stop that. Turn on the lights. Do you have a conclusion slide in there somewhere? Okay. Get to it. Tell me what it is, why we need it, and how much it costs." And then we'd move on to the next guy.

I've never been a big proponent of glorified panels to study issues that are clear. I don't appoint task forces or committees. If something is right, I do it. I do it that day. My staff quickly grasped this. One of my first days in my new office, I mentioned that I liked a certain plant. I came back from lunch and my office was a fucking jungle. There were plants everywhere.

Of course, replacing cars and couches was a good start,

but improving morale over the long term required some of the same measures that we took in improving community relations. So I opened my office to union leaders, commanders, and rank-and-file cops, and we asked them all how to do a better job.

Once a month I held a dinner in my office and invited a random selection of cops. They reminded me of myself fifteen years earlier, just street cops who came to work every day, wondering how to make their block or two a better place. While we ate, I asked them, "If you were commissioner for a day, what would you do to improve the city?" We went around the table and heard about the problems and hypocrisies that they spotted on the job every day. One cop said he'd like to have red lights put in his unmarked car. "I'm stopping cars by shining a flashlight out the window." The next day there were lights in his car.

When it became clear that more cops were needed to handle 911 calls on patrol, we transferred administrative people out of headquarters to help. To ease some of the burden on the detective squads, we added two detectives to every precinct detective squad, transferring them from Narcotics Units and the much-maligned Street Crime Unit.

As with community relations, the early signs were good. One Hundred Blacks in Law Enforcement, a hard-to-please fraternal group, gave me a B grade after thirty days. "He hit the ground running," Police Lt. Eric Adams, cofounder of the group, said. "He accomplished in thirty days what other individuals failed to accomplish in years." The other union leaders praised our openness and our desire to improve the working conditions of officers.

Community affairs and officer morale are terribly important, but in New York, public safety is the most important measure of a police commissioner. Everything else could be perfect, but if the crime rate goes up, the perception is that the commissioner has failed.

When I took over in the second half of 2000, the historic

crime reduction of the 1990s was beginning to level off. The most watched number—the murder rate—actually went up a bit in 1999 and 2000. This was the case across the country, as the economy slowed. Many experts said New York had cut crime as far as realistically possible.

As 2000 became 2001, the challenge was crystal clear: reenergize the New York Miracle, buck the national trend, and keep lowering crime in the city.

We jumped right in. One of the most effective programs was the expansion of the warrant squad, those officers who chase fugitives. Also key was the improvement of the Intelligence Division, helping different boroughs, divisions, and even jurisdictions share information to fight crime. Many of the steps we took in other areas also helped with crime fighting. New cars and improved morale encouraged officers to make arrests; better relations in the communities convinced people to help the police; and the new style of leadership may have set a tone that contributed to the improvement.

We also worked to cut response time—the time it takes cops to get to a call. When I took over, the average was twelve minutes—a minute slower than the year before and as high as it had been in nearly a decade. We attacked the issue through the improved Comp Stat process, monitoring response time daily and holding supervisors responsible. The response was tremendous. One supervisor tracked the busiest times in his precinct and then ordered more coverage during those times. Another manager lowered his precinct's response time from more than twenty-one minutes to less than sixteen. Citywide, in just six months, we cut the response time by 25 percent, to less than nine minutes.

After six months, our results spoke for themselves. While crime leveled off or rose in other cities, we cut the overall crime rate by 12 percent in the first half of 2001—more than twice the rate that it fell the year before. Crime fell in every major category, even the bellwether murder rate, which fell 13.7 percent in the first half of the year.

The mayor and I had identified three fronts and we seemed to be winning on all of them. As the *Daily News* reported, "Crime is still going down, the unions and line organizations love Kerik, the several police shootings that have occurred during his watch all appear justifiable and no cop has been seriously injured in the line of duty."

But while everything was going well in the spring of 2001, I found myself thinking back more than a decade, to 1988, and to a promise I had made.

MINUTES after I was sworn in as police commissioner, Ted Buczek came up to me, congratulated me, and asked a favor.

"Anything," I said.

"You have to promise you'll get Pablo Almonte back."

Back on that awful day in October 1988 Michael Buczek and his partner had gone into a building to help an old woman, but when they came out they encountered Daniel Mirambeaux, Pablo Almonte Lluberes, and a third man—allegedly preparing to rob some drug dealers. While Michael fought with Almonte, Mirambeaux shot the twenty-four-year-old cop and killed him. The two men then fled to the Dominican Republic.

For years Ted burned up the telephone lines trying to get the two men extradited to the United States for trial. In 1989 Mirambeaux was arrested and about to be handed over to the United States when he plunged over a railing in the Dominican prison and fell three stories to his death. It was ruled a suicide. But the other man, Pablo Almonte, remained on the loose for more than a decade. Twice he was located but remained under the protection of his brother, a general with the Dominican National Police. Almonte flaunted his freedom, running a large bakery and living in a gated compound with his family.

In the early 1990s, when I worked with him on the Michael John Buczek Foundation, I helped Ted Buczek write letters about the case. Throughout the decade he pressed politicians and police officials—even the president of the Dominican Republic—to extradite Almonte. Finally, in November 2000, Dominican police arrested the fugitive outside his bakery. I cautioned Ted Buczek not to get too excited. Until Almonte was on American soil, anything could happen. In the meantime, I pushed Bill Allee, my chief of detectives, to make sure we did everything we could to get Almonte back here.

Finally, on March 6, 2001, Pablo Almonte Lluberes was placed on a jet bound for the United States. Bill Allee called me, and I called Ted.

"Ted," I said, "remember how I told you all those months ago not to get too excited?"

"Yes," he said.

"Now . . . you can get excited."

It was cool and rainy as the jet taxied up the runway of Teterboro Airport in New Jersey. I stood on the tarmac next to Chief Allee, NYPD ball caps pulled down to our eyes, as the plane door opened and a dazed-looking Pablo Almonte descended the steps. The 250-pound fugitive kept his eyes on the ground and mumbled, possibly praying. His hands were cuffed and connected to a waist chain. Deputy U.S. Marshal Matthew Healey and NYPD Sergeant Tom Barrett, of the High Intensity Drug Trafficking Area Fugitive Task Force, escorted Almonte from the aircraft to a waiting van. Healey secured him in the rear seat of the van, then removed the handcuffs from Almonte and replaced them with his own. He handed me the cuffs that Almonte had been wearing.

"Here," Healy said. "I figured you might want these."

In the motorcade back to the city, I called Ted. "He's here," I said.

I drove straight to the Three-Three Precinct, which covered the area that Michael Buczek used to patrol. I arrived in time for the 3 P.M. roll call and stood up in front of a roomful of cops—a few of whom had served with Michael. I held up the silver handcuffs for them to see. "These are the cuffs that

Pablo Almonte was arrested in," I said. "Today sends a clear message to anyone who kills a New York City cop: We will hunt you down. We will bring you back to justice." The room broke into applause.

We had accomplished much in my first year as police commissioner—lowering crime, improving morale, and beginning to mend the rift with minority communities. But in all honesty, it would have felt incomplete without this moment.

A few weeks later Ted Buczek arrived in New York. Sgt. John Moynihan, who runs the Little League funded by the Michael John Buczek Foundation, had gotten together with David Hunt and Peter Walsh, the owners of a popular restaurant called Coogans, to celebrate Almonte's return. I could see it was a bittersweet day for Ted. I'm sure he was thinking of Michael, and of his wife, Josephine, who had recently died of cancer and hadn't lived to see Almonte extradited.

Ted and I hugged. I gave him the handcuffs. "These belong to you," I said. The room was filled with familiar faces: cops who had worked with Michael, people who had worked on the case, local politicians and civic leaders. They all cried, staring at the ceiling or covering their mouths as Mr. Buczek held those handcuffs in his shaking hands. Then he leaned over to me, his eyes welling with tears.

"Thank you," he said. "I'll never forget you."

I have found myself thinking often of Ted Buczek, of the amazing tenacity he showed in bringing home his son's killer. I would remember his courage just a few months later when I finally came face-to-face with my own injustice—buried thirty-seven years earlier in a place that I once called home.

25

OHIO

AUGUST 2001

LENNY Lemer hates to fly. So when my plane touches down in Columbus, Ohio, Lenny and Bobby Hom are already on the ground, waiting for me in the car they have driven from New York.

I climb into the backseat and stare out the window, losing myself in the flat Ohio landscape. Maybe somewhere inside of me, I've always known that one day I would have to come back.

It's been forty-one years.

We make our way east of Columbus until we hit the town of Newark, the last stop on my mother's descent. It's an old midwestern rail town of almost fifty thousand people, built along the slow-moving Licking River and the network of little streams, creeks, and runs that feed it.

Newark is a company town now, home of the Longaberger Corporation, a billion-dollar-a-year manufacturer and distributor of wooden baskets and other home and lifestyle products, which are sold through home parties. Longaberger inspires almost religious fervor among the people who buy and sell its products, and it is linked so strongly to Newark that the company's home office—a giant replica of a wooden basket built to scale as a seven-story building—is the town's most recognized landmark.

Longaberger even owns the hotel where we're staying, A Place Off The Square. As we stand in the parking lot of the hotel, preparing to retrace my mother's steps, I tell Lenny that I want to start at the end. I want to see 62 Brice Court, the apartment where—according to the news story and the death certificate—my mother was found murdered.

Lenny and Bobby shift their weight.

"What? What is it?" I ask.

Lenny says, "The house isn't there anymore."

"Okay, let's just go look at the street."

Lenny and Bobby catch each other's eyes.

"What?" I'm starting to get upset.

"You're standing on it," Lenny says.

The building at 62 Brice Court and whatever ramshackle buildings surrounded it have all been torn down to make way for this 117-room hotel and parking lot. I shiver as I realize we are standing on the very spot where my mother was killed. I look from one end of the parking lot to the other, trying to picture what it looked like then, what my mother would've seen as she staggered along this street.

Lenny has a detailed street map of old downtown Newark that shows which houses and buildings have been razed since 1964. Almost every building has the word "gone" written on it. Brice Court isn't even on the old map. It may have been little more than an alley, a cul-de-sac, or a dark court-yard off Church Street, between First and Second. We find Brice Court in the reverse city directory, however, with only three addresses listed on it: 58 Brice Court, the home of the enforcer and pimp Jay W. Allen; 60 Brice Court, which is listed as vacant; and 62 Brice Court, the house where my mother died and where William E. Byes is listed as the sole resident.

In the newspaper story, my mother's home was listed as $194^1/_2$ Main Street, maybe half a mile from where she died.

She probably walked back and forth between Main and Brice. I can almost see her shuffling down Second to Easy Street—I wonder if she saw the irony in that name—and then across a bridge over the Licking River and into East Newark.

Lenny reminds me that this was the part of town called Little Chicago because it was so wild and lawless, a stretch of old buildings filled with bars and hookers and drug dealers. There are still a handful of people who remember it that way. A bartender and a couple of women who worked as prostitutes remembered my mother as a tough street girl. The madam at the main brothel in town, the Chicken Shack, looked down on my mother because she "popped pills and begged for money" and turned tricks with black men. Ironically, the madam was black herself.

They remember William Byes and Jay W. Allen as mean and violent, but when Lenny tried to get the arrest records for the two men, he found that the county had destroyed all its old records. The handful of surviving former prostitutes and barmen that Lenny has tracked down all have different memories, but again they all agree on one basic fact: the cops never came into East Newark. They left it to thugs like Byes and Allen to enforce their own kind of street justice.

Railroad tracks frame East Newark like two lines of stitches; Little Chicago lay on the wrong side of two sets of tracks. The buildings that remain along East Main are two-story wood frame storefronts. The reverse directory gives an idea of the businesses that filled these buildings—used furniture stores and service stations, a Laundromat and beauty parlors. There were apartments above the businesses, and a good number of the apartments were above bars—Barney's Grill, the Church Street Billiards Club, the Cellar Door, and the Lucky Seven. The few people who remember my mother say that she drank and hooked mostly at the Lucky Seven, the toughest, meanest bar in a tough, mean town. On an old map, 194$^1/_2$ Main Street appears to be in the same building as the Lucky Seven, so the apartments must've been above the tavern. In the 1964 directory, 194$^1/_2$ E. Main Street has four apartments. Two of them are listed as vacant.

It's all gone now, of course. The buildings have been torn down, the strip cleaned up. What the police couldn't—or wouldn't—do, good jobs finally did. In the mid-1960s, companies like Rockwell and Owens-Corning moved into the area, along with the Newark Air Force Base, and when the economy turned around, Little Chicago faded into the prosperity of another middle-class American suburb.

Standing on the street, I realize that this Newark is far different from the place my mother haunted thirty-seven years ago. It's not just the people who are dead; her whole world is gone now.

PLAIN City is a speck of a town on the other side of Columbus, home to fewer than three thousand people. Lenny and Bobby and I go to the office of Police Chief Steve Hilbert, tall and solidly built, like the state trooper he once was. On his desk is a sign that catches my attention: "Teamwork is the fuel that allows common people to attain uncommon results."

One of the early mysteries in this case was exactly where my mother was buried. When I started searching for her, I knew she had died in 1963 or 1964 and I knew it was around Columbus. But we had no more information than that. Lenny and another NYPD detective, Jimmy Nuciforo, started checking every cemetery within a twenty-mile radius of Columbus, but found nothing. Eventually they tracked down my Uncle Bob's wife, who remembered my mother being buried in Forrest Grove Cemetery in Plain City, under the name Patricia Bailey. But when they called Chief Hilbert, he couldn't find a Patricia Bailey registered in the Plain City cemetery either.

Then, during a Memorial Day event, Chief Hilbert gave a

speech at the cemetery. Afterward, as he walked among the gravestones, he stopped to talk to someone and happened to look down. The stone at his feet read: Patricia J. Kerik. He was stunned. He immediately called Jimmy. "I found her."

It turned out that her brother Bob had registered her at the cemetery with Claude's last name, as Patricia Curtis. But my namesake, Bernard Bailey, made a decision that would lead me here today. He had the name Kerik placed on her gravestone, maybe because he believed that Donald Kerik, my father, was the best man in her life. But I think he must have had another reason in mind. He must have known that one day the son Patricia lost would come looking for her. And so she is buried under my name.

I ride in Chief Hilbert's car to the cemetery, Lenny and Bobby behind us. From the highway, a dirt road leads toward the flat, austere cemetery. It's eerily quiet as I get out of the car and follow the chief a few steps off the path. He stops in front of two small, simple stone markers set next to each other in the worn grass.

I step around Chief Hilbert, heart racing, stomach knotted. I read the name on the first stone.

John Bailey.

It is my mother's brother, beaten to death in 1952, three years before I was born. This is the Bailey family legacy— brutal childhood, drug and alcohol problems, horrible death, buried in a simple, unattended grave. Next to him lies the other stone, and I know what it says before I even look at it.

Patricia J. Kerik.

It takes my breath away, seeing her name etched in granite. I can't believe I've finally found her. If I were alone, I would fall down on her grave and cry. I don't know whether to feel sad or angry. Here I am, finally standing in the place where my mother rests. Here I am, so close to the woman who gave me life, and yet in some ways I'm no closer than I've ever been. Her grave doesn't help me remember her. It doesn't help me understand why she left or why she didn't come when I called for her all those nights. It doesn't explain the boy waiting in that dark room for his mother to return.

There are no answers here, just letters etched onto a cold, unadorned stone.

I look from my mother's grave to my uncle's and back. Tears fill my eyes, hidden behind my sunglasses.

Two lost souls are buried side by side here, forgotten in this small Ohio town. I am their first visitor in decades, a son who has come home to reclaim his past, to discover his own shadowed legacy, and maybe to give them—the abused child, the battered woman, the lost and forgotten— a voice.

I stand over the graves for a few minutes more, quiet and bewildered, desperately wanting to resurrect, in whatever way I can—by my words or by my deeds—the goodness that must have dwelled in their hearts, the innocence stolen from their lives, the love they never knew. I pray for them in silence.

Bless them, Father.

"HOLY hell," my uncle James Bailey says when I ask him to describe my mother, his sister Patricia. "She was a holy terror, a runner. And when your dad told me he was going to marry her, I said, 'Beware, brother, you're in deep shit.'"

James meets us at the front door of his apartment building. He is painfully thin and frail but with a trace of the Bailey fight left in him. The last of my mother's generation, he lives in a tiny apartment in a senior residence. It reeks of cigarette smoke. He is alone, estranged from his ex-wife and children. His kitchen counter is lined with small plastic bottles of medicine. My Uncle James confides that his stomach is in constant pain. What he cannot stomach is the horror of his own life.

"I guess you could say we didn't have any parenting," he begins. But he stops short of criticizing his and Patricia's mother, Dorothy Butler Bailey. "No, she wasn't violent. No, she didn't drink." Like so many abused children, he still feels some irrational need to protect her, to deny what happened to him. But within an hour he relaxes, and the awful stories begin: *My mother threw my brother down the stairs . . . My mother threw a shoe at me and hit me in the head and split it open . . . I had blood pouring down my face . . . She would hit you, kick you, anything . . . We were always getting beaten on.*

His hands begin to shake when he talks about his sister Helen. "She was a sadist. She'd beat us for no reason at all. She'd make us strip and beat us until we bled. She'd beat us with a metal belt buckle."

James and Patricia were the youngest, and after their father ran off, they caught the full force of their mother's rage and their sister Helen's violence. The Bailey home was a house of horror and neglect, and when Dorothy couldn't deal with her eight children, she'd dump the youngest two at a children's home.

When I bring up the children's home, James asks if he can smoke a cigarette. His hands twitch. This seventy-two-year-old man is reduced to a frightened five-year-old when he talks about that period of his life. Sixty-seven years later, the terror has still not left him.

"I hated the children's home. We were so young. I hated going there." He can't even talk about it. His face twists up, and over and over he says that the Bailey kids raised themselves. "There was never any love. Never."

Suddenly he points proudly to a picture on the coffee table in his tiny living room. It is his daughter Bobbee with her husband.

"She's very smart. She wrote me a letter. Do you want to read it?"

When he talks about his own life, he's like a child again, unable to comprehend the years that—according to his kids—he spent in an alcoholic rage. I ask about his five kids, my cousins. One daughter died of a heroin overdose at thirty-two, leaving behind two young, beautiful daughters. One of his sons, James says, "I threw out of the house. I couldn't have *that* with the other children."

That was his son's heroin problem. With no acknowledgment of his own drinking problem, James calls his boy "a hopeless addict."

And the other son? "I never saw him sober." Again he makes no connection to his own drinking problem. Instead he looks at me with childlike innocence, excited to have company. He is lonely, still haunted by the memories of 248 South Clarendon Street, the Bailey childhood home. He has spent a lifetime getting drunk and screaming into the night at his sadistic sister Helen, at his coldhearted mother, at his abandoning father—venting it all on his innocent wife and children.

In his chair, he is bent and frail. His mind wanders. He tells me about the scar tissue in his stomach and then wants to know why his daughters won't speak to him. He is desperate to reconnect with them, but he has no idea how. He doesn't know how to acknowledge the pain he caused his family, how to express his own complicated love. At seventy-two, he has what he thinks is his pride.

Yet he seems to want to close the gap with his daughter Bobbee. "Maybe I should call her," he says. "No. She should call me."

Before I leave, I ask once more about my mother, if there are lessons to be learned from her short sad life. He tells me what I've heard from others, what I already know.

"She was so smart, so beautiful. She was so much smarter than me. She'd get all A's. She'd take her books and study and she'd go to school and get all A's."

"How should I remember her?" I ask, searching for my own answer.

"She could have been someone. She could have really done something with her life. Drinking ruined her. It was the drinking."

"And—" The words catch in my throat. "What kind of a mother was she?"

"Beeze," he says earnestly, "you was a really good baby. A *happy* baby. But she wasn't a mother."

"But did she love me?"

"I don't think she loved anybody," he says. "I don't think she could."

IT'S startling to see her, my cousin Bobbee. She is James's daughter—my first cousin—and when we meet for dinner that night, I do a double take. She is very pretty, with dark hair and dark eyes and a tired, pained expression that looks all too natural. The resemblance is unmistakable. She looks just like my mother.

Bobbee fills in some of the gaps in the sad story of my Uncle James's family. After her sister died of a heroin overdose, Bobbee agreed to raise her two daughters. She hasn't seen her father in years. While her brothers have had chronic addiction problems, she and her sister Kelly have soldiered on. These two cousins of mine are clearly the survivors of this family, the strong ones. They witnessed hell and fought their way out. I know the road they've traveled. I've been there.

When dinner is over, we walk out to Bobbee's car. I catch myself staring at her. Out here, in the low and glowing evening light, she looks just the way I pictured my mother looking. Bobbee walks over to her car, opens the trunk, and gestures for me to come over. When I look in, I feel the air go out of me. Her trunk is filled with wrapped presents, just some small things: a few picture frames and photographs.

"These are for you," she says. "For all the Christmases. All the birthdays that we missed."

The sorrow that has been welling inside of me for the last twenty-four hours finally bursts. As she smiles and hands me the gifts, one by one, I have to bite my tongue to keep from crying.

* * *

I am quiet as we drive through a poor neighborhood in Columbus, Bobbee in her car behind us. Out the window something catches my eye and snaps me out of my thoughts.

"Stop!" I say to Lenny. "That's it!"

He swings the car back around.

It's the house my mother grew up in. I'm not sure how I know, but I know. I haven't been there since I was three or four, but it is definitely the house. We get out of the car and look at the address: *248*. That's it: 248 South Clarendon Street. It's been renovated, but somehow I know that I've been here before. Now, standing in front of it, I can imagine my mother inside. I can almost see her as a little girl in this house—feisty, bright, and beautiful, about to be destroyed piece by piece. No love or affection. No escape.

No one to protect her.

Bobbee has pulled up behind us, and she climbs out of her car, her eyes glued to the house in front of us.

"I remember," I say to her.

"So do I," she says.

The violence and addiction that were born in this house are the closest that she and I have to a shared family history. It is our legacy. It makes Bobbee think about her own house, about her father and the beatings that her mother took, about the years Bobbee spent trying to protect her siblings and her mother, trying to keep it all together. Finally, she looks away. "I can't forget what my father did," she says.

"You should call him," I say. But I stop short of asking her to forgive him. I don't know why.

THE phone rings in the car on the way back to the hotel.

"We've got a problem." It is John Picciano, my chief of staff. This has been a tragic night in New York. A bunch of cops were drinking outside the Seven-Two Precinct in Brooklyn the morning after their shift ended. Some of them moved on to a strip club and kept drinking, and then one cop, Officer Joseph Gray, got into his minivan and drove off. *After thirteen hours of drinking,* he ran a red light and hit a woman, her four-year-old son, and the woman's sister. All three were killed. The woman was eight months pregnant. The baby died as well.

"Jesus," I say. I tell Pitch I'll be on the next flight to New York—which unfortunately doesn't leave until morning. It makes me sick. A drunken cop has killed four people. One of *my cops* has killed four people. While I'm in Ohio dredging up a world in which alcohol ruined three generations, it is destroying more lives in New York.

Back at the hotel I pace around the room, my head spinning. I have never been one to look back at my life. I've always been too busy clawing ahead, just trying to survive. And the truth is, I've been *afraid* to look back, afraid to open the door to a room where a big part of me has been locked away for more than forty years.

But here in Ohio, all there is for me is the past. And this trip—which really began last spring, the day I finally decided to find my mother—has changed me. I set out to find her, and what I've found instead are the pieces of her that still live in me. I think about what everyone says when they describe her: *She could have done something with her life. She could have been someone.* And yet, when she needed them, where were all these people who believed so strongly in her?

I pull the curtains back in my hotel room and stare out the window at an old stone church across the street from the hotel. I wonder if my mother saw the same church from her own window on Brice Court.

Maybe you can only move forward for so long before you have to look back. When I look back, I see that from the scraps of my mother's sad life and from my own abandonment, I have built a man from the values I admire most: courage and strength and honor. And most of all: loyalty.

In just three months, Mayor Giuliani's second term will end and someone else will take over the city. For the past two months the newspapers have been filled with stories speculating that at least two of the candidates will ask me to stay on as police commissioner. According to historians, an incoming mayor has only retained the police commissioner once in the last hundred years. Although it would be flattering, and an honor to remain in command, I've made my decision.

When Rudolph Giuliani moves on, I plan to move on as well. Part of it is respect for the job he has done for the city, but there is another, more important reason: my unending respect and compassion for him, and my loyalty for what he has done for me. Not only did he take me from the level of third-grade detective and catapult me beyond my expectations, not only did he provide for me an opportunity that I could only dream of, but what he gave me, in the end, was something I had been searching my whole life. He believed in me. He had unconditional faith in me. At a time when I doubted myself, when no one else believed I could do it, he believed. He went against the advice of members of his own cabinet and said something that my mother and father and Mr. Johns and so many others never said to me: "You can do it."

That simple faith, I have come to understand, those few simple words can inspire a man to rise to any expectation. Those words can change a life. They changed mine. I think about my mother and how different her life might have been if someone, anyone, had simply said to her, "You can do it."

Leaving my post will be extremely difficult because I love the NYPD. I love its men and women, and I know I could do much more if I stayed at the helm.

But the New York City police commissioner is only as good as his commander in chief—the mayor. Without his support and backing and committed resources, the police department could fail, and as those who know me know, I'm not big on failure.

As I watched the recent mayoral candidates chase one another around the city during the election of 2001, I became demoralized by the way they used the police department—and the city's safety—as just another political tool. Some of these men have bashed the police department for their entire political careers, yet all of a sudden they emerge as law-and-order candidates. One minute they pose with former police commissioner William Bratton, and the next minute they're campaigning side by side with the department's biggest critic, Al Sharpton. To me, it's not about Bratton or Sharpton. It's about the candidates and their lack of ideals and principles, their lack of loyalty. Their political pandering is an indication of a lack of character, conviction, and manly honor. Their beliefs change depending on their audience and the weather: that is, on whether or not they'll get your vote.

This is not what politics should be. This is not what men and women should be. This is not what I will be.

So that's it for me. Although I'd die for this job, and at times nearly have, I won't work for someone who has little respect and regard for the men and women who go out every day and put their lives on the line.

When I get back to New York, I plan to announce that I will not serve as police commissioner under the next mayor. When I turn away from the window, I am at peace with myself.

EARLY Sunday morning, before my flight, I meet two Newark police officers for breakfast—Detective Steven Vanoy and Sergeant Ken Hinkle. They are the investigators Chief Pennington assigned to my mother's homicide. They've worked hard searching for new information in the case, for old witnesses and anyone who might have known my mother. But the years, booze, and drugs have left few witnesses. Most everyone is long dead. A few old prostitutes remember Patricia, and some of the women remember her death, but they don't want to talk about it. "Why do you want to dig that up?" an old madam asked the detectives. "Bury it and let it go. Forget about it."

Vanoy and Hinkle echo what Lenny and I found on our own: William E. Byes, who claimed to have found my mother having convulsions in his apartment, was a vicious criminal. His partner, J. W. Allen, may have been even worse, as one woman described him, "as violent and mean as a rattlesnake." Both were pimps with long histories of brutalizing women. You could say the same about Claude Curtis.

As we tracked them down, we found that Claude Curtis lived the rest of his life in Dayton, Ohio, and died in 1992. J. W. Allen and William Byes are dead too. Byes died in February 2000, just eighteen months ago.

And so the question continues to haunt me: What happened in the early morning hours of December 14, 1964?

Who killed my mother?

After looking back at her life and mine, I know that her death began long before that morning. It began with a brutal, lonely childhood, and it ended at the hands of three violent, evil men who beat the life out of her, bit by bit, until one of them struck the final blow. When I ask, "Who killed my mother?," I now know the answer.

They all did.

Dorothy Butler, Helen Bailey, Claude Curtis, William E. Byes, J. W. Allen. Every one of them killed her.

What disturbs me is that none of them are alive to answer for her death. I've spent a life in pursuit of justice, and yet in this case, in the case of my own mother, it will never come.

I thank the detectives for their time, dedication, and perseverance. I get into the car and begin the hour-long ride to the Columbus airport.

My mind fades, and exhaustion from the last forty-eight hours sets in. I close my eyes.

Light streams through the crack in the door. I hear voices on the other side. I can see her face. It is the face in the photo. I recognize her eyes. They are my eyes. I try to reach out to her. I want to talk to her. Just once.

I want to tell her I understand. I understand now why she wasn't there for me. Why she never came for me. I want to tell her it's all right. I want her to look at me. To see the man I've become. I want her to be proud of me.

For forty-one years I've been haunted by a dream of that four-year-old boy left alone in a room. I know where I was now. And I know why. And for the first time I can finally say to my mother: "I forgive you."

The phone rings in the car. I open my eyes and my mother's image fades into the trees and pastures along the highway.

It's John Picciano calling from New York. I listen to him and ask a few short questions. "When?" "Where?" "Does the mayor know?" I thank him and hang up.

"What is it, Commissioner?" Lenny asks.

"Jack Maple is dead."

Jack Maple—the architect of Comp Stat and much of the New York Miracle—has died of cancer. He was a real man, a true hero to me.

At the airport I board a plane for New York, settle into my seat, and stare out the window. Ohio shrinks beneath me. As we descend out of the clouds above Manhattan, I am still thinking about Jack Maple and about the other men who have been heroes to me along the way: *Keith Keller. Tibor. B. J. Turner. Jerry Speziale. Lenny Lemer. Hector Santiago. Eddie Aswad. John Picciano. Rudy Giuliani . . . and so many more.*

But one hero stands above all others. He's the man who quietly and without accolades went to Columbus, Ohio, and found me in that room—a lost four-year-old-boy—a man who fought for me and brought me home.

That hero was my father.

And now, forty-one years later, and knowing the truth, it

is my turn to take the hand of that four-year-old boy and lead him from the room. There will be no more light coming through the door in the darkness and no more fear.

I have finally come home.

AFTERWORD

GROUND ZERO

SEPTEMBER 11, 2001

AT 1:30 A.M. on Tuesday morning, I finished the final chapter of this book. I reread the last section and then leaned back and sighed, relieved that this emotionally draining journey into my past was finally over.

At 6:00 A.M. I got up and went downtown to my office at One Police Plaza, arriving a little before 7:00. I looked over the day's schedule of meetings and obligations. In bold letters at the top, it read TUESDAY, SEPTEMBER 11, 2001.

I went in the back room of my office to work out. At 7:45 A.M., just as I was finishing my workout, American Airlines Flight 11 was taking off from Logan Airport in Boston, bound for Los Angeles with ninety-two people. Thirteen minutes later, United Flight 175 took off from Logan for L.A.

I walked out to my desk to go over some paperwork, talked to John Picciano about the day, and then went in the back room to take a shower. It was about 8:25, and Flight 11 had just notified the ground that it had been hijacked.

Twenty minutes later, Hector Santiago, standing in the outer offices, heard a muffled explosion. He didn't think anything of it. A minute later he heard an NYPD Emergency Services officer scream into the radio, "An airplane just hit the World Trade Center!" Every phone in the office seemed to ring at that instant. Hector answered his own phone, and it was Lenny Lemer: "Hec, we got a plane just crashed into the towers!"

I was in the shower and the door to my back office was locked. Hector began kicking the door. "Boss! Boss!" Pitch joined him.

I came out in a towel, with shaving cream all over my face, and Hector and Pitch told me what they'd heard. "They're saying a plane hit the building," John said, "but you should see the fuckin' hole! It's unbelievable." Still, I thought it would be manageable. A small airplane—a prop plane, a twin-engine—had smashed itself harmlessly against the side of the building, tragic for the handful of people on the plane but certainly something we could handle.

I walked through the outer offices to my conference room, which had a window overlooking the World Trade Center. What I saw—what millions of New Yorkers and Americans saw—was terrifying. There was a huge hole in the top portion of the north Twin Tower and black smoke was pouring out of it. This wasn't a twin-engine plane. But at that point I couldn't grasp how a commercial jet would hit the tower. I didn't know, of course, that I was staring at the gaping hole caused by Flight 11—the 767 hijacked and flown into the building by radical Muslim terrorists.

"Get the mayor's car on the phone," I said. I was dressed in less than two minutes, and Hector, Craig Taylor, and I raced to the elevator and down into the garage, where we jumped in a car and began screaming through midmorning traffic toward the towers, lights flashing and sirens blaring.

My office at One Police Plaza is less than half a mile from the World Trade Center. We were there in less than three minutes. We squealed up to the intersection on the northwest corner of the World Trade Center, at West Broadway and Vesey, near the mobilization point that my chief of department, Joe Esposito, had set up. I climbed out, leaned back, and stared almost straight up to take in the top of the 110-story smoking tower. I couldn't believe my eyes. A black cloud poured from the side and the fire—fed by a full tank of jet fuel—was burning up to the higher floors. Debris was raining from the sky. We stared at larger things falling from the windows of the higher floors, and it took a moment to realize those were the bodies of people who had jumped. I can only imagine the horror of what they faced. The jet had hit between the ninety-sixth and one-hundred-third floors, and anything above those floors was an inferno. They could burn alive or jump to their death. A few held each other as they jumped. It is a vision that I will never forget.

I caught Hector's eyes. This was beyond anything we could have imagined. People on the ground were yelling and running away. Paper and ash and bits of debris were falling everywhere. People were moving away from the buildings, but way too slowly; encumbered with briefcases and bags, they were turning to look back. "We gotta get that building evacuated," I said. "Now!"

John Picciano and Chris Rising had arrived at the scene too, and we began trying to establish a command center, a place to coordinate our efforts for the next few hours. The city had built a $13 million state-of-the-art command center at the Office of Emergency Management in 7 World Trade Center, right next to the towers, and Mayor Giuliani was on his way to meet us there. But I wasn't sure how safe it would be, since it was so close to the tower.

It was just before 9:00 A.M., and a call went out over the radio for a Level 4 mobilization—the most serious situation we could have in the police department. I didn't know it yet, but it was about to get even worse. The second hijacked jet, Flight 175 with sixty-five people aboard, had just begun its dive into New York City airspace.

As we tried to set up a command center on the northwest side of the towers, over on the corner directly opposite from us—at Liberty Street and the West Side Highway—the captain of my detail, Sean Crowley, and my special assistant, Eddie Aswad, were scouting for a closer command post. They pulled their cars up on the sidewalk in front of 1 World Financial Center, a smaller building across the street from the south tower. It seemed to them the perfect spot: close, with a pedestrian skywalk that would provide some cover. Behind the Financial Center there was room to land a bird— a helicopter—and Sean ran behind the building to see what kind of access we'd have to the river if we needed to bring in police boats. "We got harbor!" Sean yelled to Eddie as they set up there.

And then there was a loud boom. It was 9:06.

On our side of the World Trade Center, I had just turned my back to give an order when I heard the explosion. I turned again. A massive orange and black fireball rolled up the side of the second building as smoke billowed and glass streamed from it. The second hijacked 767 had hit the south tower between the eighty-seventh and ninety-third floors. I had no idea what had happened.

First I had believed that a small plane hit the first tower, and then I thought that a passenger jet *accidentally* hit the first tower, but now, with both towers engulfed in flames, I could see this was something else entirely. Terrorism. I didn't know about the second plane, so for an instant I thought there were bombs. The second jet had entered on the other side of the south tower and debris was shooting out the side.

The wreckage was coming right at us.

"They're blowing up the fucking buildings!" I said.

What had been a light rain of debris was now a torrent. We turned and ran up West Broadway to get away from it. We were only a block away, right under the towers, and pieces of the building and the jet fell all around us. Behind me, a two-foot chunk of metal caught Hector in the leg and nearly dropped him to the pavement. Craig Taylor had pulled my car into a garage and he went to retrieve the car, stopping to pick up the piece that had hit Hector.

It was a piece from a jet engine.

We were a block away now and the radio traffic confirmed it: a second jet had crashed into the World Trade Center.

Now my mind raced as I tried to get my arms around this situation, tried to think of what to do. In the NYPD we have contingency plans for every imaginable problem. But this . . . was unimaginable. This wasn't a police job anymore. This was a military situation. We were under attack. I had to concentrate: What would the next target be? City Hall? The United Nations? Police headquarters? The Empire State Building?

"Hector!" I yelled. "Evacuate City Hall and One Police Plaza. Call Aviation and have them restrict this airspace. And get the military on the phone."

Hector, still smarting from the chunk of metal that had clipped his leg, was shaking his head and holding out a cell phone. "Sir, phones are dead! The radios are dead! We can't get anything!"

I looked back at the buildings, the flames burning their way up to the top, more desperate people leaping out to their deaths rather than enduring the 2000-degree inferno.

"Then let's get a command post. Right now!"

Whatever questions we had about the safety of the Office of Emergency Management bunker at 7 World Trade Center before, now we knew it wasn't safe. We were on Barclay Street, a block from where we'd just been standing. A man ran out of the main floor of 75 Barclay Street and told Hector that he was a retired cop and that we could use his office. Hector ran in to make sure the phones were set up.

The mayor's car was racing down West Broadway toward the scene. I flagged him down. "They're driving planes into the buildings! We gotta get everyone out of City Hall," he said.

There was so much going on, so many people yelling and asking questions. And still the bodies were falling. The mayor and I talked about setting up a command post, and someone suggested again that we go to the bunker at the Office of Emergency Management in 7 World Trade Center. The mayor and I agreed that it wasn't safe, so we walked toward the West Side Highway, where firefighters and cops from the Emergency Services Unit had set up a deployment area and were suiting up to go into the buildings. A steady line of them was moving toward the burning towers. We saw Peter Ganci, the fire department's chief of department; William Feehan, the first deputy commissioner of the fire department; and Father Mychal Judge, the beloved sixty-eight-year-old fire department chaplain. We spoke to them briefly about the rescue. All around us, brave firefighters were putting on their gear, our cops were doing the same, and the Emergency Services guys were pulling on their masks and marching off toward the buildings. I passed Sergeant John Coughlan and some other ESU cops. "Be careful," I said. All around the buildings, police officers—like their brothers in the fire department—were ignoring the danger and leading people from buildings and out of the area.

We walked north on West Street as the ESU teams started off toward the buildings or the Office of Emergency Management across from the north tower. In ten minutes those courageous men and women would all be lost, along with so many more.

The fires were burning up the buildings, and the smoke and debris were getting worse. I knew the mayor shouldn't stay there any longer.

"Mayor," I said, "we've got to get you out of here and set up a command post."

Someone again suggested City Hall. I was worried about City Hall, and Tony Carbonetti, the mayor's chief of staff, agreed. "City Hall could be a target," he said.

But still people suggested going there. Hector leaned over my shoulder. "Boss, don't let 'em go to City Hall."

There was a rumbling. Another jet? "We got a third plane coming in!" someone yelled. There wasn't another jet, but by then Hector had grabbed me by the collar and was pulling me north, away from the burning buildings. The mayor was running next to me. I was thinking about the cops down there and wondering how a city police commissioner goes about getting military air support. I told Hector to call Aviation and have them notify the military. I wondered how many planes the other side had. And I wondered who the hell the other side was.

Our immediate problem was setting up a command post, someplace close enough that we could keep an eye on what was happening and far enough removed that the mayor wasn't in danger. We moved back toward the building on Barclay Street, and I sent Hector and Pitch inside to get it ready. I talked to Chief Esposito on the radio to make sure our people were being deployed at the scene and to see if he needed anything.

We moved into a small internal Merrill Lynch office at 75 Barclay, two blocks from the World Trade Center, where I huddled with the mayor, Joe Lhota, the deputy mayor for operations, Tony Carbonetti, and Denny Young, the mayor's counsel. "We need to get the president on the phone," Mayor Giuliani said. "We've got to get the Department of Defense." Then Joe Dunne, my first deputy commissioner, limped in. I thought of his courage and dedication. He was on crutches because of a severed Achilles tendon, and still he had come in to work.

But while we had a number of top officials, we didn't have any federal numbers with us and we weren't sure we had any phones that would work anyway. Throughout this, I was very impressed with the mayor and his cabinet. Patty Varrone and John Huvane, his detail, were unflappable. No one panicked or showed any sense of defeat. It was the same with Joe Dunne, Joe Esposito, Hector, Pitch, and the rest of my guys. We just went to work. Unfortunately, at that point, there was absolutely nothing we could do to get a complete picture of what was really happening. We couldn't even find a television to turn on the news to see what the media was reporting. Finally, someone found a radio.

Then in the background someone yelled, "They hit the Pentagon!" I thought these people had lost it; there was no way. I walked into the office where the mayor was on the telephone, and Joe Lhota and Tony Carbonetti signaled for me to be quiet. "The mayor's on with the White House," they said. He was talking to an aide to President Bush. As the mayor hung up, he had a puzzled look on his face.

"What's wrong?" I asked.

"The Pentagon has been hit, and they're evacuating the White House," he said.

I didn't have time to get my mind around what he was saying, because a few moments later there was a low rumbling that sounded like it came from everywhere at once. "What's that?" someone asked. The building shook. It was 9:55 A.M. Outside, 2 World Trade Center leaned slightly to the side and then began coming down, floor by floor.

There was screaming outside. The windows around us began popping like popcorn. *Boom! Boom! Boom!* "Everybody, hit the deck!" someone yelled.

And then there was a great whooshing explosion— *FWOOM!*—as the south tower pulled into itself and then blasted smoke and debris out in every direction, as if it had taken a deep breath and then blown it out. In 75 Barclay people dove under desks and tables.

"Move!" someone yelled, and again Hector was pulling me, through the hallways toward the back of the building. I could hear the rumbling and smell the smoke. People screamed. We ran toward the back of the building, Hector calling into the radio the signal that I was in danger: "Code black! Code black!"

ON the West Side Highway, Sean Crowley and Eddie Aswad had just about finished setting up their area for the command center. Sean looked up the West Side Highway and saw the cops in the Emergency Services Unit putting on their gear and getting ready to go into the buildings. Like another member of my detail, Bobby Picciano, Sean used to be in that unit, and he felt a tug of responsibility—he should be going with them. He'd responded to the bombing of the twin towers in 1993, in which six people died and more than one thousand were injured.

Eddie looked over and saw firefighters putting on their masks and oxygen tanks and moving single file toward the burning towers. He also saw Glenn Pettit, a young video photographer who works for the police department; the camera on his shoulder was trained on the south tower.

"I'm gonna get closer," Glenn said.

"Just watch yourself," said Eddie. "Be careful."

Eddie and Sean met in the street to make sure they were ready to start up the command post. Like all of us, Eddie and Sean assumed that since the towers had survived the crash of the airliners, they were structurally stable. But unbeknownst to everyone, the fires inside were being stoked by as many as twenty thousand gallons of explosive jet fuel from each jet's tank, running through the building and burning at 2,000 degrees—until the steel itself began to give way.

About ten seconds after Glenn Pettit walked away, Eddie and Sean heard the rumble.

Someone yelled, "Here it comes!"

Eddie turned to look at the south tower dissolving from the top into a massive column of smoke. Sean didn't need to turn. The look on Eddie's face was enough. They both ran. They crossed the street and ducked behind their cars, then ran toward the pillars that held up the sky bridge leading to 1 World Financial Center. Behind them was the thick, double-paned glass wall of the building. As they crouched behind the pillars, other people ran toward them, seeking shelter as the first wave of debris flew at them—chunks of concrete and steel; and then the second cloud rolled over them—black dust and more steel.

The people hiding behind the pillars had nudged Eddie against the glass wall, and he was struck by debris and by people who banged into him as they were hit. The air grew thick and stifling.

Eddie and Sean knew they were going to die.

The only question was whether they'd be killed by a blow to the head from a piece of steel or by choking in this cloud of soot and blasted concrete. The debris pinned them against the glass wall. Elsewhere every window had been blown out, but for some reason this one thick pane of glass held, and Eddie could hear—in the darkness—people banging their fists helplessly against it, trying to break into the building.

The debris was rolling in like waves, coming up to their knees and their thighs. They worried that they'd be buried by it. They were suffocating. In what they knew would be their last moments, both men thought about their children. Eddie said their names to himself so they would be his last thoughts.

Still the window behind them held. Eddie reached down for his gun, as did Sean and a couple of other cops huddled behind the pillars. Eddie couldn't get to his gun because he was covered in debris. One of the guys was finally able to fire over his shoulder, up into the thick glass behind them— two shots, three, four—until the glass cracked, buckled, and gave way. The people hiding behind the pillars surged over the window frame and into the building. The air inside was a thick charcoal gray.

"Sean!" Eddie called as he bumped into someone.

"Eddie, is that you?" They linked arms and began moving through the darkness, their hands in front of their faces. They were in the ornate lobby of the building and crashed into palm trees and desks, slowly making their way through the littered and dusty wasteland.

It was eerily quiet in there. They came to a wall and then a kind of round glass with the strangest thing in the center— a pie-shape bit of fresh air. They had found a revolving door that hadn't been turned and so there was a pocket of air that didn't have any of the choking dust in it. They pushed through the revolving door, gulping the air, and came outside—where it was darker than it had been inside the building.

They continued walking slowly, arms linked, as the air cleared just a little bit. They didn't see any other people. They walked until they came to the North Cove Yacht Harbor. A boat was there, and its captain looked at them as if they were ghosts. He gave them bottles of water and they tried to wash the fiberglass and dust from their eyes, but there was so much concrete in the dust that it muddied up their throats and faces.

People began gathering at the docks, and Eddie and Sean took charge, loading them onto the boat to be ferried across the water to New Jersey. There were so many people that they limited passage to children accompanied by a parent and to the injured.

Eddie saw the NYPD physician, Greg Fried, hunched over and clearly injured. "We gotta get you on the boat," said Eddie, but Dr. Fried said no, he had to go back and help people. Eddie and Sean grabbed him, and put him on the boat. Later, when he arrived at the hospital, the doctors told him that his blood pressure was so low he would have died in an hour. Eddie and Sean saved his life.

The boat that Eddie and Sean had found ferried two loads of people over to New Jersey, and they had just pulled up to the shore for another boatload when they heard the rumbling again.

The second tower was coming down, with the same thundering cloud of smoke and grit. The captain of the boat slammed the throttle in reverse and the boat backed away from the shore. Eddie watched as black smoke swallowed everyone on shore.

ON the street near the trade center, Craig Taylor was parked next to the mayor's driver. Both cars were facing the towers. When the first one started to go, people in the cars around them panicked, jumped out, and ran away on foot. But Craig slammed his car into reverse and backed up West Broadway, the mayor's driver right next to him, as the black cloud surged toward them. They both made it to safety.

At the same time, Mayor Giuliani, Joe Lhota, Denny Young, Tony Carbonetti, the mayor's communications director, Sunny Mindel, other members of his cabinet, Joe Dunne, and I were being led by our staffs through the narrow corridors of the lower level of 75 Barclay Street. In one dark hallway, we looked down to see smoke coming at us and we moved another way. We went down one corridor that was a dead end and then another, until finally a door opened and two janitors appeared almost from out of nowhere. They led us through a maze of hallways beneath the street and up into the lobby of a building on Church Street, where we checked to make sure our people were okay, then tried to figure out what to do next.

A man walked into the lobby, and I didn't recognize him at first. He was covered with ash, his whole body gray and white. His eyes were brimming with blood, and there was a long, deep cut on his hand. It was Tibor. We sat him down and got him some water. He'd come down to help and had been on the street when the buildings collapsed. I knew he was one of the lucky ones. We got Tibor settled, and started out again, hoping to find someplace to set up headquarters and begin getting a handle on this disaster.

We came out on Church Street and found ourselves in a gray fog of ash and smoke. Paper was coming down everywhere, like some horrible ticker tape.

We began walking north and east, joining thousands of people, a ragtag parade of people covered in ash and soot, looks of sheer disbelief on our faces, the cloud at our backs. Slowly we emerged from the ash and looked back to see gray knots of smoke where the towers had once stood. I couldn't believe what I was seeing. I didn't even know yet that the second tower had come down.

As we walked, people joined us, reporters who wanted to question the mayor and me, and regular New Yorkers who were just looking for something to join. It was a terribly sad and devastating moment, and yet it was powerful to see the way people reached out, comforting one another, offering water—anything. With the worst thing people could imagine smoking behind us, we were witnessing the best that people had to offer—their compassion and help. At some point, the fire commissioner, Thomas Von Essen, was with us, a vacant look on his face as he wondered how many men and women he might have lost when the buildings came down.

As we continued up Church Street, we called to the people around us, "Keep moving, keep going north. Get as far from the buildings as you can."

I kept thinking, How many more targets are there? We had to get somewhere and start figuring out what we were going to do. At one point, an F-16 flew overhead and we all looked up. It was quiet, and then someone from the mayor's office said, "I think that's one of ours."

Hector, Pitch, and I walked with the mayor and his staff. As we walked, we debated whether any place might be safe to set up a command post. We considered businesses and schools and precinct houses. Hector said we should go to a low-income housing project; whoever was crashing jets into our buildings would never bomb the projects, he argued.

Someone else suggested a hotel—the Tribeca Grand. We walked into the lobby. The mayor and I both looked up at the same time. The whole top of the building was made of glass. We imagined that glass flying in an explosion, and shook our heads. We went back out in the street and continued our march north.

Finally we came to a firehouse at the corner of Houston Street and Sixth Avenue. It would work, but we couldn't get in. The firefighters had all gone down to the World Trade Center and had locked the building behind them. Hector broke his knife trying to get us in, but finally we jimmied the lock, got the door open, and burst in. There were thirteen of us, a dusty, tired group of people trying to get the city back on its feet.

For about an hour this was what the top echelon of city government was reduced to, a dozen people covered in soot, standing behind a guy as he tried to break into a firehouse.

Still, I was amazed at the focus and strength of these people. Military jets were streaking across the sky, and for the first time I wasn't feeling as hopeless as I had for the past hour.

Once we got inside, we found two telephones that worked, and for the first half hour our only other source of communication was the police radio. But finally we got more phones set up and we began to organize the city's response. When there was a free phone and a free minute, Pitch called his wife to tell her he was fine, but when she answered he abruptly hung up, afraid that he would lose his composure. He didn't want her to worry. He had to call back twice before he could tell her that he was okay. He asked her to pick up the kids from school. "They're not in any danger," he said. "Just go get 'em, okay?"

I didn't realize it, but during our retreat north police headquarters had no idea what had happened to us. The last anyone had heard of me, I was in the area that was now a blast zone, the buildings just on the fringe of the World Trade Center. And no one could raise me on the phone.

For twenty minutes I was missing, but now I contacted the office and began to find out how the department had responded and to hear about my staff and my detail. I didn't know about any of them other than Tibor, who had gone to the hospital to have his hand treated, and Hector, Pitch, and Donny Trenkle, who had been with me the whole time. There were early reports that we'd lost Joe Esposito, who had been at 7 World Trade Center when the buildings collapsed, although he survived and continued to work.

In the interim, the entire New York Police Department had mobilized. All the procedures we had in place kicked in, and cops went where they were needed and acted with amazing courage and resourcefulness.

I wasn't surprised to find out that the cops in my detail were in the center of it all. Guys like Eddie and Sean acted with heroism, and everyone in my detail was right there, ready to put themselves in danger as well. I was proud of each and every one of them. Vinnie Gericitano and Mike

Jermyn, for instance, had been at the airport for separate flights and immediately raced back to help. Sonny Archer caught up with us at the firehouse, and John Picciano told him to take the department priest, Father Robert Romano, over to Bellevue Hospital to see if anyone needed spiritual counseling or last rites.

But, in a glimpse of the horror to come, there just weren't very many injured people at the hospitals. So Sonny drove the priest down to Vesey Street, where I had just been. It was still raining white ash and paper, and fires were burning in the rubble. But it was so quiet. There were overturned fire trucks, burned-out cars, but not a soul was around. That's when Sonny saw a bit of blue shirt under a pile of rubble. He pulled the rubble away. It was an emergency medical technician. The man was dead, his chest split open.

Sonny and Father Romano walked to the West Side Highway, where so many cops and firefighters had staged their rescue efforts. They passed only a few people—ghosts like Tibor, dazed and covered with gray-white ash.

Then they came to a car from the Six-Two Precinct; it had been crushed by falling steel girders. A sergeant covered in ash was staring at the car. "I was in that car," he said.

"Your guys," Sonny asked, "are they okay?"

The sergeant wouldn't look away from his car. "My nightstick is in the car."

Sonny gently took him by the arm and led him away "Sarge. Don't worry about your nightstick. Come on."

It was so desolate and dead; they could smell it, feel it on their skin. Someone approached Father Romano, recognized him, and told him that he had been with Father Judge just before the building came down. Father Judge was giving last rites to a firefighter who had been struck by a falling body.

"Father Judge is dead," the man said. Father Romano began to cry.

THE firehouse had been a good emergency command center, but we needed something bigger and more secure. I suggested the police academy, a centrally located building of modest height and design, and an unlikely target if the terrorists should strike again. It had phones and meeting rooms and could be secured easily.

So our little emergency government piled into cars and moved over to the academy to begin the work of responding to the greatest crisis in the city's history. We gathered other city officials there, coordinated our emergency response, and made sure we had cops where they needed to be.

We also made sure the airports were locked down and the airspace closed. We didn't know how many casualties we might have; some people were saying ten thousand and more. We wanted a chance to stop the bleeding even before we figured out how to begin protecting and healing the city. I think that process began with the press conferences, where we tried to calm fears and let people know what was happening. We did not sugarcoat things—"It was the most horrific scene I've ever seen in my whole life," the mayor said—but showed Americans that we were not defeated by so cowardly an attack.

Like everyone else, I was completely impressed with my friend Rudolph Giuliani. And I was proud, but I certainly wasn't surprised. We tend to take a great leader for granted, but in times of crisis we don't have that luxury. I know the last year had been hard on him: a difficult divorce, questions about his relationship with Judith Nathan, his battle with cancer, and his shortened run for the U.S. Senate. It was a horrible year made worse by the constant glare of the New York media.

But now, with the city literally under attack, Rudolph Giuliani was the mayor he'd always been, solving problems, inspiring and comforting not just New Yorkers but Americans everywhere. It made me proud to serve next to him.

The police department had no shortage of its own problems. We didn't know yet how many police officers had died in the collapse of the towers. The telephones were out at police headquarters, as were most cell phones and pagers. That meant all communication had to go over a crowded radio system. We quickly ran phone lines into the police academy and began doing what we do best—solving problems. That afternoon we deployed about a thousand officers to southern Manhattan to help at the scene, and we sent about ten thousand others—detectives and officers from special units—to handle patrol duties elsewhere. One of the first phone calls that Mayor Giuliani made was to the head of the New York Stock Exchange, Dick Grasso, to find out when he could reopen the exchange. The mayor was determined to send the terrorists a message: YOU FAILED.

And the people of the city cooperated. Luckily, even criminals aren't immune to the shock and depression that came with that horrible attack. Crime dropped 30 percent in the days that followed, and there were only a few incidents of looting.

We worked all afternoon and evening getting a handle on things, shutting off the southern part of the city, getting rescue workers in as close as possible, coordinating with the federal government. We had been doing telephone interviews with reporters, but we knew it was important that people see the mayor, that they realize the city was still working. We had press conferences but asked the media to keep our whereabouts secret, in case there were other attacks planned. For five years Mayor Giuliani had led the nation in disaster preparation—and had often been criticized for it. But now our security changes after the 1993 World Trade Center bombing and our preparations for the millennium celebrations were paying off.

At 11:15 P.M. the mayor and I went to Bellevue Hospital to visit the first victims, people with horrible burns, broken bones, cuts, and internal injuries. Among those we visited were a Port Authority police officer and two firefighters. But there simply weren't as many injured patients as there should have been.

Next we went to St. Vincent's, the hospital nearest the twin towers. It was the same story. Dozens of doctors and nurses stood around in scrubs outside the hospital doors, waiting for injured people to treat. All day triage stations, clinics, ambulances, and hospitals waited. Boats stood ready to ferry the wounded to New Jersey. But the people never came. That was the really hard part. It was eerie, seeing just how *few people* were being treated at the hospitals. In the 1993 bombing of the World Trade Center, about one hundred eighty people were injured for every person killed. Here the ratio was a lot different.

As horrible as the attack was, it's terrifying to imagine what could have been. The first building was struck at 8:48 A.M., and while many financial workers had been at their desks for hours, attorneys and many other professionals hadn't come to work yet. It was also the first day of school for many parents and primary election day, so some people were dropping their kids off or voting. If the attack had come two hours later, there might have been thirty thousand people in those two towers, and who knows how many might have died. While we must focus on those thousands who lost their lives, the stories of calm, steady evacuation from the buildings are heartening, and the bravery of firefighters, cops, and regular citizens saved thousands of people.

Then, just after midnight, the mayor and I began to make our way south through Manhattan, toward the fallen buildings, toward what would become known as Ground Zero.

A thick layer of ash and paper covered southwestern Manhattan for blocks on all sides of the World Trade Center. On the streets approaching Ground Zero, cars had been crushed by falling debris, store windows were blown out, traffic lights crumpled over. The buildings all around the World Trade Center were damaged, their windows blown out, huge steel beams from the towers thrown through them like spears. Six other buildings near the World Trade Center had collapsed and a dozen more had suffered serious, maybe even structural, damage.

Everywhere there were piles of ash and paper that had been blown out of the trade centers—memos, résumés, orders, business cards, legal documents.

Spotlights in the center of the wreckage cast an eerie glow on the rubble as we got nearer. Piles of steel girders and concrete smoked, and fires burned deep in the core, where the two 110-story buildings had been reduced to piles of rubble six stories high in some places and at nearly ground level in others. Steam rose from the piles, and smoke from the seams in the rubble. Every time a thick girder was removed, oxygen fed the smoldering fire, and FDNY trucks doused the flames with thousands of gallons of water.

Pictures can't fully convey the enormity of the devastation; the thickness and weight of those steel beams, for instance, twisted and tossed aside like toothpicks, simply elude them. And even the numbers—by some counts, more than a million tons of rubble over sixteen acres—are inadequate to the task. When I finally saw it firsthand, all I could do was put my head in my hands.

As we walked around the massive piles of debris, the mayor and I tried to comfort firefighters and police officers. They were working around the clock because so many friends and coworkers were down there. I understood how they felt; those were my people down there too, my friends. We thanked the tireless search and rescue workers. Slowly we made our way closer. At the horrible center of the destruction, rescue workers formed long lines—bucket brigades—and sifted through the rubble by hand, filling five-gallon orange-and-white buckets that were then passed back through the lines. When any sort of gap was found, rescue workers descended with flashlights and outdated maps of the stores, subway tunnels, and basements that once lay beneath the towers, now just a tangle of steel and disappointment. Workers covered the mounds of debris, and in the lines of people I saw something familiar. I remembered, as a kid, lying on the ground and watching ants swarm over a hill. That's what it looked like. Body bags sat in boxes nearby, ready in case a person or some part of a person was found, and giant bins were used to collect anything that looked like a jet engine part or some other piece of evidence.

Hundreds of cops were at the scene, and I watched them with pride as they helped the rescue effort, looking for evidence and protecting the scene from looters, sightseers, and potential threats. We still didn't know exactly how many of our officers were buried in the rubble; the numbers ran between twenty and forty. Firefighters slumped against walls or sat crying, thinking about the hundreds of brothers they'd lost.

All over the site rescue workers climbed over mounds of wire and steel and dust, peered into destroyed cars and devastated buildings, desperately looking for people but finding more parts than actual bodies, more bodies than survivors. Even that first night it was clear that finding survivors was not going to be easy.

People have struggled to find a way to describe the devastation at Ground Zero. Some have said it resembled a movie set or a war zone or some vision of Armageddon. Those things are true enough, but when someone asked me what it looked like, I didn't hesitate to find another picture in my mind.

"Hell," I said. "It looks the way I imagine hell would look."

The mayor and I were quiet when we saw 7 World Trade Center, where the Office of Emergency Management had once stood. Tuesday afternoon the building had collapsed. We could see that if we had gone in there, we would have been among the dead. Behind it, at 75 Barclay, where we'd been working when the south tower came down, the windows were blown out; outside, the streetlights were bent and cars demolished. The van in which Joe Dunne had been riding now rested on a pile of rubble about thirty inches high. This was the war zone, the buildings a block, two blocks, three blocks from the towers. The towers were just a field of rubble, unrecognizable as buildings; the buildings surrounding the World Trade Center were the ones that looked like they had been attacked.

That morning, I went to bed at 3:30 A.M. on the couch in my office, hoping to catch a couple of hours of sleep before I headed out again.

I remember lying there, staring at the ceiling, hearing every airplane that passed overhead, every creak in the floor. I could visualize the TV pictures of those towers coming down, and I started to put them together with what we had gone through on the ground: the debris shooting from the side of the building when the second plane hit, the thunder of smoke and debris when the south tower fell to the ground. And it dawned on me—for the first time, really—that we had almost been killed twice; so many of my staff and detail had nearly died, and yet we were the fortunate ones.

All day I had organized and ordered, reacted and responded, and now I lay back and considered the magnitude of what had just happened to my city. We had worked so hard to make New York safe, and we had accomplished so much, and now, in one day . . . this. In one day, terrorists had killed as many as six thousand people, half the total murdered last year in all of the United States.

I felt waves of sadness roll over me, followed immediately by anger—rage toward the people who had done this, the religious zealots who somehow believed that killing innocent American civilians would further their goals. I hoped our country would see this as a military attack on our people, and that we would respond with the full force of the U.S. military to make sure that our people were avenged, and that this would never happen again.

Coincidentally, just a few weeks earlier, in August, I had toured Israel, where I met with military and police officials there to talk about terrorism and other aspects of policing. Having lived in the Middle East when I was younger, I was more than familiar with the violent history of that region and

America's place in it. I told reporters there that Americans stood behind Israel's long battle against terrorism and that we would not—that we could not—back down from it.

As I toured religious sites and Israeli cities, I thought about the way we lived in the United States and the way Israelis lived with the constant fear of terrorist attacks. No one enters a mall or a big building or, certainly, an airport, without a serious security check. I wondered even then how Americans would respond to having their purses searched before they went into a store. Now, just three weeks later, we were living in a very different country, and we would find out how much the American people were willing to give up and compromise to win this battle. I believed strongly that we had to strike back decisively and heavily, to inflict damage worse than we had received.

Like other former soldiers who served between wars, I've always known how fortunate I was to be a soldier during peacetime; my service didn't require me to give my life for my country. Yet I've also always believed that I would have performed well in combat. Well, I thought, as I rolled over to try to sleep, you've got your war now.

WEDNESDAY morning I woke up an hour and a half after I'd gone to bed, at 5:00 A.M., though I don't really think I slept at all. I got my staff organized and met with the mayor and the other city officials at about 8:30. The mayor looked as tired as I felt. We gathered around a long table on the seventh floor of the police academy for what would be the first of our daily strategy meetings, a chance to compare notes and get ready to tackle that day's challenges.

There certainly would be no shortage of challenges.

We talked about the massive rescue effort, about police presence, about getting counseling to the families, food and supplies to rescue workers. The task before us was immense. The media called what had happened in the 1990s the "New York Miracle." Well, this would be the real New York Miracle, if we could somehow get the city back to some semblance of itself. The mayor was desperately looking for symbols, and he still wanted to open the stock market right away, both to spark investor confidence and to show the terrorists that they couldn't beat us, that they could blow up buildings but not stop our free markets.

But it was simply too soon. The chairman of the stock exchange wasn't ready, the financial community wasn't ready, the emergency and building people for the city weren't ready, and I think the mayor realized the American people might not be ready yet as well.

These roundtable meetings with the mayor, the other commissioners, and other city leaders would form the backbone of our recovery in the coming days, as we threw the full weight of the city and the federal government at the worst civilian catastrophe in the history of the United States. The meetings were frank and productive; the participants were decisive. There was very little debate. People presented problems, and we solved them and moved on to the next one.

At 10:20 that morning the mayor took a call from the president's chief of staff. They talked about airport security and getting the stock market open. As he spoke on the phone, the mayor—who had probably gone as long as I had without food or sleep—ate Cheerios out of the box.

At the site twenty-six hours had passed since the first plane had hit the north tower. The rescue work was ongoing, but it was painfully slow. Workers rappelled down ropes into "the pit," a thirty-foot-deep hole where much of the debris was being removed. Still, the bucket brigade continued, hundreds of people lining up to do their part. The piles of debris were scoured by evidence teams and then put into the dump trucks. Ironworkers arrived to begin cutting the massive steel beams. Cops and firefighters had to be told to go home; if their brothers and sisters were alive somewhere in there, they weren't about to leave. And yet, with all those committed people, only five survivors had been recovered from the rubble alive, and only a few dozen bodies had been removed. It was becoming painfully apparent that many bodies would never be recovered. Refrigerated trucks, to be used as makeshift morgues, sat empty along the West Side Highway.

Again, we visited the hospitals, where doctors stood waiting for injured victims from the World Trade Center, people who would never come. Friends and relatives poured into south Manhattan, covering park benches, walls, and streetlights with pictures of the missing. Moving around the city that day and seeing all of the people, I was overwhelmed by the grief they carried, and the resiliency as well. New Yorkers were going about their lives, refusing to let the terrorists have the last word.

As for the NYPD, we had started with a number as high as forty people missing, but we eventually tracked down officers who weren't accounted for, and came up with a total of twenty-one police officers missing and presumed dead. Our final number was twenty-three missing. Among them was Glenn Pettit, the officer with the video camera who had talked to Eddie Aswad and Sean Crowley just moments before the south tower collapsed. Also missing was Joseph Vigiano, who had twice been awarded the Combat Cross and whom I had so happily promoted just months earlier. His brother John, a firefighter, also was missing. Sixteen of the missing cops were, like Vigiano, members of the Emergency Services Unit, a group that always went beyond the call of duty, even in the face of such terrible danger. Other cops were simply in the area and rushed to help, like John Perry, a cop from the Bronx who was at headquarters that day to file his retirement papers when he saw the explosion at the World Trade Center and ran down to help. He was last seen trying to get people to safety.

There were dozens of stories like John Perry's, and every one was about a hero. The stories of my missing police officers were so heart wrenching, I couldn't imagine what Fire Commissioner Thomas Von Essen was going through. He had lost 343 of his firefighters, including some of his top brass, the men we'd seen on West Street: Chief Ganci, First

Deputy Commissioner Feehan, and the department chaplain, Mychal Judge. I've known Tommy Von Essen for years, and to watch him struggle with the loss of so many of his people every day was one of the worst parts of this entire tragedy.

At One Police Plaza we opened up the auditorium as a family center for the survivors to grieve and talk to department chaplains. The pain in the family center was raw and overwhelming. I met with Joseph Vigiano's mother and father, two amazingly strong people. His father, Joseph Vigiano, Sr., was a hero firefighter himself and understood the dangers of the job. But to lose two sons goes beyond anything that any of us should have to bear. I found myself drawing resolve from the Vigianos' strength. Even in later days, as it became less likely that we would find any survivors, I wanted to keep looking—for people like the Vigianos. We assigned officers to drive and take care of each family who had lost a son or a husband or a daughter or a wife. When I talked to them, I just tried to listen, to speak simply and clearly, and to tell them the truth. I warned them not to take in too many press accounts: "As soon as I find anything out, I will tell you right away."

When I finally returned to my office Wednesday afternoon, there was something waiting for me on my desk. I recognized the tight military fold, the white stars on the blue field, the red and white stripes. It was a large American flag, torn and covered with ash. The smell of fire and smoke filled my office. A note was tucked into the crease. I pulled the note out and walked behind my desk. I took a breath and opened it. It was from Sergeant Gerry Kane and Detective Pete Friscia, assigned to the protocol unit in my office. As I read the note I stood at my desk, crying.

"Boss," it began.

This is the flag that flew in front of WTC at Church St. It was blown off the pole and was tangled on a streetlight.

We as well as some firefighters and soldiers recovered it. The soldiers folded it.

In Israel you said that we can't back down to terrorism. You are right. You lead and we will follow.

PRESIDENT George W. Bush stepped out of the black Suburban and walked toward us. The motorcade stretched out behind him. They had flown over with helicopters, and now the president, the mayor, and the governor walked toward 75 Barclay Street, where we had been working when the south tower came down. It was Friday afternoon, three days since the attack, and much of the rubble had been cleared away on the blocks extending away from Ground Zero. He greeted us warmly and put his arm around Tommy Von Essen's mud-stained shoulder. The president looked at the broken windows and damaged facades of the buildings as Mayor Giuliani and I explained where we had been standing during the disaster. We showed him 7 World Trade Center, which had been badly damaged and finally collapsed hours after the towers.

President Bush listened, shook hands with everyone, and offered condolences. He seemed genuinely awed by what he saw, and when it was time to move down to West Street, he climbed into his truck and gestured for us all to join him. There were seats for only four people, so we wedged in like buddies going to a ball game—the president, the mayor, the governor, Tommy Von Essen, Richie Sheirer, who directed the Office of Emergency Management, and I.

On the way, the president looked out the window and spoke about what a tragedy this was. "The people responsible for this have got to pay," he said.

At Ground Zero he moved around easily, thanking rescue workers and asking them questions. He climbed on top of a burned-out fire truck and put his arm around a retired firefighter, then grabbed a bullhorn and began speaking. When someone yelled that they couldn't hear him, the president turned. "I can hear you," he said. "The rest of the world hears you, and the people who knocked down these buildings will hear all of us soon!" The rescue workers, firefighters, and cops began chanting "U.S.A.! U.S.A.!" It was exactly what we needed. After two days of burrowing into the piles of steel and concrete, the people wanted to hear that America would strike back for what had happened. I know I wanted to hear it. Flags were everywhere, and I found myself thinking about the strength of America, how we had taken the worst the terrorists had to offer, and now we would respond.

Cardinal Edward Egan led a prayer and we departed, moving up the West Side Highway to the Jacob Javits Convention Center, where rescue workers and family members of some of the missing firefighters and cops were waiting. The president was amazing with those people, listening, offering condolences, promising that the country would do what it needed to support the relief effort in New York and to bring terrorists everywhere to justice. We were told that the president would stay forty-five minutes, an hour and fifteen minutes tops. But he seemed overwhelmed by what he saw, and he stayed more than four hours, posing for pictures, consoling the families, and bringing a much-needed boost to the city.

An amazing transformation had come over New York and, I suppose, the whole country. The grief and shock were still pervasive, of course—on the walls of photographs of missing people at the train stations and parks; in the boroughs, where children went to bed without their parents; and at the site, where rescue workers hoped against hope that somewhere in the dust and twisted steel, someone—anyone—was alive. But in addition to the grief, other feelings emerged; patriotism and an amazing amount of support for the firefighters and police officers. As I drove down the West Side Highway, police lights flashing and siren blaring, people lined the street, three and four deep, waving flags and signs. It was hard to believe that just a few weeks earlier, we had considered morale and community relations one of our most serious problems at the NYPD.

The outpouring of affection for police officers and the job that they do was overwhelming for the officers out on the lines and for me. In the coming days baseball players and entertainers wore NYPD and FDNY ball caps and T-shirts, and the courage and dedication shown by the cops and fire-fighters inspired people around the country. People kept talking about what good might come out of this horror. I think the good came out in the people.

SOMEONE was alive! We couldn't believe it when we heard. It was Thursday night at about 10:00 P.M. and I was down at Ground Zero with Pitch and my detail, watching as the bucket brigade continued to remove debris, one plastic pail at a time. Every few minutes a signal would go back through the lines, and the rescuers would all pause, listening for tapping or cries or anything that might mean someone was down there. A hand would go up, and then another, and the whole line would be quiet. It was an amazing thing to watch.

Suddenly Thomas Lawless, the borough commander of Queens South, ran up, charged with good news. A nurse had come into a precinct house to say that her husband, a Port Authority police officer, had called from the rubble to say that he was alive. He was in level 1B of the basement with another nine officers. The word raced through the lines of rescue workers, and they dug feverishly and carefully, not wanting to cave in whatever void in the rubble these people had found.

A patrol car came screaming up to the site with the woman in it. Still wearing her surgical scrubs, she climbed out of the car, crying hysterically. I gave her a hug and assured her we would do whatever we could to rescue her husband and the others who were still trapped. Apparently, he had just called her again while she was in the car, but they kept getting disconnected. We had crisis counselors and detectives ready to talk to her, and they brought her to the fire department's site headquarters to get from her any more information that might help us pinpoint where, among the acres of basements in the former trade center towers, the officers might be.

All night there was palpable excitement as we waited for word. The media quickly found out about it and ran with the story, and families clung to the hope that their missing loved ones might be among the trapped survivors.

But right away the details of her story seemed suspect, and the closer we looked, the worse it became. The badge number she gave for her husband didn't match the name she gave, and her details seemed fuzzy, as if she hadn't thought of them all yet. When we checked her cell phone records, we found that no calls had come in to her phone at all.

At the site this brief bit of hope had been an adrenaline shot to rescue workers who had worked feverishly without sleep. Now word seeped through the lines that it was a hoax, that the woman was disturbed or worse. It was the cruelest thing someone could have done, for the rescue workers who risked their lives going into dark crevices and tunnels looking for survivors, and for the families who were still holding out hope.

On Friday we found out that the woman had been allowed to go home. At the morning meeting with the mayor and the other commissioners and officials, I turned to John Picciano. "I want you to get her," I said. "I want this woman locked up."

In the hallway Pitch reached out to an inspector who said the woman had gone home to New Jersey. "Get your best people on it," Pitch said. "We need to arrest this woman."

During the press conference, while the mayor was speaking, Pitch's phone rang. "John?" the cop on the other end said, "We got her." Detectives had grilled her, and finally she'd given it up. She had invented the whole thing.

I announced that the woman had been arrested and charged with three counts—reckless endangerment, falsely reporting an incident, and interfering with fire operations. If I could have thought of any other charges, I would have asked that those be added too. She had done one of the cruelest things I could imagine—that is, giving false hope to the thousands of rescue workers and family members, and to the millions of Americans who were watching every detail of the rescue effort on television.

That's why I announced her arrest at the press conference. It had to be made public. We couldn't afford to have anyone else think they could get away with this. I felt the same way about looters. Considering the huge area that had been affected, there wasn't very much looting, but when we found it, we had to deal with it quickly and decisively. Someone had tried to break into the safes behind automatic teller machines, and some clothing and jewelry stores were targeted. Tibor even caught a couple of men in a jewelry shop at Fulton and Church Streets. They had grabbed three thousand dollars' worth of watches and were charged with burglary, grand larceny, and impersonating officers.

Many firefighters and cops had thrown off their uniforms during the chaos, and a few people picked them up and posed as rescue workers to gain access to the scene. It was a disgusting thing to do, and we arrested everyone we caught doing it.

But considering the vast size of the area and the scope of the destruction, it was amazing how few problems there really were in the first week. Most New Yorkers were patient, respectful, and helpful. It was as if the whole city was united behind the rescue and recovery effort.

Eventually we moved the city's emergency headquarters to a pier just upriver from the disaster site. There, we continued tackling the problems one problem at a time, and began discussing how we were going to prepare the families for the disappointing news that the rescue part of this rescue and recovery was very likely finished.

For those people digging through rubble, Thursday and Friday stretched into the weekend, and expectations that we would find anyone alive began to dim. Rescue workers were struck by the hopelessness of going through a million tons of rubble by hand, one bucketful at a time. By the weekend, only one line of workers was using the orange-and-white pails—maybe to keep up the symbolic belief that all hope hadn't been lost. At the same time, most of the buckets were stacked alongside the piles of rubble. Larger equipment was brought in, and ironworkers torched the heavy sections of steel so they could be lifted away by cranes and put on flatbed trucks to be hauled away. Smashed cars were stacked three and four deep and then hauled off, and most of the streets leading into the World Trade Center were cleared of debris.

Dump trucks took the debris to Staten Island, where it was spread over the Fresh Kills landfill. NYPD detectives, FBI agents, and National Guardsmen used rakes to sift through the glass and grit and steel, looking for any evidence or for human remains that a family could put into a coffin and bury. It was horrible work, but as with all the horrible work that week, I don't recall anyone complaining.

WHAT chilled me most was imagining how nineteen terrorists could have planned and carried out this horrible attack without anyone finding out. As a law enforcement issue, that was the most troubling thing for me in the days after the attack: just how little we knew about the terrorist cells that did this. These were described as "sleeper cells," groups of people who infiltrated the United States and posed as ordinary citizens for periods of time until they were called into action. If so, the cells managed to stay undetected, amazing for such a large operation. There must have been funding and coordination at higher levels. I recalled the sleepers planted by the cocaine cartels in the New York area in the 1980s, operatives set up in houses in the suburbs to look like normal Americans. Those cells were self-contained, that is, designed to keep an investigation from leading to the top. But even if people on the ground in New

York were in charge of the day-to-day operations, it was the drug kingpins back in Colombia pulling all the strings.

In the same way, the terrorist cells in the United States seem designed to sneak in under our radar and protect the individuals and countries funding and training them. It wasn't that we weren't looking. We spent ten billion dollars on fighting terrorism last year and, as it turns out, we were completely vulnerable. And while the September attack was a shocking event, it was not isolated and it was certainly not without warning. There were 423 international terrorist attacks in 2000, an 8 percent increase over the year before. Almost half of those attacks, 200, were against the United States, an 18 percent increase over the year before. And we have known since 1993 that the World Trade Center was a tempting target for terrorists.

Of course there are no easy answers, and it's only in hindsight that we can see the signs leading toward the September 11, 2001, attack. But protecting our citizens in the United States and preparing for terrorist attacks—the homeland defense, as President Bush called it—will be the country's biggest law enforcement challenge over the next few years. Bush made a wonderful choice when he picked former governor Tom Ridge to head the office of homeland security, but there is much work to be done.

Obviously, the first step is airport security, where improvements are long overdue. I agree with the push in Congress to make airport security a federal law enforcement function. Security officers should be highly trained peace officers with access to FBI and INS watch lists and should run the names and aliases before boarding every plane. Information from all airlines needs to be made available to security officers, and the public should have only limited access to that information. Magnetometers need to be more sensitive and new technologies have to be explored as we look for better ways to identify potential terrorists. In the meantime, armed sky marshals must be plentiful enough to provide real deterrence, and cockpits need to be made more secure.

After airport security, I look at immigration as the next natural area for improvement. It appears the terrorists in the September 11 attack flowed back and forth across the Canadian border. We need to start by reassessing the way we look at our borders. Right now they are simply corridors of trade and transportation with almost no thought for security. I can only remember one time the borders were used for actually securing the United States, and that was in preparation for the millennium celebrations, when security was heightened and we actually caught terrorists before they acted. That needs to be the rule, not the exception. Right now we have too many agencies with a hand in protecting our borders, everyone from the border patrol to the customs service, the Coast Guard, the National Guard, and local police and sheriffs' offices. There is no coordination at the top, no agency ultimately responsible.

With secure borders we can establish a comprehensive watch list of security risks—a database of hundreds of thousands of people ineligible for admission. We can train our border people to spot forged documents and make sure immigration laws are actually followed. Enforcement of those laws is imperative.

I also fully support Attorney General John Ashcroft's recent antiterrorism package, which would heighten the priority of terrorism investigations. Ashcroft's proposals would greatly improve the intelligence and law enforcement community's ability to use wiretaps, would eliminate the statute of limitations for terrorism crimes, and would put teeth in the prosecution of terrorists and their accomplices. They would also criminalize the possession of certain chemicals that could be used in acts of terrorism, and expand the definition of terrorist crimes to include the people who harbor terrorists, finance them, or give them expert advice.

But whatever we do as a nation, much of the responsibility will rest with Americans as individuals. Our entire country has been transformed. The reality is that we have to live now in the same world that European countries have been living in, the same world that Israel and Arab nations have found—a world in which some individual rights are sacrificed for security. We have to prepare for that. Local and state governments will have to be willing to spend the money to help their citizens feel safe.

Terrorism represents a challenge for police departments as well. We will have to change the way we police our cities, following trends that were created in places like Italy, which had to learn to battle the Red Brigade; England and Ireland, where the Irish Republican Army has been a major law enforcement priority; and, of course, Israel and the Arab nations, where terrorism is a fact of daily life. American police departments will need to improve in almost every area, from intelligence to explosives, from crowd control to emergency training. No American city was as prepared for a terrorist attack as New York, and yet, in hindsight, there was more we could have done.

We will do more now, as will other American cities. And if taxpayers don't want police work to suffer in traditional areas, we will have to pay more for this protection. In New York, I know that we are up for the challenge. There is no police department anywhere that is more ready to face this new world.

ON Friday, September 14, I sent a Teletype message to all the precinct houses and boroughs. "I wanted to take a moment to express the pride and gratitude I feel for what you have done over the past two days," I wrote.

I know you are concerned about the heroes that went into the attack site and still haven't been found. . . . The City of New York, the NYPD and our brothers and sisters in this city have suffered a tremendous loss.

Our nation has never been hit harder and it is going to take days and perhaps even weeks to know the full magnitude of this cowardly and despicable act. I don't have all the answers yet, but I can tell you that a total

of 23 members of the NYPD remain missing. I promise
you that we are doing everything to get them out.

   This is an unimaginable period for you and your
families, but this city will survive and we will be the
ones who make it happen. You are all heroes and I
have never been prouder to be a member of the NYPD
than I am right now.

   Be careful, rest when you get a chance and stay
strong. God bless you, God bless America and God
bless the NYPD.

Each day that passed brought the tragedy home more
completely. As the number of missing crept up past four
thousand, five thousand, six thousand, the scope of the attack and its aftermath was becoming harder and harder to
fathom.

By the weekend the first funerals had been held. More
than two thousand people packed St. Francis of Assisi Ro-
man Catholic Church on West 31st Street for the service for
Mychal Judge, his casket draped with an FDNY flag and
carried by disheveled, crying firefighters. At St. Kilian Ro-
man Catholic Church, Peter Ganci was laid to rest. When the
command post had moved north to safety, Ganci had gone
back toward the towers to check on the rest of his men. At
the service the mayor recalled seeing Ganci just before he
and I returned to the building at 75 Barclay: "I quickly said,
'God bless you,' and thought I would see him later."

But it may have been even harder for the other families,
the ones who had no body to bury. A week after the attack,
there were still no bodies of NYPD officers to bury. And
hundreds of firefighters were still missing. On September
17, six days after the attack, a service was held at St.
Patrick's Cathedral for the missing firefighters, police officers, and other rescue workers. I sat in a front pew, next to
Tommy Von Essen and the mayor, praying that some of our
people might still be alive.

"Death, it proclaims, has and must have two faces," said

Cardinal Edward Egan. "One of sadness and pain, and the other of peace and triumph."

I have felt raw in every way since the attack. My anger at the terrorists and their sponsors is raw. My grief for the families is raw. Even my own personal feelings are raw and unformed, bitter in my throat.

I think I will feel this way until the people who planned this horrible, cowardly attack are brought to justice. As a cop, justice for me has never been something abstract. It is very real: the drug dealer in handcuffs, the murderer behind bars. It is the time for justice now. It is the time for heroes.

I spent my life studying with and emulating men I saw as heroes—from my father to Rudolph Giuliani, from the cops who walked a foot post in Paterson to the martial arts teachers I studied with, from retired Green Berets in the Middle East to undercover cops in the drug wars. Yet I'd never encountered anything close to the honor and bravery I saw on September 11. We have, as Cardinal Egan said, been living with sadness and pain. But let us now live in the courage and strength of the people we lost; let us follow their example to triumph and then to peace.

Someday soon, when we have won this war we are embarking on, we will build a monument to the people lost in its first battle, the attack of September 11, 2001. It should be a monument not to terror but to the honor, courage, and decency displayed by everyday citizens caught in events beyond their control—a monument to the police officers and firefighters whose courage and sacrifice must now light our way.

Until then, our actions must be their memorial. As witness to their courage and honor, let us offer our own sacrifice and bravery. And our humanity.

The day after the attack, Eddie Aswad returned to the place where he and Sean Crowley had almost died. He walked amid the rubble, the dust, and the bent steel. He shook his head, amazed that he had survived. Three bodies had been found in the place where Eddie and Sean had been standing. He looked inside his smashed car and into the window of the building where they'd been trapped.

Inside the building where he'd taken refuge, Eddie couldn't believe the devastation. Three inches of ash and paper blanketed the hallways. Windows were blown out, and steel girders from the towers had pierced the facade. Still in shock, and trying to make some sense of it all, Eddie walked alone down the halls until he saw, in the rubble, a small photo. It was a baby picture, folded and torn. He bent and picked it up, then wiped the ash away. Somehow, through all the violent fires and chaos, it had endured.

He studied the face of the baby in the photo and didn't know what to do. He didn't want to take the picture, but he knew he couldn't leave it in the piles of debris either. A sculpture stood in the entryway, covered with dust and debris. He took one last look at the photo, then carefully placed it on the sculpture. No one was there. No one would see it. Eddie's small gesture was a great act of defiance against a monumental act of evil.

In the middle of the rubble, covered in ash, and searching for some understanding of it all, Eddie Aswad was a hero. A quiet man, he taught me, in that simple act, the meaning of human dignity and nobility. His humanity, our humanity, despite the devastation, will endure.

IN REMEMBRANCE

THE events of September 11, 2001, robbed the New York Police Department, and the city at large, of twenty-three extraordinary human beings: police officers, sergeants, and detectives; twenty-two men and one woman who were beloved by their families and valued by the communities they served. But in their sacrifice these fallen heroes gave the world something truly great in return: a demonstration of unshaken courage in the face of death, and of the nobility of the human spirit. In a city of superlatives, theirs was an ultimate act of virtue; let their lives, and their bravery, never be forgotten.

JOHN COUGHLIN
Sergeant, ESS #4

MICHAEL CURTIN
Sergeant, ESS #2

JOHN D'ALLARA
Police Officer, ESS #2

VINCENT DANZ
Police Officer, ESS #3

JEROME DOMINGUEZ
Police Officer, ESS #3

STEPHEN DRISCOLL
Police Officer, ESS #4

MARK ELLIS
Police Officer, TD #4

ROBERT FAZIO
Police Officer, 13th Precinct

RODNEY GILLIS
Sergeant, ESS #8

RONALD KLOEPFER
Police Officer, ESS #7

THOMAS LANGONE
Police Officer, ESS #10

JAMES LEAHY
Police Officer, 6th Precinct

BRIAN McDONNELL
Police Officer, ESS #1

JOHN PERRY
Police Officer, 40th Precinct

GLEN PETTIT
Police Officer, Video Unit

CLAUDE RICHARDS
Detective, Bomb Squad

TIMOTHY ROY
Sergeant, S.T.E.D.

MOIRA SMITH
Police Officer, 13th Precinct

RAMON SUAREZ
Police Officer, TD #4

PAUL TALTY
Police Officer, ESS #10

SANTOS VALENTIN
Police Officer, ESS #7

JOSEPH VIGIANO
Detective, ESS #2

WALTER WEAVER
Police Officer, ESS #3

Listen to

BERNARD B. KERIK'S

New York Times bestseller

THE LOST SON

A Life in Pursuit of Justice

Performed by
RON MCLARTY

ISBN 0-06-008393-X
$25.95 ($38.95 Can.)
6 hours/4 cassettes

**Available wherever books are sold,
or call 1-800-331-3761 to order.**

HarperAudio
An Imprint of HarperCollins*Publishers*
www.harpercollins.com

LOA 0902